CW00551610

Punch

23-27 TUDOR STREET, LONDON EC4Y 0HR

Telex LDN 265863 (Unipapers) Telephone: 01-583 9199

Jeffrey Bernard

c/o Private Eye

34 Greek Street

London W 1

Nov 23 1977

Dear Jeffrey,

Are you going to do the fucking article orearen't you ?

yours

Miles

Miles Kington

PUNCH PUBLICATIONS LTD. Directors: A V Caudery N A Whinfrey W Davis B P Knox-Peebles R Tookey R E Forrester
Registered office: 23-27 Tudor Street London EC4Y 0HR Telephone: 01-583 9199 Registered in England No. 797363

Jeffrey Bernard's (1932-1997) column in the *Spectator*, which began in 1978, chronicled his various medical, alcoholic and sexual adventures, invariably with wit and honesty. His unconventional lifestyle attracted the attention of Keith Waterhouse, who turned his life story into a hit play called *Jeffrey Bernard is Unwell*. He famously vomited on the Queen Mother's feet at the Royal Ascot and later collapsed drunkenly, unable to deliver his speech at the national point-to-point dinner.

LOW LIFE:
IRREVERENT
REFLECTIONS FROM
THE BOTTOM
OF A GLASS

Jeffrey Bernard

DUCKWORTH

This edition first published in the United Kingdom by
Duckworth in 2019
Duckworth, an imprint of Duckworth Books ltd

First published by Duckworth in 1986

1Golden Court, Richmond
TW9 1EU, United Kingdom

www.duckworthbooks.co.uk

For bulk and special sales please contact
info@duckworthbooks.com

A catalogue record for this book is available from the British Library

Text design and Typesetting by Geethik Technologies

Printed and bound in Great Britain by Clays Ltd, Elcograf S.p.A.

9780715653814

For Isabel Bernard, with love

Contents

viii

Contents

Foreword

At 11am, Jeffrey Bernard would enter the Coach and Horses from Greek Street by the door at the far end, the shallow end, where the Italians and shoplifters drank. In the 1980s he'd often take a paper napkin from a bunch folded and tucked into a glass on the counter by the landlord Norman Balon's aged mother. As he blew his nose, dripping with the exertion in the fresh air of getting to the pub, his hand would shake. It was, he remembered being told by a medic, a benign tremor.

His muscles were beginning to waste. 'I'm as weak as a kitten,' he'd say, as he climbed onto the high stool by the bar at the deep end, by the gents'. By 1990, when he was in his late fifties, his knees were thicker than his thighs.

His once stylish dress was a little dog-eared and out of fashion. He'd wear a blazer and slacks, as in Trevor Leighton's photograph now in the National Portrait Gallery, and sometimes grey leather shoes – a mistake. He hadn't lost his hair and his eyes were part of the charm of his smile. His cheeks were sinking in.

He would take the change from the night before from his pocket and dump it on the counter: perhaps thirty 10p pieces, a pile of coppers, and assorted small silver coins. This we regulars called drunkard's change or shrapnel. In the time before lunch he was at his best, reaching a narrow plateau with the help of a few large vodkas, ice and soda. He had stopped taking lime – because of diabetes, he said.

'Unfortunately,' he wrote in one of his columns, 'that peak only lasts for up to two hours and then the wheels fall off, the memory evaporates, repetitiveness sets in alongside aggression or melancholy or both.'

It was in those shrinking hours that he gave himself to the conversation that served as a rehearsal for his columns, typed crisply in the chill early hours of press day on Monica his electric typewriter with hardly a correction. The smoky Coach and Horses was his rehearsal room. In his time, it was one of a handful of conversation pubs in Soho where painters, poets and actors gathered, some, like Francis Bacon, Lucian Freud, Elizabeth Smart, Tom Baker or John Hurt, famous. Most of us not. Stagehands, failed actresses and the man who invented cat-racing talked and shouted at each other, too. This little republic of radical democracy admitted anyone but bores.

Jeffrey once quoted a leading authority on alcoholism who marked a station of the descent of the alcoholic with the telling sign: 'Starts drinking with social inferiors.' For all his hero-worship of the successful, Jeffrey did count as friends some of the flotsam and jetsam of Soho: Mick Tobin, the stage carpenter, Graham Mason, the drunkest man in the Coach and Horses, or Gordon Smith, the limping stage-door keeper, who generally attracted more sympathy than comradeship. If he fell out with them, it could be a more definitive breach than with some women who had once been his lovers, such as Marsh Dunbar, who recovered, as it were, from being in love with him and remained a friend until his death forty years later.

Some of his heroes were long dead: a small bust of Nelson stood on his desk in his lodgings. Another was Byron, and Jeffrey made his life an audition for the role of Byronic hero.

In his room at the art-writer Geraldine Norman's flat, where he'd lodged since 1981, there were framed photographs covering a whole wall, showing Jeffrey alongside a series of greats, including Graham Greene, Lester Piggott, Francis Bacon, Richard Ingrams and Peter O'Toole. At a party at the flat, a woman asked his brother Bruce whether that was Jeffrey's room. 'Either that,' he replied, 'or someone who likes him *very much.*'

Keith Waterhouse perhaps made Jeffrey famous, with his hit play *Jeffrey Bernard Is Unwell* (1989), to which Peter O'Toole took with such sympathetic gusto. But Waterhouse simply presented on stage almost word for word some of Jeffrey's 'Low Life' columns from *The Spectator*, where they had been appearing since 1975 opposite 'High Life' by Taki Theodoracopulos. Norman Balon, the awkward, cross-grained, warm-hearted landlord, had made those columns possible by providing his eccentrically hospitable pub as Jeffrey's inconvenient office and treacherous refuge.

Jeffrey had ranged more widely, in Soho and at racecourses, in earlier decades. By the Eighties he was never seen in the French pub in Dean Street, with whose landlord, the great Gaston Berlemeont, he must have fallen out, and seldom in the Colony Room Club, with whose proprietor, the monstrous Ian Board, he had an edgy relationship. In any case the Colony remained mostly an afternoon drinking club, and Jeffrey was increasingly sleepy in the afternoon. So he had come to rely on the Coach as a sort of day centre where anyone who wanted to give him work knew to find him.

One element in Jeffrey's conversation that fascinated me was his store of memories of people who might be called the Sacred Ancestors of the kind of bohemianism that survived in the Soho of the Eighties. These dead presences figured in such memoirs as Daniel Farson's *Soho in the Fifties* (1987), the launch party for which was held across the street at Kettner's, where Oscar Wilde would dine.

In the depths of the Soho Valhalla lay the poet Paul Potts, the principal enemies of whose popularity were his constant cadging of drinks and money, his theft of friends' books and shirts, his wounding outbursts of verbal abuse and, later, his strong and offensive smell. But Jeffrey had got the better of him by somehow managing to steal one of *his* shirts.

A little less monstrous among the Sacred Ancestors were the 'Two Roberts', Colquhoun and MacBryde, the pair of painters who'd died young in the Sixties. According to Jeffrey's account they hadn't really started drinking until they were thirty. Then they made up for lost time. 'There must be some bloke who's ended up in a nut house because something very terrible happened to him when he was a little boy,' Jeffrey said in conversation one morning. 'He was standing outside a pub in Notting Hill while his parents were having a drink inside, when suddenly Robert Colquhoun came out and was sick all over him. Imagine it: two pints of Guinness and shepherd's pie all over you.'

I don't think that particular memory found its way into the Low Life column. But another remark did, I think. 'You know those haddock in Richard's fish shop,' Jeffrey Bernard once said to Graham Mason. 'You can tell if they're fresh by the eyes. Well, if you were a haddock, I'd leave you on the slab.'

Jeffrey did not exactly remember everything that was said in the pub, even if it was said by him, but elements would come back to him. One morning I talked with him about Dickens's account in *The Uncommercial Traveller* of a visit to the 'Foul Wards' for women at Wapping workhouse. He was fascinated and resolved to read it. In conversation one evening later that week he mentioned to me Dickens's visit to a women's dosshouse, unaware that I had been his source. In his next column, he had himself become the object of Dickens's attentions, or lack of them: 'It's wet and cold and I suppose if I had been walking along Old Compton Street a hundred years ago Charles Dickens would have snubbed me.'

It was astonishing that, under the daily disablement of alcohol, any work got done at all, but Jeffrey's columns built up week by week to become respectable volumes. The subtitle of the book *Low Life* was well chosen: *A Kind of Autobiography*. He was commissioned to write an autobiography but never did. His columns serve as a compelling version of his life. In November 1986, the party for the publication of *Low Life* was wisely held at lunchtime when more people would be functioning.

Only a critical mass of well-wishers at the venue was capable of overcoming the chill atmosphere of the room upstairs at the Coach and Horses (where *Private Eye* held its fortnightly lunches), which had once been the Balons' dining-room and bore a strong sense of abandonment. As Jeffrey remarked, the austere decor might have been designed by Stafford Cripps. He was pleased that day to see a sprinkling of well-known friends such as John Osborne, Keith Waterhouse and Beryl Bainbridge; Charles Moore the editor of *The Spectator*, no great toper, raised a glass; the most regular of the regulars enjoyed the spirits, a rare offering at a publisher's party as an addition to wine. Even Oliver and Bruce, Jeffrey's brothers, made the most of a sunny spell in their stormy relations with him for the day. Only Graham Mason refused to come upstairs on the curious grounds that 'I don't like drink unless it's paid for.'

Looking back, these were precarious years of outward success. Collections of columns elevated Jeffrey from the journalistic to the literary world; the play was in the offing; there was even a horse race at Lingfield named after him. Though he had nowhere to live that he could call his own, Jeffrey found enough money to make use of the Groucho Club as a bolthole. It had been founded in 1985 and quite a few Soho regulars disapproved in theory of its clientele of advertising types who seemed to have few marks of hard-won authenticity.

In practice I was perfectly happy when Jeffrey said one day, 'Follow me,' and took me to the Groucho for lunch. I was practically homeless, having spent some nights on the hearthrug of a kindly regular, and I was definitely hungry enough to appreciate breast of pheasant and sorbet and a good bottle of claret shared with Jeffrey. He asked the head waiter what he'd had for lunch the day before and now ordered the day's special. Before it came he'd forgotten what it was going to be.

I was unrealistic enough to assume the wild atmosphere of the Eighties would last for ever. I couldn't have thought about it much. If in Soho we were all in the same boat, which was a comfort, it was becoming clear that the vessel was Géricault's *Raft of the Medusa*. When the sea became rougher, people fell off.

Michael Heath the cartoonist perceptively remarked that Jeffrey's hobby was observing his own physical dissolution. He was drinking a bottle and a half or two bottles of vodka a day. He dreamt, when he could sleep, of being eaten by giant maggots. Diabetes led to gangrene and later a leg was amputated below the knee, by the same brilliant surgeon that had removed the cysts as big as tangerines behind his ears.

Jeffrey could now, when annoyed, wave his stump. A prosthetic leg was left standing in the bath at home. I sometimes wheeled him back to the high-rise council flat in Berwick Street he'd now got.

As a youngster Jeffrey had dived into the deep end of the long-running tragi-comedy of Soho bohemia, played out nightly in pubs and drinking clubs. I've tried to capture what it was like in my book *Soho in the Eighties*. I've never laughed so much as I did in those years, despite everything.

Jeffrey died in 1997 in the same week as the Princess of Wales and Mother Teresa. Daniel Farson, the writer and photographer, died later that year. Bacon was dead. Ian Board the proprietor of the Colony Room Club, was dead. Soho was dead.

I don't know if Jeffrey's writing was ever relevant. It was universal and timeless, though some of the male conventions of those days, such as sexism against women, now seems rather shocking. Of course, he often did it to annoy, because he knew it teased, and it came as little surprise when the feminist Dale Spender moved to have him barred from the Groucho Club for his language. For Jeffrey, who had once had a boxing licence, words could be an alternative to fisticuffs. Yet his most deadly weapon was withdrawal of affection, which only worked against those who had not learnt to love him.

It was precisely because Soho was a dead district walking that a revival of *Jeffrey Bernard is Unwell* was staged 'immersively' in the Coach and Horses in 2019 to draw attention to the ending of the tenancy of its landlord by the decision of commercial brewers who preferred, it seemed, compliant managers without the hazard of Soho bohemianism. The Low Life columns have acquired a beguiling historical dimension, yet there is more of that strange extinct life in these pages than in the grid of Georgian streets that survive today as the parish of St Anne, Soho.

Christopher Howse
Author of *Soho in the Eighties*

LOW LIFE

Introduction

I suppose I first got hooked on the low life as a child of about twelve and well before I really understood the meaning of the phrase. My initial taste and immediate liking for forbidden fruit was, I suppose, not simply a reaction against authority and rules but an instinctive feeling that there was something very, very exciting and possibly glamorous going on outside and beyond the walls of my playroom and schoolroom.

I'd had hints of it from an early age. My parents were what you might call middle-class Bohemian. My mother was an opera singer who came from a working-class family with vague gypsy origins. She had a touch of class when she sang and, although she toured America successfully with a company run by Sir Nigel Playfair, children and what she claimed was my father's jealousy cut her career short. My father was a stage designer, architect and designer of all sorts. He was quite an extraordinary man. He came from a family called Cornwallis-West who specialised in keeping skeletons in cupboards. There was a scandal connected with Jenny Churchill and they changed their name to Bernard. He sailed before the mast at the turn of the century and then got a job at the Manchester Opera House and taught himself to draw. At the end of the day he would take on local tearaways on the stage for nobbins – thrown in coins – at the instigation of the stage staff. Somehow, by his own grit and talent, he got to the dizzy heights of an office in Park Lane and a house in Cheyne Walk. Among other things he designed the Lyons Corner Houses and the entrance to the Strand Palace Hotel which now stands complete in the Victoria and Albert Museum. But my parents treated their children with some severity, and from the time my father died when I was seven years old my mother was hell-bent on giving me a good education in the hopes that I might become an officer and a gentleman.

But, as I say, during that time I saw too much evidence to go along enthusiastically with that venture. My mother gave occasional cocktail parties for musicians, actors and actresses and stage people of all sorts, and I didn't have to be more than twelve to see that they were getting a little more fun out of life than the Latin master at my prep school or the local grocer in Holland Park. There was an atmosphere of a low life of sorts at home and it filtered down to me. I became aware of wickedness, and that's exactly what excited me about it. It needs to be said, to put it in perspective for readers too young to be of an age of awareness in the late 1940s, that almost everything one hankered for was considered wicked.

For us of course – not for parents or schoolmasters. Take sex. It was the age of suspender-belt and stocking. Only what they called 'broad-minded' people went to bed with anyone apart from their husband or wife. It was also extremely difficult indeed for a teenage boy to get a girl to bed at all, and if you were lucky enough it was quite something to boast about among your friends. You became an instant Jack the Lad. I used to think that only theatrical people and the working classes got drunk and that racing was strictly for the upper classes and villains. The prospects were sheer heaven and I couldn't wait to grow up.

Anyway, that was the backdrop for the first act of this farce called the low life. The second act opened with my discovery of masturbation. I knew nothing at all about sex and simply thought that masturbation was a unique discovery on my part that was a lonely hobby of a sort that produced a pleasant sensation. I introduced it to my incredibly innocent prep school the next term – feeling like Marco Polo returning to Europe with the new inventions of gunpowder and paper – and soon the entire school was rocked to its foundations both metaphorically and physically. Shortly after that I discovered the facts of sex itself: not so much life – sex. I found a handbook in some nearby woods issued to American GIs at the time. It was called *The Red Light*. Shortly after that I kissed a girl for the first time and what you might call the rot set in.

I passed my common entrance to a ghastly naval college called Pangbourne in the nick of time before being expelled for being what they called a bad influence. But, from then on, sex was uppermost in my mind and I spent two years sitting in the back row of a classroom with a picture of Veronica Lake and another of Ava Gardner pinned under my desk lid and speculating as to my first woman and the rest that, I hoped, might follow. Not a lot of work got done.

Now, it was at the same time that I discovered the Turf. I was barely aware of racing, but I did know that there was one boy who made a book and took sixpenny and shilling bets. Anyway, he was found out one day and the heavens opened up. He got no less than twelve cuts – cuts they were called in the navy and cut they literally bloody-well did because even wearing trousers my bum was bleeding. I was amazed. With schoolboy logic I thought anything you can get that lot for must be marvellous. Probably nearly as good as sex. So I started reading the racing pages.

At the same time as this I discovered the demon drink which, I hasten to add, wasn't to become any sort of a problem until years later. It wasn't a pleasure then, and nothing and no one is a problem until you get to need and love them.

At the beginning of one term, one of my friends brought back a bottle of rather disgusting cherry brandy. We sipped at it gently with two other boys at weekends in a hut in the woods we'd built. We used to sit in this hut, roll cigarettes and smoke while we discussed the various merits of Veronica Lake, Ava Gardner, Rita Hayworth, Gordon Richards and Charlie Smirke.

Looking back on those ghastly days I suppose one of the things that also attracted me to the low life eventually was the fact that I most enjoyed the company of boys who were always in trouble. I still do. But the future as an officer and gentleman came to an end when I was asked to leave. The Captain of the college sent my mother a letter asking her to take me away and in so doing paid me the greatest back-handed compliment I have ever received. 'While I consider him to be psychologically unsuitable for public school life,' he wrote, 'I consider he has a great future as a seam bowler.' What more could any low-lifer ask for setting out on the great journey of life?

So that was that. Authority and rules were slipping away fast, and suddenly all that delicious wickedness I had been dreaming about for years was within my reach: girls, pubs, clubs, racecourses and a room of one's own – bliss. With a pinstriped suit, all the rage in those days, I thought I could conquer them all. But then, for the first time, I became painfully aware of the business of money. I didn't yet realise that money meant something far more glorious – freedom. I was just acutely aware of the need for what we call 'moving-around' money.

But the base of operations I chose was Soho. I'd been there before in the school holiday when my brother, a student at St Martin's School of Art, asked me up there for coffee one day. It was instant magic to me, a sort of Disneyland for low-lifers. There was a café they used that was full of artists, poets, amateur and professional philosophers, writers, actors, bums, layabouts, a few genuine Bohemians, eccentrics, lunatics and pretty girls. There were also thieves, who then as now plundered Foyle's bookshop, ponces, bookies' runners and con men. It was heaven. Not the dreadful dump it is now. You can imagine what it was like suddenly to be plonked down in that after years of Dickensian schooling! But of course the endless cups of tea, the modest rent and the half pints of bitter even at only 8½d a half had to be paid for, and what on earth does an expensive but bad education equip you to do? Very little. So I began alternating between navvying and dish-washing, jacking the jobs in when I'd got hold of a few bob and then bumming around for a while until it was time to go to work again.

Now, let's get one thing straight about jobs like navvying and dish-washing. There are still people about who think that there's something vaguely romantic about hard graft like that. There isn't. Neither is there very much dignity in manual labour. If there was, the Duke of Westminster would be digging his own garden. The myth of the beauty of sweating your guts out comes from the romantic school of D.H. Lawrence-worshippers – and look where he ended up. Mexico. I worked in the coal mines in 1953 and one day on that wretched face I swore I would never look a page of his in the face again. People who like their jobs, people who – to use that awful sociological phrase, have 'job satisfaction' – may regard a stint on a building site as fun, but one of the first things I realised in those days in Soho was that there is no virtue in *work for its own sake*.

But anyway, between those lousy jobs there were some amazing times in Soho. It was extraordinary to go to Fitzrovia and drink with the faces of the Fifties. There were the painters John Minton, the Roberts Colquhoun and McBryde, Francis Bacon – still with us. There was George Baker, Louis McNeice, the dreaded Dylan Thomas, Malcolm Arnold, Alan Rawsthorne. John Davenport, Tom Driberg, Maurice Richardson, Robert Newton – and one could go on. Actually, I'm not name dropping but simply pointing out the duality of that life. And it was the undercurrent of that life which was so incredibly appealing to me, the real low life, the misspent youth. There were snooker clubs and there was Jack Solomon's gym in Windmill Street. I got hooked on both snooker and boxing in those days. There were some marvellous fighters about then. I have met all sorts of sportsmen and I can tell you that boxers are the nicest. This may have something to do with the fact that when you can do it you don't have to be nasty. Boxing has gone to the dogs now, but then it had a touch of gladiatorial glamour about it. I used to train with champions in those days, world champions from America too, and they were all lovely men outside the ring. I progressed to working in a boxing booth in Tottenham – a very bent business except for taking on naive boys who wanted to show off in front of their girl friends – and for that I got the princely sum of ten shillings. Then I got a professional licence for a while – Jack the Lad again. The last fight I had was at Slough Town Hall. I got flattened and paid a fiver. Out of that I paid the return fare to Slough, ten bob to my manager and ten bob to my second. I shared the change with the loser of the main event on a bottle of

Gordon's gin which we drank on the train home. This is the life, I thought. What a fool.

Of course, if I had listened to my mother I could have been a naval officer or learned how to become a bank manager or worked as a solicitor's clerk. And who the hell would I have met? As I've often said in the *Spectator*, I've met a better class of person in the gutter than I have in the drawing-room. That's not inverted snobbery, it's just that I prefer the company of people who know what it's like to be in the shit. Skating on thin ice keeps a man on his toes. My colleague Taki who writes the 'High Life' column in the *Spectator* once said the only thing the rich can't buy is better company because, by virtue of being rich, they have to stick with each other.

But skating on thin ice wasn't a sport I took up seriously until I took up writing about racing professionally. As I said, I always liked it, but when I first had the expenses actually to go to the racecourse instead of the betting shop it gave me a hell of a buzz. In fact, until I got used to it, it almost made the hair on the back of my neck stand up. It's not easy to explain that. It has a sort of glamour. It has a sort of romance. A race can be extremely exciting. It's very colourful. It has a sort of electricity for me, but as usual words fail me. It's always difficult to communicate an enthusiasm or love. The people are something else. There are very few grey areas in racing. It's a black-and-white business. Racing people are either tremendously good people or they are out-and-out greedy sods. But there again, like my gutter – I use the word metaphorically, of course, and intend no insults – there are successful people in racing, not the privileged few, who started absolutely potless and who know just what it's like to be on the floor.

Now the whole point of mentioning this is to point out that the experience makes people *kinder*, and that's important.

There's also the behind-the-scenes area in racing. You should go up on the Lambourn Downs early one spring morning when they're on the gallops riding work. If you stand on the top looking towards the village you can pick them out in the distance coming out of the mist. As they get closer the noise of the hooves comes through, and then as they slam those hooves into the turf it's like small thunder intermingled with the jangle of bits, bridles and stirrups, and the bellows of the horses' lungs, the air coming out of their nostrils like plumes on a cold bright morning. And they call *that* low life? If I was a poet I could convince you. Then, after that, you go down to the yard and have breakfast, and maybe Joe Mercer's there, or even Lester. Then it's cocktail hour and then off to the races. It's something of an alfresco drinking club, and that's the trouble.

When I was the *Sporting Life* columnist in 1971 you could say it was my downfall. Booze is the main artery that runs through the low life. Anyway, the column took off. I had my picture at the top of it twice a week and so strangers recognised me. They used to send me over everything from large Scotches to bottles of champagne, and I'm afraid it went to my head in both senses of the word. In 1972, having been sacked from the *Life* because of my drunken behaviour, I ended up in what's politely called an alcohol and drug addiction unit attached to a lunatic asylum in Ealing.

It was pretty depressing. I had been a pretty heavy drinker since 1960, but with my involvement with racing five years later I really went over the top. At the time it all seemed rather jolly, but then I cracked after working for the *Sporting Life* and got carted off. The procedure in these places is to sedate you quite heavily on arrival, so that you avoid nasty withdrawal symptoms, and give you loads of vitamin B complex. You get woken up from time to time to get fed and they put you physically on your feet, so to speak. Even this trauma has its absurdities and lighter side.

When I did eventually come to on day three, I discovered that the man in the next bed to me was a BOAC pilot. I actually laughed after a week of tears. He'd landed a Trident at Heathrow so drunk that he'd passed out over the controls as soon as the plane had touched down. (This would make a fantastic television commercial.) Anyway, they grounded him in their infinite wisdom for a while, and later; would you believe, put him in charge of traffic control at Nairobi, where he somehow contrived to get two aircraft to land on the same runway at the same time, both coming in opposite directions. One of them had sufficient power to rise above it all at the last moment. I'm not sure whether you would call that high life or low life.

Anyway, Jumbo as he was aptly called, had had a rough time in the war and his drinking had been escalating ever since. But the funny thing was that nearly everyone in that place had an *excuse*. There was a singular lack of personality defects. Alcoholics are fantastic self-deceivers. The only prerequisite to stop drinking is to *want* to stop. The success of group therapy is wildly exaggerated, but then the medical profession don't really understand what goes on in an alcoholic's mind. Even Max Glatt, a world authority on the subject, once said to me, 'If you want to know about alcoholism ask an alcoholic.' But, over the years, it's a personal problem that I have come to accept without dramatising it – I hope. For me, it's just a bloody nuisance because it does interfere with the smooth running of one's day-to-day existence.

On the other hand, I wouldn't like day-to-day existence to be too smooth. That wouldn't go with low life at all. Perhaps the worst aspect of boozing is that it becomes one's first loyalty. And that's no exaggeration. That's why marriage is impossible. Drink is the other woman. Four times I've fooled myself into thinking I wanted to make a commitment of that sort, but I suppose what I'm really committed to are all the things I've been talking about. I'm never quite sure whether it has all been rather sad or rather ridiculous. It's certainly all absurd. A friend of mine who killed herself in a fire when she went to bed drunk and lit a cigarette used to say that you can't get through life without a highly developed sense of the absurd. I go along with that but, by God, she certainly had an absurd ending. I often think about her and two other friends who killed themselves falling down stairs and I'm sure that in a strange way people die when there simply isn't anything at all left for them to do.

The other thing I ponder sitting on my stool in the Coach and Horses is the alternative. The idle pub cliché-ridden chat often becomes unbearable when friends are absent and only the bores are holding the fort. 'How are you today? God, you look awful. What on earth was that fight about last night. Did you back Lester's in the last at Windsor? How did you get on with that woman I saw you talking to? Same again? Yes, I think I'll have just the one.' It makes me want to scream. And then I have this strange fantasy. You've seen those old posters advertising insurance. Well, I'm the man in one. I'm with my wife, a sweet, harmless, devoted little thing and we're striding forth purposefully into the future under a symbolic umbrella. We're safe because we're prudent and responsible. We've got the obligatory two children with us, a boy of fourteen and a girl of twelve – decently spaced out – and they're beaming, he under his school cap and she in her gymslip. Behind us there's our little mock-Tudor house. I think we live either in

Chislehurst or Haslemere. Apart from my loving family I love my lawnmower and my Ford Escort, which I lie under most Sunday mornings. I may have a glass of whisky and soda when I get back from the office, but I don't chew the cud with the lads down the local. I may have fifty pence on the Grand National, but both my feet are firmly on the ground. But, best of all, I am not in the slightest bit frightened of opening buff envelopes. In fact I'm not frightened of anything except possibly Mrs Thatcher losing the next election or there not being enough rain for the herbaceous border.

Now I'm not knocking this family, in fact I grudgingly envy them in some ways. The trouble is I can't find the family halfway between that fantasy one and this single low one here that I've opted for. And speaking of families brings me to the delicate subject of women – although, heaven knows, they're about as delicate as an SS Panzer Division. Over the years it's been a strange sort of war between us, but now, well into the second half of the ridiculous game, they're leading me by the equivalent of six nil. But we've had some terrific truces. The sad thing is it nearly always ends in tears – mostly mine. In spite of that I must say that I've been very lucky in knowing some marvellous women and they've been very good to me. The clashes have been mostly over my selfishness and the fact that I can't bear the way most of them are so firmly in touch with reality. It is fairly typical of them that my favourite woman and wife said to me, when we split up, 'I thought you'd change and settle down.' I was drunk for most of the time I was wooing her, and surely you can see a train coming if you're standing on the line. Anyway, you don't change and settle down at forty-six.

Another trouble, I've always been at first attracted by the packaging, only to discover there was another person inside and not the one I'd dreamed of. Perhaps I'm caught in some sort of sartorial time warp, or perhaps my tastes for appearances are somewhat dated. It's odd that winning stays in a gambler's memory for longer than losing does and I find it a little depressing that all the fringe miseries of being unable to make a relationship work stick vividly, whereas happy times in the mind's eye are now in soft focus. Perhaps it's because of that that I write so much, probably too much, about loss. This may be why some people enjoy reading about low life in the *Spectator*. It probably makes them feel safer. If you're living where the grass is greener it must be reassuring to glance occasionally at a rubbish dump.

Some women, though, seem to want to turn rubbish dumps into gardens. They also seem to like little-boys-lost. Well, at fifty-two I'm afraid that game's over, but I used to be quite good at it. But dear, oh dear, the things this obsession with women and sex led to in the past. It's utterly absurd, ridiculous and laughable to think that I've been through two spates of drunken suicide attempts over two different women. But then for years and years I was terrified of living alone and of the desolation of being left. It wasn't until quite recently that I discovered that being alone can often be a luxury.

The other thing I'm getting the hang of is building enough necessary arrogance of a sort to defend myself. It has to be reciprocal. If a person doesn't like you as much as you like them then they are quite simply, by definition, the wrong person. Playing Dante to a Beatrice isn't my idea of fun.

So what is my idea of fun? A lot of people can't understand why the idiom of low life interests me, since not a lot actually happens to me. I'm like a bee buzzing around finding flowers that have already had the honey taken. But it's not quite true. I make things happen if I can. For that matter what the hell actually *happens* in a bank, insurance office or to a shopkeeper? Not a lot.

I think the thing is to try to turn the day into an event somehow in whatever small way. Even being trapped by my addiction in a few pubs, clubs, restaurants and racecourses is a freedom of a sort, and I do, after all, like my friends, which is more than I can say for lot of the high-life brigade.

Anyway, from time to time I get tastes of the high life and I can't say I envy them for much except of course their money and that's only to provide more freedom. Steering a course between the high and the low is the best journey I know. A double life is my ideal, keeping them separate from each other. And that ideal is lived by a friend of mine, a famous contemporary painter. He works very hard from the crack of dawn and then mingles with low-lifers after lunch in the afternoon. Then, most evenings, he goes home, cleans up, puts on his Savile Row suit and goes out to very up-market or at least expensive clubs and restaurants, where he mingles with the aristocracy, rich and famous. I like the mixture. Meanwhile it's back to the Coach and Horses for me.

Slightly rhyming verses for Jeff Bernard's 50th birthday

Elizabeth Smart died on 4 March 1986. This poem first appeared in *In the Meantime* (Deneau, 1985).

My Dear Jeff,
I can't say enough
how much I admire
the way you have
conducted your entire
life, and the way you have
used your marvellous Muse.
And how right she was to
choose you. Because
she's a Rare Bird who would
have retired or died
if you hadn't known how
to amuse
her, and her you.
That's one non-bogus
marriage made
on Parnassus
and *true*.

She knew
exactly what and who
she was letting herself
in for: the real You.
Drink, betting shops and pubs
are the sort of thing that rubs
her up the right way;
she'll always stay
and make you more beautiful
and witty
every day.

This is a loose love
Ode, owed
to one of my friends
who is in my special
collection of people
who make amends

for endless excruciating
boring hours
so often lived
when foolishly pursuing
stimulation,
and none occurs.

Sterne, Benchley, Leacock,
Carroll, and Nash, and Lear
are not more dear
to me than bedrock
Bernard(3).
(Do I not pay 65p
ungrudgingly weekly,
for a fixative laugh,
uniquely Jeff?,
who has become
a consolatory
addictive to me?)

Wilde would have smiled
and been beguiled
and bright enough to know
that *you* had a better
Muse in tow
than he.
Could he see
the angelic emanations
from gutters where we
all fall, while
trying to pee,
and rise, or try to rise,
unwisely, in majesty?

And Swift is bitter
and cross
and doesn't make us
feel better
at bearing our lot,
and, in his rage
at the odds,
misses the old adage
that recurs to me
often, in every mess:
'against stupidity
even the gods
are helpless.'
He
lifted furious fists
but had no effect
on the jibbering idjits.

Your subject is not mean,
Who's up, who's in,
or jockeying for position
(what a dreary sin).
Funny but kind,
your subject is justly seen
as the inexhaustible one
of nude mankind:
Yourself, in fact, drinking,
amidst the alien corn,
and explaining the amazing
joke
of being born.

Your sources–
grief and love
and the Coach and Horses
and all the things we're
thinking of
but don't admit,
because they don't fit
our grand ideas of
our own importance.
You hit the
soul on the head
when it rises
out of its lying bed,
pompous with portents
above its station,
and greedy for rewards
above its ration.

But you're never snide,
and you never hurt,
and you wouldn't want to win
on a doctored beast,
and anyhow the least

of your pleasures
resides in paltry measures.

So guard, great joker God,
please guard this great Bernard,
and let 1982
be the most brilliant year he
ever knew.
Let him be known
for the prince of men he is,
a master at taking out of
himself and us the piss.

If you will do this, God,
I'll be good all year,
and try to be better-dressed,
and soberer, and keep my
prose-style clear, (for this great
man is embedded in my heart)
I'll remain, Sir, then and only
then,
Yours sincerely,
Elizabeth Smart.

Happy days

I've just spent two days sitting on the floor surrounded by remorse-inducing memorabilia. Backache and boredom propelled me from my sick bed to clear up boxes and drawers full of old letters and papers, but it was the postcards and snaps, evidence of holidays and seemingly happier times past that ended up at grey Heathrow or with the slamming of a door – front and then car – that had me rooted to the carpet wondering for the millionth time what could or might have been. If you have tears, prepare to jerk them now. No, don't. It's been quite a laugh. I found an old divorce petition actually complaining that I was morose, sullen, non-communicative and shunning any social contact when I was *not* drinking; but what surprised me was the expression on the faces of those ladies in the holiday pics. You're standing there, a Mediterranean Jack-the-Lad under a palm tree with a long drink in one hand, peeling shoulders and self-conscious grin, and she, in spite of her sunny smile, has that look in her eyes, almost smouldering, denoting that all the while she can count the bills dropping on to the doormat at home. Fill in the balloon over her head and it would read, 'Why am I with this idiot?'

Pictures in which she or they are actually looking at you and not the camera are an even bigger giveaway. But what breaks my heart are the snaps that were taken at the time or just after you first met. Actually, they don't break my heart at

all, they just make me cringe with embarrassment. There's
that awful look of pride in new ownership that reminds me
of a salesman with a new car or a child with a new dog.
You're both sunny side up then and you think the process
of hard-boiling is going to take a hundred years. But, sitting
there on the carpet, pushing the snapshots to one side for a
minute and dipping into the old letters, the tale unfolds itself.
'Miss you terribly.' 'So looking forward to next weekend.'
'We must try harder.' 'We can't go on like this.' 'I must have
been mad to think it could work.' 'I think we should say
goodbye.' Yes, your dinner might not be in the oven but, by
Christ, your letters and snapshots are in your old drawers
and scrapbooks.

Almost as sad is the sight of those old friends. There's Fred
on the beach pulling a silly face, Jim pissed in a nightclub
and Bob waving frantically from the balcony of his room.
If you see Fred now – bump into him in a pub – he looks a
little embarrassed. He assesses the situation, peering into your
pocket with his X-ray eyes and asks, 'What are *you* doing now?'
'Oh, the same old thing,' you reply, resisting the temptation
to remind him of the time he took you aside with tears in his
eyes to tell you that Maggie was leaving him and that life was
no longer worth living. 'Still scribbling?' he asks, adding, 'No,
no. I insist. This one's on me.' The largesse is so offhand and
who'd think the four of you once squabbled over a restaurant
bill in Paris?

With luck and in two or three weeks' time I'm off to get a
breath of sun-drenched hot air into the offending lung. Alone.
But I shall still take a camera. Three years ago I got a Russian
soldier in Red Square to take a picture of me standing outside
the Kremlin. It's deeply moving. I look like another alcoholic
defector. But however awful one looks the memory banks and

scrapbooks need to be kept stoked up. The holiday show must go on. This time I'll get a snap with the local barman. We'll have our arms around each other's shoulders and if you look carefully and closely into his eyes you'll see that he's thinking, 'God, how I loathe these boring, drunken, peseta-less tourists.' The only trouble is that I may not be drunk. At the moment I can hardly keep one down, so you'll forgive me I hope if I remain yours, morose, sullen, non-communicative and shunning any social contact. That wife was quite right about not drinking. It's a disaster. If you're born two or three drinks under par you just end up with your old snaps snapping at people.

Lone Christmas

Turkeys, I suppose, spend the major part of their lives being lulled into a false sense of security and well-being. Their final demand, so to speak, comes but once and lack of rehearsals must make the final crunch an unexpected and painless event. No, I can't feel sorry for them en masse but I couldn't help shedding a tear for the one I nibbled at in the Park Lane Hilton on Christmas Day. The idea of being stuffed daily only to end up being eaten by me and an assorted bunch of fairly revolting Arabs and Iranians makes me feel that a turkey's life lacks meaning. And, talking of getting stuffed, it occurred to me as I eyed the menu that had the Last Supper been held in the Hilton the bill would have come to £500, VAT and tip included.

But it was a pretty good lunch as lunches go, even though conversation was limited to exchanges with a trainee wine waiter who'd just learnt the phrase 'full-bodied' and who kept repeating it like a parrot. I had a nice little table by the window on the first floor restaurant that overlooked Hyde Park. The grass there was like icing on an enormous cake. To my right the sun was setting over Byron's statue and to my left a hideous Arabian couple were looking down their amazing noses at me and getting high on Evian water. You can hardly blame Arabs for making their women cover their faces but you can certainly blame the men themselves for dressing in those horribly common, expensive Yves St Laurent suits that still have flared trousers. They marinate themselves in Fabergé aftershave and talk constantly of money. The idea of being whipped by these people for having the odd drink gave me the most dreadful daymares, and I shall be turning down any offers from the *Kuwait Times* to syndicate Low Life.

The population of the Hilton made me feel I was residing in the Gaza strip and they could have saved themselves fortunes if they'd put down sand instead of carpets. Behind me, a Jewish couple spent the lunch talking, not to each other, but to the waiters. 'A sausage with your stuffing, sir?' – 'Ooh, no. My husband won't eat sausages – will you, Cyril? No, he's always hated sausages, haven't you? I've tried him on sausages time and time again, but he just won't eat one – will you, darling?' In the background an incredibly naive and old-world pianist was getting little response from the ivories he was tickling heavy-handedly. He played a strange non-stop medley that comprised such leaden oldies as 'Old Man River', 'Hearts of Oak', 'Polly Wolly Doodle' and 'Rock-a-Bye Baby'.

I kicked off with an avocado, which was followed by some excellent chicken consommé. With the last sip of that, between 'Jingle Bells' and 'You Made Me Love You', a big table in front of me was taken over by a very flash Italian family. The woman immediately put me off the forthcoming turkey. She was one of those blonde icebergs I'm irresistibly drawn to and who make me feel like the *Titanic*. The packaging is obvious. Butter wouldn't melt in their mouths but gold ingots might. They wear on their backs what they've earned on them and at forty the skin begins to wrinkle around the eyes with the effort of trying to acquire even more wealth and ease. Even the children have blow-waved hair and are allowed to snap at waiters. Well, I staggered through the main course eyeing the lady's excellent legs, but my food was out of focus since I'd lost my reading and eating glasses. Over three hours at my table I consumed a modest bottle of Moulin à Vent and one large vodka. That lot came to £19.05, which I thought was pretty strong, and I also thought I was being rather nice to the *Spectator* accounts department by eschewing the wine that cost £200 a bottle. The lunch was £25, by the way. I came back to earth over the pudding. As I say, I'd lost my glasses and the waiter didn't bother to tell me that the first mouthful was still on fire. But the Hilton food is good, and the simple meal I had that night – a hamburger and chips followed by a fresh fruit salad and two drinks – was even better, although I thought £10.85 a trifle steep with 15 per cent on that.

No, where these people get you is over trifling items like 30p for a very brief telephone call. Also, another entry, 'Room service dinner – £5.40', was simply a drink and a piece of cake, if my memory serves me, which it doesn't often. And although the room was very comfortable, I thought £77 a little much. But then I'm not, like the foreign guests, in a position to regard loot as mere pieces of paper. As a lone Christmas I preferred it to being alone at home. After all it was amusing to watch other people putting such an enormous effort into a ritual that's double Dutch to them. They looked quite incredulous when Father Christmas walked into the restaurant ringing a bell and actually giving the children presents. When I signed the bill on

Boxing Day morning, all I could think of was the fact that had Pontius Pilate had any sense at all and simply put Jesus Christ on probation for a couple of years or given him a suspended sentence, then none of this would have happened.

Heroes

Let us now praise the heroes of 1985. First there was Stanley. Now Stanley's a good man. True he drinks a little and true his marriage was on the rocks because of it, but he made an effort, did Stanley, and one day last summer he told his long-suffering wife that he'd bought tickets to South Africa where they'd go for a holiday. A second honeymoon if you like, a new start, a new leaf and the slate would be clean. Well, why not? Give it a go, she thought.

Came the day they were to depart from Heathrow and Stanley had just one more little thing to do and that was to take his office staff to luncheon. His good wife was to pick him up at the restaurant at three p.m. and off they'd go. Of course, by then dear Stanley was legless having had, by the wine waiter's reckoning, twelve Remy Martins on top of the obligatory plonk. Never mind, she thought, give him one more chance. Once on the flight and once in Africa he'd be all right. Off they drove to Heathrow, Stanley hiccupping gently all the way and nodding off from time to time, and eventually they got to the check-in point where Stanley was promptly sick all over the girl who was doing the checking in. Still, his wife went along with him. Not so the airline people. At the last moment they refused Stanley a boarding pass. Now, I for one would give Stanley ten out of ten for effort. Whether or not a safari by water wagon would have saved Stanley's marriage is neither here nor there. The fact remains there was true nobility in Stanley having bought two tickets to South Africa, let alone leaving the safety of the restaurant for the hazards of flight, and I'd willingly go into the jungle with him and probably will.

And let us not forget the heroines of yesteryear. What about Eva? This extremely practical and sensible woman seduced one of England's leading bookmakers after the last race of the Royal Ascot meeting. A nasty man who refused me credit once when I was under tremendous pressure, he fancies himself as being a staying satyr brimful of stamina. In fact, as Eva later told me, he's a sexual bore. Anyway, into bed they got and after an hour and a half of making love to her he was still making love to her and, as she shrewdly observed, you can have too much of a good thing. So she turned on the bedside light and began to read *Middlemarch*. Came the dawn and the collapse of the revolting penciller she'd ploughed through five chapters. A tremendous compliment to George Eliot, don't you think?

Another who did well last year was Michael Nolles who fell down the concrete stairs to his basement flat. Yes, he fell head over heels, breaking a leg badly and landing outside the door of his flat. His wife, hearing his moans, opened the door – which opened outwards – and smashed his head in. Then, assuming he was drunk, she closed the door and left him there. By morning, hypothermia had set in. He now limps with a touch of humility and is hoping to buy a bungalow.

And, lest we forget, Jeremy. Since I reported trying to get him back into the Queen's Elm he has been barred from the Cadogan Arms, Finches, the wine bar next to it and been shown the yellow card by the Coach and Horses and the Man in the Moon. As a psychiatrist once told me, geographical escapes are futile, but I can see no alternative for Jeremy and I must recommend Northampton which has, I'm told, more pubs to the acre than any town in England.

And I'm still getting reports of the late lamented and lovable Michael Dempsey. Last week a colleague told me that on the occasion of Michael's last visit to Ireland he stayed in a town which boasted some thirty pubs. Within two days, Michael was considered to be a poet, gentleman and scholar in five of them and barred from four others.

Dempsey's last bow was more spectacular in my opinion than Sherlock Holmes at the Reichenbach Falls. One of his last public appearances was made at the Lamb and Flag in Lamb's Conduit Street. Faced by a bevy of the Right to Choose Party, he said, 'I'm glad to see that you are all wearing your Right to Choose badges. This means that you are all opting to have abortions. In that case, you will not be producing children who are as hideous and revolting as yourselves.'

Cards

It's been a perfectly dreadful week relieved only by the reappearance of Tom Baker, who's finished his stint in *Treasure Island* and survived the dreadful parrot, and I've decided definitely to give up playing poker on Thursday nights. Everyone thinks they can play poker. It's a sort of Mitty thing. The green baize, the cigar-smoke haze, the occasional clink of ice in the glass breaking the tense silence or the flick and snap of a card and the superb feeling of filling a straight before pulling that pile of money towards you. Well, my Thursday night games haven't been quite like that. For one thing we have a Spanish waiter who's quite mad and who can turn a pair of fives into a drama on a par with *Aïda*, and for another there's a tendency for people to turn up at eight p.m. far too smashed to make any sense of the game. Admittedly it's a friendly game in so far as we all start with a lousy £10-worth of 10p pieces but where's the romance in winning – no, losing – £10? I felt so ghastly the morning after the last game I thought I would go in search of one card who could cheer me up, Peter Langan. Sadly he wasn't in his little brasserie – he's driving the population of Los Angeles mad at the moment – but I had a drink at the bar and reflected on what an extraordinary man he is. He has style, you know. Some time ago there was a fire in the kitchen. They dialled 999 and sent for the fire brigade. While they awaited the firemen Langan tried to keep the fire under control with champagne. I'm not claiming that it was Louis Roederer Cristal Brut, neither is he, but it does indicate a certain amount of imagination and a healthy contempt for wine with bubbles in it.

Which reminds me of the story I heard of another card who shall have to remain nameless, but a restaurateur as well. This man arrived home at six in the morning after a night on the tiles, totally legless and bursting for a pee. He fell out of his taxi and just as he was about to urinate in desperation into the gutter he spotted a dear old couple approaching who were taking their dog for an early morning trot. A vestige of decorum prompted him to do the decent thing and he turned away. As the seconds went by he became more desperate and stumbling up the steps to his front door he aimed his keys at the lock which he missed and missed again. He was now at his wits' end – no great distance to travel – and he inserted his member through the letterbox. Now, it so happens that at that precise moment his landlord, an angry man who had been trying to evict our hero for some time, was walking down the staircase with his dog, with the perfectly reasonable intention of taking some exercise. You may imagine his and Fido's horror when confronted not with the terror of a buff envelope but with our man's member. The hound backed snarling and steaming, the landlord – one can only imagine – clasped his fluttering heart and our man politely turned his head to say 'Good morning' to the couple he had originally tried to avoid offending. There has to be a moral somewhere but I'm damned if I can see it.

Yes, the Soho cards are a lot better than the ones I've been dealt at the tables recently, which reminds me… Brian's just been sprung after sixteen months inside. I hear he didn't have too bad a time of it since they put him in charge of the kitchen – surely, the library apart, the cushiest job in the nick and the best place in which to fiddle therein. It'll be cheering to see him again. Meanwhile, here in the Coach and Horses depression sets in again. As I write to you at my desk in the saloon a Maltese gentleman at my side is actually studying the Crayford and Bristol greyhound racing cards in the *Sun*. I ask you. Dogs – Crayford – Bristol – the *Sun*. Is this the end of civilisation as we know it? You could slam the letterbox on the member of such a man.

Unbalanced

The past few days have been just about as bad as bad can be. I'm still getting some nasty twinges because of the man who cut off his penis. Yes, if you didn't happen to see it in the papers this man cut off his penis and threw it on the fire so that he could devote the rest of his life to God without any distractions. It seems that he and his wife had been discussing the horrific business for the past twelve years and last week he took the plunge. With her blessing, wouldn't you know. Well, I've been pondering aspects of this bizarre do-it-yourself surgery and some interesting points arise apart from the very obvious fact that the wife must be a *Guardian* reader (she's probably already received her 'Jill'll Fix It' badge).

But why did the wretched man choose his perfectly harmless penis? Surely he must have realised that sex is in the head and that his penis was merely his solo instrument in a far bigger concerto than you or I will ever comprehend. I mean, if I wanted to devote the rest of my life to any one thing at all without being distracted I'd cut off my head. Then, of course, I can't help wondering what their sex life must have been like during the past twelve years of disarmament talks. Pretty tentative I should think and, with the thought of the dreadful redundancy to come in the back of his mind, maybe non-existent. And another thing, why dispose of the black-balled would-be member on a fire? What on earth does he think wastepaper baskets are for? I suppose he was committing it to hell. And then, in spite of what must have been considerable post-operative pain, he discharged himself from hospital after only three days – that is, if a man sans penis can discharge himself at all.

The fact that God didn't intervene in the matter proves my theory that He is a woman after all. But what a typically selfish woman that wife. You wouldn't want to go into the jungle with her. I mean, she could have cut off something herself, even if it had only been her hair, just to show willing. What a Grimm business. If the silly man had never got married in the first place he would only have had to cut off his right arm, assuming he's right-handed that is.

What a mug. Wouldn't you be suspicious? I can just imagine a wife saying to me, 'Now, come along. Be a darling and cut it off.' I'd think, 'Now hang on a minute. Is she trying to tell me something? Is this some sort of clue?' I'm not daft, you know. And another thing. If you were in his boots having done the deed how would you feel if you saw your renegade wife chatting up the milkman? There's a possible television comedy series in this.

Another criticism I have to make about this now top-heavy evangelist is that to take twelve years to make up one's mind about anything shows a certain lack of resolution. If I was lying in my bath feeling slightly disgruntled and pondering a penisectomy I'd do it there and then. Or would I? Perhaps not. Whereas his pruning was quite ruthless, I'd probably chicken out and take it an inch at a time.

So, where will he go from here? What will guide him? Speaking for myself – a bad habit I must get out of – I'm where I am today having followed for thirty-odd years the direction in which my penis has pointed. The resultant emotional aggravation has been colossal, but I wouldn't have done without it. The aggravation I mean. How slow, calm and tedious would the rat race be if none of us jockeys had whips.

Yes, as I say, it's been a horrid week and I can't help wondering whether our man has had second thoughts. Dear God, it's a sad life. What people do to each other is bad enough. Now I'm beginning to think that madness is self-inflicted. Never trust a man who's not grateful for small mercies.

Poles apart

For a moment I thought I was going mad. There I was, sitting quietly in the Coach and Horses minding my own business and having my eleven a.m. gargle, when this man walked up to me and said, 'D'you remember Peter the Pole who worked in the dirty bookshop in St Anne's Court? You know, the bloke whose father is an ear-nose-and-throat surgeon in Warsaw? Well anyway, he's just moved to Hounslow.' There's no answer to that. It has to be the most extraordinary address I've ever had aimed at me. Not only do I not know Peter the Pole, have never even heard of him, nor care greatly how his father scrapes a living,

I also have very little time for a man who moves to Hounslow
and wouldn't trust him an inch. But what an amazing thing to
walk up to someone out of the blue and ask them that.

So I said no, I didn't know the said Peter the Pole, and I
turned my back on the man – feeling distinctly apprehensive
– and continued to ponder the meaning of life and man's
incredible ascent from the discovery of fire and the invention
of the wheel to Hounslow.

Well might I have been apprehensive. Just as I was beginning
to feel a little calmer the charming Mrs Balon, Norman's
unfortunate mother, snuck up behind me and whispered, 'I
bet you didn't know my grandfather had an umbrella shop in
Gower Street.' Oddly enough the possibility of Mrs Balon's
grandfather ever having had an umbrella shop in Gower Street
has never crossed my seething brain, although, God knows,
I'm a broad-minded man. Well, after a short but emotional
discussion on the subject of the 1890 umbrella boom in Gower
Street, Mrs Balon and I went our separate ways: she to the
snack bar and me back to what was rapidly becoming a strictly
medicinal drink. Just as I was draining that, a man approached
me and said, with a thick Glaswegian accent, 'Hey Jimmy, I bet
you've never seen a black man's funeral.'

Then it clicked. I was in the middle of some dreadful plot.
These mad utterances were codes or ciphers like the *Thirty-nine
Steps* or the *Five Orange Pips* or the *Dancing Men*. Obviously I
was to meet a man with a Polish accent in Hounslow who
would give me a message to deliver to a dead black man in
an umbrella shop in Gower Street. Nothing so extraordinary
about that after all, is there? But it called for another drink,
and just as I ordered it the Glaswegian sprang at me again.
'No, you haven't,' he said. 'When they die they make them
into tyres.'

Long-distance

If one needed proof of the stupidity of Americans beyond the democratic election of both Mr Carter and Mr Reagan then surely Heaven's Union, the celestial telegram service run by a Gabriel Gabor, is just that. In case you didn't read about it the idea is that you send a telegram of up to fifty words to relatives and friends who've heard the guvnor in the sky call 'last orders' and who've subsequently departed for the Great Beyond. The messengers who carry these mad messages are terminally ill patients who memorise them before they snuff it and Mr Gabor cops £23 for each one. I find it fairly sick.

'How d'you do. I hear you're dying. Jolly good. Well done. Look, I wonder if you'd do me a favour and ask my wife where she left my gold cufflinks. I'll pay for a reply which you can give to a baby that's going to be born after you get there. And oh, by the way, while you're there ask her was she being knocked off by Bill Smith. Thanks. Have a good trip.'

But that's not all Mr Gabor has up his sleeve. He's got talking tombstones. Before your missus pegs out she records a message on to tape and then, when you visit her grave on a Sunday afternoon to put a vase of dandelions on it, you press a button and, lo, you hear the same old story again. 'Hello, is that you, Jeff? I'm amazed you managed to tear yourself away from the pub to come and visit me. Your dinner's in the oven. Honestly, I thought you'd change and settle down. Don't you ever think of the future. Christ, this headache is killing me. I suppose you lost it all at the betting shop. Stop staring at that woman at the next grave. You're drunk again. You make me sick. Don't bother to come next Sunday. I'll be all right. Don't worry about me. I don't suppose you ever have, anyway.

Always thinking about yourself. Me, me, me. I told you you make me sick, didn't I? Yes, of course I did. Well, good bloody bye.'

Mind you, the chances of outliving a wife are pretty remote, so I don't think the question will arise and I'm wondering if Mr Gabor has any messengers bound for hell. I'm delaying the trip there for as long as possible myself but should any readers care to send me £23 I'm willing to drive over Beachy Head after one final fling. Yes, I'm definitely not going to heaven. I'm sure it's very white and cold, sparsely furnished with maybe a bit of shining chrome here and there and altogether rather like a modern hospital. I suppose they sit about in little groups talking about the old days and gesticulating limply with their wings and enquiring of all newcomers, 'Any messages?'

Yes, I don't think hell will be a lot different from where I'm at now. In fact I'm fairly well convinced that I died in 1932 and this is it. I mean, just look at Norman in the Coach. All he needs is a trident in one hand – I must get him to take his shoes off to see if he's got cloven hooves – and there's your devil. God knows, most of the customers are griffins and gargoyles or advocates and I'm certainly getting my fair share of messages. I particularly like the ones I get on the phone when Mum Balon answers it and asks me across the room, having forgotten to cover the receiver, 'Are you here?' 'Who is it?' 'I don't *think* he's here but he says who is it.'

But this American business; they've got to be mad. A psychologist who counsels the terminally ill in Los Angeles says of Mr Gabor's message service: 'It could provide the dying with a sense of purpose.' That's a great bloody comfort. I'm pretty sure I'm dying and my purpose is to hang on to life. Like grim death.

Questionable

Two weeks ago *The Times* carried another of those silly, melodramatic features on the subject of alcoholism. It was headed by the usual old questions which, if you could answer yes to any of them, showed that there was 'serious cause for alarm'. Well, the more I looked at these questions the less alarmed I felt. In fact I've now come to the conclusion that I don't drink enough. Just look at this nonsense.

Q. Do you find that you drink embarrassingly quickly and have finished your drink long before those around you?

J.B. The speed at which I drink embarrasses others. That's to say I am frequently outfumbled. Peter Owen, for example, last bought a round in 1971. Such men need to be reminded that one swallow does not make a summer.

Q. Do you have time off from work because of drinking; or has your work performance suffered because of alcohol?

J.B. The situation is very much the reverse. Work frequently interferes with my drinking. Last week I spent an hour drinking Perrier before going to see a publisher, while all around me were falling down. And another thing. Drinking *is* my work. I was once paid £500 for an article on that very subject.

Q. Do your family and friends express concern over the amount you drink?

J.B. Well, as my big brother says, 'Concern is a very elastic word.' I think they express a mild surprise at where on earth the money comes from and they simply look into their glasses a little harder. My friend, the philanthropist and thespian Tom Baker, is concerned that I don't drink enough. He says that if I could get a bit more vodka in I might spew up a novel.

Q. Have there been family quarrels because of your drinking? Are you becoming difficult, irritable and testy after drinking?

J.B. I believe there was a tremendous row in 1934 as to whether I should be fed Nestles or Cow & Gate milk. Am I *becoming* difficult, testy and irritable? You must be joking. I'm impossible. After closing time last Tuesday I hit a Greek greengrocer in Goodge Street who asked me not to feel his cucumbers. I also have three ex-wives who can testify to my testiness. Especially *before* drinking.

Q. *Do you find that your memory is getting worse? Have you ever had loss of memory after a heavy drinking session?*

J.B. Quite honestly I can't remember ever having had a heavy drinking session. Can you repeat the question please?

Q. *Do you order yourself a double when the rest of the party are drinking singles, or do you order yourself a quick extra drink while collecting an order from the bar?*

J.B. None of my 'party' drinks singles. They do have some style, you know. As to ordering a quick drink I can tell you that there is no such thing in either the French pub or the Coach and Horses. Both the barman in the French and Michael in the Coach take more time to serve a drink than it took the Royal Navy to get to the Falkland Islands.

Q. *Do you have an uneasy feeling that you are drinking too much; that you no longer have control over your drinking; that you can no longer take it or leave it?*

J.B. No, but I do have an uneasy feeling that I won't be able to take it for much longer. I live in dread of hepatitis and the obligatory six months' abstention that follows it.

Q. *Has your sexual drive and ability suffered because of your drinking?*

J.B. Mind your own fucking business. Actually, I find alcohol to be an aphrodisiac. Especially for the duration of a hangover. Unfortunately, since I discovered Smirnoff – and this is an unsolicited testimonial – I no longer get hangovers.

Q. *Do you…?*

J.B. I'm sorry, I can't answer any more questions. It's nearly opening time.

Wanderlust

I'm thinking, quite seriously, of retiring. The list of things I haven't done is far too long and I'm well into the second half of this ridiculous game. While I was sitting on a train last weekend and gazing out of the window at Oxfordshire and Berkshire it occurred to me, for example, that I've never fished or lazed my way up the Thames in a luxury cabin cruiser crewed by voluptuous young women. Who needs a desk and a typewriter? Neither have I whiled away the day on a golf course and in the club house. Yes, the sight of the River Thames, even in dreaded Pangbourne of ghastly memories, had me dreaming of picnic hampers in bee-loud glades by quiet waters, chilled white wine and pâté under summer skies, no deadlines just fishing lines and distant girlish laughter, but not too distant of course.

Weather permitting, my intention this summer is to take a boat from Reading to Oxford, stopping at every pub and decent restaurant on the way. Whether I shall make the trip before or after my Greek holiday I'm not sure. Yes, a delightful friend of a friend I met at the weekend has put his villa and yacht at my disposal and I think I might throw this typewriter out of the window in a few minutes' time. Neither have I sipped raki in Istanbul or fed peacocks in Kashmir, and Mexico beckons. True, I've eaten bread and dripping in Camden Town and downed a half of bitter in Notting Hill, but I shall be fifty in two weeks' time and I haven't sailed up the Nile or seen Hong Kong – in fact, the highlights so far have been pretty dim. Had I video replays to command, the choices would be fairly sparse. They certainly wouldn't concern *any* work I've ever done, except for three months with Joan Littlewood, but I would like to see playbacks of my wedding days just to remind me of the fund of optimism I once had. Why the sight of the Thames should trigger off these middle-aged meanderings I'm not quite sure, but it did and I'd very much like to tie an apple in my handkerchief and take a walk around the world. I suppose the sight of the water got me thinking of boats, then ships, and I can stare at cargo ships all day dreaming and wondering where they've been and where they're going. As for staring into the mirror, a pastime less compulsive than it used to be, I can see exactly where I've been and where I'm going and the impending birthday which has recently become an obsession is concentrating my mind horribly.

Readers wishing to commit suicide are invited to apply for berths on the good ship *Miss Right* sailing up the Thames sometime in July. Whether there'll be room for you all I'm not sure, but if you're feeling anything like me we might have to get a bigger boat, as the man said in *Jaws*. In that event we could conclude this entertainment in the blue of the Mediterranean. Dave in the French pub has suggested time and time again that we hire a bus and drive over Beachy Head, but I think it lacks style.

It could have been a glimpse of the boathouse at Pangbourne where I used to smoke illicit cigarettes that got me going for, after all, time's stood still since then. One's still smoking illicit cigarettes, so to speak, but it's just that one no longer cares about being caught. Come to think of it quite a few of us were caught a long time ago. So, is it too late to take early retirement and trail our hands in the waters of the Thames? Not if we hurry and act now. I call on all of you who aren't enjoying your work to give up. Take the cotton wool out of your ears and *listen* to the sirens. Join me on the rocks. Meanwhile, I shall contemplate further on the business of being fifty, have a good cry and a drink. Not necessarily in that order.

Candidates

If you answered that extraordinary Dateline computer dating ad with absolute honesty I wonder what on earth you'd get. Well, I don't. I mean I wonder what *I'd* get. They ask, in the bit you fill in and send off to them, 'Do you consider yourself Shy, Extrovert, Adventurous, Family Type, Clothes-conscious, Generous, Outdoor Type, Creative, Practical, Intellectual.' Then the loons go on to say, 'Indicate which activities and interests you enjoy' etc, and they list a load of guff whereby you could con anyone from a distance and land yourself a meet with something really awful.

Now, one is fairly civilised and likes classical music and poetry and knows that there's nothing like half an hour's chat with the barman on the subject of the polyphonic motets of Lassus, but who on earth wants to meet a woman whose idea of a swinging weekend is two hours in the British Museum Reading Room followed by a nut cutlet picnic in the park reading Keats out loud before setting off for an archaeological dig with knapsacks stuffed with tapes of the Matthew Passion, *Under Milk Wood* and the late quartets? I have a vision of pitching a tent by the dig, diverting her attention by pointing out a lesser crested grebe, quickly going through her handbag and discovering she's not on the pill. Thank you and goodnight. You could tell a woman like that that it was opening time and she'd think you were talking about the British Film Institute.

On the other hand, if you ticked off, in the list of activities and interests, Pubs and Clubs, Jazz, Sport, Good Food and Travelling you'd be landed with an equally ghastly disaster area. She'd almost certainly have laddered stockings, eyes that had worked overtime at crying, a handbag containing a rubbish dump, thrush, a smoker's cough, an Equity card, and a bedsitter with a single bed in Clapham. (Sorry about the Clapham bit, Sheila.)

But the list of what you may consider yourself to be is a trifle daft, not to say short. Shy? Extrovert? Well, both of course. Generous? Yes, and mean and selfish too. Outdoor type? Well I've never found a secret tunnel to the Coach and Horses, but I have occasionally managed to unwind in the gutter after a hard day's work. What about Family Type? I've tried to start more families than you've had hot dinners, madam. Clothes-conscious? I am aware of the fact that they're mostly on the floor and under the bed, if that's what you mean. Creative? Yes. Freud tells us that all babies are creative. Practical? Well, I'm still breathing but I believe that walls should be painted by decorators and windows cleaned by window cleaners. Intellectual? As an ox.

Two other things that strike me as a little odd are, first, that there's no mention of sex. It still takes place I'm told and, come to think of it, I hope it's like riding a bike. You'd be odd to want to date and meet someone through Dateline who wasn't in a possible legover situation, I should have thought. I mean, it is in the back of one's mind occasionally. The other odd thing is the question about whether one is interested in conversation. Do they mean that there is any possibility that you *couldn't* be? Have they got mates lined up for us who've had their tongues cut out? Perhaps they've got the charwoman of the British Museum Reading Room on their books and are trying to shift her. What Dateline should do is to differentiate between conversation and anecdote and so, I'm afraid, should many pub acquaintances of mine. In fact, as the excellent poet and gentleman George Barker once told me, 'Anecdote is not a form of conversation.' (A sign should be so printed and hung on the wall of every pub in England.)

No, I shan't fill in the form, I'll simply wait and hope to bump into the stranger who'll laugh at my jokes and worship the ground I walk on, as the man said.

Titbits

I don't know why, but recently I've been wondering what on earth it must feel like to be a guide dog. I don't much like dogs but I do love labradors. They're the only dogs that are kind, soppy, forgiving and kind to children. I'd willingly guide a blind labrador. I had one once – a bitch – I called her Smedley and she was pretty extraordinary. One day – during a period when I was desperately skint – she ate an entire weekend's shopping when my back was turned. A shoulder of lamb, some chops, six herrings, the lot – you name it. I kicked hell out of her and she merely retreated to a corner and gazed at me with adoration, wagging her tail ever so tentatively and slowly. You could half kill a dog like that but it'd still love you.

But what of fish? I'm thinking of getting a fish tank and stuffing its waters with inscrutable, flat, slow-thinking things from the oriental deep. If my abode were bigger I'd get a soothing hippopotamus. Looking at them, like looking at Denis Healey, Clement Freud and Kenneth Muir, one is assured that, in spite of being up to here in shit, there's really no *hurry*. Another fancy of mine is for a bird cage. A budgie like Bernard Levin, a vulture like Enoch Powell and a canary like Mrs Thatcher. And what of ferrets like Peter Shore? Put him down a hole and he'd come up with next Sunday's lunch. Then of course there's the taxidermist-defying Cyril Smith. Badger from *The Wind in the Willows*? Not half nice enough. Moby Dick? Too pale. Shirley Williams? A poodle.

This, of course, brings me to just how you'd cook people given your Andes-air-crash-and-subsequent-starvation situation. The recipe isn't the only problem, there's also the matter of where and what part of the anatomy you'd start at. Malcolm Muggeridge is a very slender shish kebab, whereas his disciple, Richard Ingrams, the black-and-white man of television, is simply a piece of burned toast. Martin Amis and Claire Tomalin are olives. Our old friend Alan Watkins boiled beef and carrots.

And what of closer to home? What of that silly game of naming all sorts of things whereby your companion has to guess who the hell you're referring to? In all honesty, picking myself, I find it a real putdown. I know I'm shepherd's pie, a second-hand paperback, a pair of grey flannel trousers, a 1950 Austin Cambridge, a two-mile handicap hurdler, a Kleenex, a paper clip, an unsharpened pencil (HB2), and an unsolicited advertisement shoved through and up my own letterbox, but at least I'm a large vodka, lime, ice and soda and deserve grilling, marinating and serving hot.

And what about our dear contributors? How on earth do you prepare, cook and serve the likes of Bron Waugh, a man who suffers fools *less* gladly than anyone I know. I think he'd have to be garnished with capers, whereas Ingrams should be pickled. Our editor should be covered in a benign cream sauce and the readers who send letters flambéed. (Ladies, of course, may be slightly more nourishing. A shoulder of Antonia Fraser. Spare ribs of Jill Tweedie.) Should the granaries of the world run out, get blown up or go bad, we've always got each

other. Meanwhile, I lick my lips and heave in contemplation of
the passable feast involving Loren and Wedgwood Benn. May
my plane never crash in the Andes or anywhere.

Within limits

> The Middlesex Hospital,
> Mortimer Street,
> London W1

H.M. Prison,
Stanford Hill,
Sheerness, Kent

Dear Ken: Isn't it just typical that both you and I should be
in open prisons during Royal Ascot week? Perhaps we should
confine our sinning to the winter months, although, as far as
you're concerned, conditions would be a little sharper than
they would be for me. Eva told me she'd been to see you and
that you *seemed* to be bearing up. I take my hat off to you. I'm
here for just a few days and already gloom descends only to
be lifted by trifling entertainments like eating fairly awful food,
ticking off items on the following day's menu and chasing
the newspaper man down the corridor as he tries to escape
without making a sale. A sadist I shouldn't wonder. But I
shouldn't moan to you of all people, banged up as you are in
a dormitory full of what might be a very dodgy lot. My cell,
as it were, consists of four and my three companions are dead
ringers for any and all the other trios I've ever served time with
in hospitals. It's a bit like being in rep.

Mr James is the paisley dressing gown sort and the paisley
dressing gown has usually seen better days. He has silver hair,

a clipped military moustache and Tiptree jam on top of his locker and not the cheap stuff. He does the *Daily Telegraph* crossword, usually has trouble with the 'waterworks' and has a rather genteel sort of visitor. He often thinks he's dying but he's as tough as leather. On my left we have Mr Croft who has a pituitary gland disorder which seems to fascinate him as much as it does the medical staff. He's fat, farts a fair amount and is an extremely useful dustbin and waste disposal unit when my friends and visitors bring me excessive amounts of fruit. He's a *Daily Mirror* crossword man and, unlike most tabloid addicts, he's delightfully unsycophantic towards the Middlesex staff. Not a forelock tugger this one. He drinks vast quantities of orangeade and has a strangely musical snore. Last night he changed key at least four times. Very fond of telling the nurses that they're the light of his life.

On my immediate right my fellow sufferer is Mr Jones who absolutely laps up tests of any kind, blood lettings, X-rays and inquisitions from students. The Joneses of the hospital world would be nothing without their illnesses. Diabetes to Jones is what eggs are to bacon. It's just as well for him that the condition is incurable. But he's not daft. He can read a paper, urinate, smoke a cigarette and listen to Radio 2 on his earphones all at the same time and that makes some professional jugglers look a trifle green. Last night he fell asleep with the earphones in and I was tempted to wake him up with a sharp switch over to Radio 3. The funny thing about a lot of Joneses is the way their wives seem proud of them being ill: 'Ooh yes, George has been terribly ill. He nearly died last year, didn't you, George? Eight hours they said he had but he's still here, aren't you, George?'

As you may imagine, my visitors are slightly different. Norman came to see me yesterday and brought me a vast amount of fruit and cheese. He said I'd been missed that lunch-hour session in the Coach and I said how could I be missed I'd only been in the Middlesex for a few hours. 'Business is business,' he said. And I thought I'd never be loved for my money.

By the way, I gather from your letter to our mutual friend that you are incarcerated with some faily childish nuts and that there was a fracas in your hut over a Mars bar recently. It's pretty much the same here and we have a daily drama in the day room over what we'll watch on television. Normally and quite rightly it should go by a majority vote, but last night an Irishman flipped when we opted for the news and not an epic about some stolen emeralds dumped in a lake by a villain and safeguarded by piranha fish. The Irishman went quite berserk and called me and Mr Jones some horrible names. Unfortunately for him he's on a drip and it's quite difficult to hit yours truly – slow on his feet this week thanks to various drugs – when you're attached to a stand supporting a bottle of saline solution. Anyway, I had a word with him this morning – a captive audience you might say – and he's been told that we're watching Royal Ascot today come what may, otherwise he'll be in need of medical care. I hope the atmosphere is better in the nick and I hope to see you in time for the Manchester November Handicap.

Yours, Jeff.

Words of wisdom

Dear Bill,

Forgive the familiarity but if we're going to correspond with each other I can't keep addressing you as William, Prince of Wales. Anyway, what prompted me to drop you a line was that pompous balderdash Sir William Rees-Mogg wrote in the *Sunday Times* about your family and implying that you should play the great game of life with a straight bat. Take it from me, old chap, that the difference between a cow shot and an exquisite late cut is simply a matter of timing. I didn't get where I am today with a straight bat.

As to your family and ancestors I must warn you, as one directly descended from Richard Neville, Warwick the Kingmaker, don't count your chickens before they're hatched. Oh, and another warning, if you ever hear your father utter the word Gordonstoun, run for your life. And Bill, talking of life, I always say you only get out of it what you put into it.

Well, I expect you're feeling a little disgruntled, but none of us chooses our parents. Your grandmother is the one to keep an eye on and I advise you to get on the right side of her. I was sick over her tulips under the Royal Box at Ascot in 1971 when I was the *Sporting Life* columnist and you don't see yours truly mentioned in the Birthday Honours List very often. Incidentally, you could take a page out of her book and take up horse racing as a hobby. You get to meet some funny people although her racing manager, Lord Porchester, isn't my idea of a joke; but the bar is open all afternoon.

Sorry, I'm rambling on a bit and all I meant to say was good luck to you. By the way, take a tip from me and stay out of Wales even if you are the Prince of it. They're a horrible bloody lot and God alone knows what your great uncle Ted was doing chatting up those miners. Now he was a card, but more about him when you're a little older. Which brings me to marriage and a word in your shell-like on the subject, if I may, having taken the plunge more times than I care to remember. Your mum and dad are going to try and find you a right one when the time comes to get you a Queen. Hold out, Bill. Don't get stuck with any old bird from Lichtenstein, Schleswig Holstein, Luxembourg, the Gold Coast or the Falkland Islands. Marry for love, never get anything on the HP and never trust a cabinet.

I do hope this letter doesn't find you as it leaves me. I'm making another appearance in court tomorrow and your granny can detain people at her pleasure and it's a pleasure that can last for thirty years. Thank God you'll never see the inside of a nick. Not unless another Oliver Cromwell emerges from the Fens anyway. Yes, it's not all laughs being a prince or a king. You've got your Charles I getting his redundancy, your Princes in the Tower, Richard II getting his, George III going bonkers, Victoria laying the table for two and, on top of all that, you've got some twit from the *Sunday Times* writing your biography and making a bomb out of it.

Mind you, there are compensations. You've got nice accommodation and I can vouch for the shooting at Sandringham, having bagged a pheasant there one night in '69. You won't go short of a few bob and you'll be able to get away at weekends. I suppose you'll have to go into the navy, cut ribbons and open bridges, plant trees on new housing estates, stand on balconies and wave to American tourists, but at the end of the day you'll be able to put your feet up and decree the odd nightcap or two.

So there we are. We drank your health in the Coach and Horses last week – all week to be truthful – and although Norman is a bit choked that you're not Jewish he sends his regards. As for the bloke who said 'Put not your trust in princes', he didn't know you, did he, Bill?

Well, I'll say cheerio now and remain your subjective subject, Jeff.

Half measures

I'm getting a little sick of Soho. There was a time when you could always find somebody there to talk to – your actual conversation I mean – but recently it's been all World Cup and, for longer than that, money. It's really awful how money and the wretched subject of the cost of living have become the main talking points not just in Soho but everywhere. Like the man said about having had an unhappy childhood, money is not a fit subject for conversation. What's more it's the ones who are fairly well-lined – staff hacks on national newspapers and advertising people – who do the most moaning about money. The Americans have a phrase for it, 'crying poor', and it's particularly insulting to cry poor to a man who's holding sweet bugger all in his bin. But now there's yet another form of moaning and it appears in print written by journalists who get banged up when they go to report on wars. Surely it's part of the job and to be expected; I've a funny feeling that the man who got nicked after chatting to the Queen while sitting on the edge of her bed was from the *Sunday Times* Insight Team.

This one seems destined for Broadmoor. To ask the Queen for a cigarette is rock bottom and it's also being a trifle mean with your expenses. I know that most journalists live on their expenses and bank their salaries but it reeks of meanness and I expect a conversational moan about the cost of living led up to the business of tapping Her Majesty for a fag. Another giveaway was the business of stealing a half bottle of wine. It's the half that appeals to me. I have seen halves being bought by men who think they're actually entertaining some poor woman in a restaurant and I'm damned if I can think of anything less stylish. Perhaps half bottles are kept for the staff. A footman's life is terribly hard. It's also ludicrous to assume that the Queen smokes in bed. To nod off while rereading *Black Beauty* and set that lot on fire would be a major disaster, although experts tell me that heat can improve wine. (A wine merchants in Dean Street was hit by incendiary bombs during the Blitz and apparently it performed miracles for what was saved from the cellar.) And where was the Duke. Raiding the fridge?

No it must have been a very nasty experience all round and I'm no stranger to being asked for cigarettes by people when I'm lying in my bed. Usually what's happened is that I've jumped the gun by getting into bed thinking I'd be followed. But what these ladies do is light up a cigarette and then give you a hundred specious reasons for having to go home. 'My husband may phone from Paris.' 'My cat can't bear to be left alone.' 'But we've only known each other for a day.' 'Listen, I like you. I really do, but not like that.' 'The babysitter will go mad if I'm late.' Sadly I've never had a footman to summon and have these people thrown out before they smoke all my cigarettes. I resign myself to the situation, take a Valium and then fall asleep and burn the bedspread with the last fag. I now have a fire extinguisher by my bed but I never really know whether to aim it at my privates, the lady or the bedspread.

But, skint as I am, I wouldn't give house-room to a half bottle of anything. And now I'm off to Kingsclere for a ten-week rest from Buckingham Palace perils and World Cup post-mortems, but I fear they'll be discussing the cost of living in the local where I may pop in for the entire full-size bottle occasionally. I shall be reporting to you on the subject of the countryside in July, herbaceous borders, cuckoo spit, possible fairies at the bottom of the *Guardian* and with luck someone beautiful may break into my bedroom and ask me for a cigarette. If it's my favourite clairvoyant I shall give the footman the night off.

Back to nature

Typing, like eating, at a table in a sunshine-filled garden is nearly always impracticable. I am blinded by the whiteness of the paper, and wind rips the bottom half of it back into the keys and there is always a wasp lurking behind me, like a sadistic schoolmaster, wanting to see what I've written. I eat my lunch by the herbaceous border and am joined by every insect in Kingsclere. The merest of breezes cools that which should be hot, before the first bite. My Earl Grey tea is cold before I take the first sip and the bluebottle swimming on the surface is living proof of it. In desperation I switch to vodka and the ice melts away as quickly as a man you've helped. Hacks should work in smoke-filled unventilated rooms, beneath an Anglepoise. Even the charm of the rustic soundtrack begins to grate. The church bells, at first reminiscent of *the* Elegy and all that, go on for just that bit too long and the vicar next door has been giving his lawn a short back and sides for three hours and the motor mower begins to sound like one of those wretched motorbikes in London ridden by psychopathic messenger boys.

But of course it is all very lovely. The only nagging in my mind is that the friends I'm caretaking and cat-sitting for – they're gorging themselves on *fruits de mer* in and around Honfleur – should return unexpectedly and catch me with a dirty ashtray. Consequently I leap from garden to house every five minutes to wipe a surface or wash up a cup and glass. Apart from Great Portland Street not being outside the bedroom window, another bonus is the Crown in Kingsclere. It has just about the best pub food I've come across. Unfortunately, a recommendation from the likes of Egon Ronay and not me tends to fill a place with tourists, or passing trade as they are called. But the landlord's heart is in the right place and I go there every day to unwind. Actually, I don't, and I don't understand that phrase. I drink to wind *up*.

Between the Crown and writing to you, dear reader, my other work is making splendid and rapid progress. I speak, of course, of my long-awaited autobiography. Last week, when I arrived, I wrote my name at the top left-hand corner of a piece of paper and the very next day I wrote the figure '1' opposite. Sometimes my grim determination frightens me. Luckily I have enough self-discipline to stop when all work and no play makes Jack a dull boy and I took myself to Newbury races last Saturday to have another look at the human race. I took my brand new binoculars with me – Russian-made, excellent and extraordinarily cheap – and beheld strange things through them. First, a measure poured out by the racing caterers, Ring & Brymer, and secondly the wintry smile of experience on my ex-wife's face, easily the most attractive face there. She's got a new gimmick now. She keeps brushing non-existent dandruff from my shoulders. This is one of the best and simplest put-downs I know of. The other is to say to someone of me within my earshot, 'He's very sweet *really*'. It's the emphasis on the word 'really' that gets me; you might just as well say it to console a postman who has just had his leg bitten off by your Doberman. But it was nice to back a couple of winners after an excellent picnic, even though all or most of the good 'faces' like Peter Walwyn were away at Keeneland in the USA for the sales.

And now it's back to the grindstone, although the vicar has just decided to hoover the inside of his car. Twixt autobiographical paragraphs of tear-jerking sensitivity and sips of vodka and warm ice I have to write a piece for a women's magazine on 'Women in Pubs'. At least it's something I know about. But how on earth can I concentrate on anything in view of the recent events at this journal in Doughty Street? Next week I shall reveal how the *Spectator* was rocked to its very foundations when security staff discovered that No. 56 is full of heterosexuals. Expect heads to roll. I could kick myself for Mimi (500 old francs, Montparnasse, 1949). How did they find out?

Room to improve

Since Angela Levin of the *Observer* magazine has studiously avoided writing of my one and only favourite room, preferring as she does the old-world charm of Judi Dench's pad and the copper-warming-pan horror of Jean Rook's place, not to mention the ample loot apparent in both, I shall take it upon myself to give you a guided tour of the cell I scream myself to work and sleep in. (Sorry to trouble you but I need to record it as it is now for future reference.) Yes, the memory banks have blown a fuse and framed pictures and collages on the wall are standing in. But the first thing that might strike a visitor to this dark brown study is that it smells like the John Player factory. The window's been open since the beginning of June but we stink of smoke. My best friend, a Dutch cheese plant, thrives on it strangely, but I expect Nelson, whose bust stands on the window ledge, to cough at any moment.

What does appal me is the sundry crap that one collects and ends up surrounded by over the years. I have some unbelievable books – review copies plus unsolicited nonsense from publishers wanting a plug. But I think Miss Levin would want me photographed at my desk. It used to belong to my old and sadly departed friend Frank Norman. He wrote 'Fings Aint Wot They Used T'Be' at it, but, since I acquired it, it has seen no hits. On it at this moment are two summonses from Newbury County

Court – hangovers from Lambourn days – a ticking off from the Barclaycard people, a passport that's simply dying to be used, a corkscrew, an overflowing ashtray, a Jockey Club press badge, Valium and a tear-jerker of a diary circa 1979. There are six drawers in the desk, one full of determinedly virginal paper, and there's another drawer where the buff nasties go and which is never looked into. By the side of the desk there's a three-litre bottle of Smirnoff that I got on my birthday, which is now collecting 20p pieces. (It took £15 just to cover the bottom of it and when it's full it's the Aegean for me.)

But those pictures on the wall; what a strange assortment. I have to admit that I'm in most of them, but what's Francis Bacon doing with Rocky Graziano, Tom Baker, Lester Piggott, Richard Ingrams, Tony Zale, Frank Norman, my last three wives, my mum and dad, my brothers, daughter and my prep school cricket team? There's hundreds more but that school team picture somehow embarrasses me now. We look more like a masturbating team than a cricket one and probably were. By my bed, and this is not a suitable journal to discuss that old thing in, there's a fridge. Very comforting in the summer. That contains my favourite glass, vodka, lime, Perrier water, swizzle sticks and orange sorbet. I once found a slice of quiche in it too.

But I'm going to have to clear out a load of books and bung them to Oxfam. If they distribute them carefully I expect *The Alcoholic and the Help He Needs*, *Florence Nightingale* and *Clever Betting at Your Betshop* will be queued up for in French Equatorial Africa. Other books which might raise a giggle in the jungle are Juliet Mitchell's *Psychoanalysis and Feminism*, *Depression* – I've a library on that subject – and *Rule Britannia*.

Now the thing is, would I change my chambers in the unlikely event of a pools win or a lunatic legacy? I'd probably consider a penthouse flat overlooking the park and near the Ritz, but I'd have second thoughts. After all, I am semi-retired. Some might say completely so. What more does a man need other than a bed, fridge, bath, a telephone that's mysteriously stopped taking incoming calls from women, an exhausted Barclaycard, a friendly houseplant, fifteen ashtrays and a tolerant landlady? Copper bedwarming pan? Horse brasses? Not on your Nelly. But I do wish Angela Levin would pop round for a drop of the Earl Grey. The chaos here would be a sight for her sore old eyes.

Men's page

If any of you men out there have got any problems you'd like to discuss with me please feel free to write. It's high time someone got a men's page going, and I must assume that the editors of national newspapers have never heard of the Sex Discrimination Act. Last Sunday I spent most of the morning reading a piece about ovarian cysts in the *Observer*. It grabbed me so much that my own cyst-free egg got quite cold alongside the toast. Now don't worry that I'm going to write about my testicles in a sort of retaliatory way because I'm not, and anyway they still haven't returned to me. But I'm sure you get my drift. I mean why can't they devote a little space to subjects such as 'husband-battering'? And what about beauty care? Every time I look into a mirror I curse the fact that they don't make cosmetics for men. The wear and tear inflicted on one by day-to-day existence is colossal and it shows. Yes, a few beauty tips – and I for one would like to know where Bernard Levin goes to get his hair waved.

I sometimes think these female hacks think that only women have sexual problems. (When you see some of them you realise that premature ejaculation could be a blessing in disguise and I'm pleased to say that Cosmo Landesman is writing a book on the subject.) Yes, they're all so absorbed with their own problems that they can't be bothered to help us find the *male* multiple orgasm. I'd very much like to know just where the hell that's been hiding all these years. It would kill the man who found it, but where's the spirit of Dunkirk? Which reminds me: all the medical advice columns in print are for women only. There's no doctor I can write to to ask why my hands shake, why I forget my own telephone number and why the bed keeps catching fire. And, speaking as an orphan and bachelor, where is there a word of cheer? Women think that only women get depressed and lonely, and as I write this, the tears streaming down the channels of my face, it occurs to me that if I don't get laid this weekend then I may have to make a cry for help. Probably in the Man in the Moon.

There's also very little advice in print for men with career problems. My own is that, quite simply, I'm virtually unemployable, and it's no joke, although I sometimes manage to put on a brave grin. I mean, what the hell can I do? I'm too old and weak now to do anything strictly physical like dig holes and if I got a job as a bank clerk I'd probably get a bit fidgety round about eleven a.m. I couldn't even get a job as a barman since it's assumed that anyone over forty is on the fiddle. Both Oxford and Cambridge Universities have rejected my proposal to inaugurate a chair of cracker-barrel philosophy and that would have suited me down to the ground. I must admit that the press does indulge in a bit of male fashion, but once a man's got a pair of jeans and a jersey, a suit for the races, what on earth more can he want?

My dear friend Irma Kurtz was willing for me to take over her agony column in *Cosmopolitan* for the duration of her holiday but they won't hear of it. You see, they think men can't feel agony. God almighty, if they knew what it was like to have a menopause that lasted twenty years, to have cold flushes and morning sickness for twenty bloody years and to be under the moon every night! And what about those endless interviews they do in women's magazines on the likes of Robert Redford? I don't give a toss for Robert Redford but I'd very much like to know for example whether or not Cyd Charisse has got varicose veins after all these years. Yes, we men must counterattack the 'women's page' and do the opposite; namely, alienate men from women. The only danger though is that we could end up as a nation of wankers and the trade union movement would never allow that.

Rambling

Help! Help! I'm drowning in memorabilia. I want to jump into tomorrow but how big is the drop the other side of midnight? I'm sorry to go on about my wretched possessions but they've become an obsession and I might go mad if I don't get this room cleared up shortly. Everything I approach, every book, photograph and scrap of paper I want to throw away holds up its arms and screams 'Wait, remember me?' and we sit down together and talk of past times. In desperation I asked my last wife to help me clear out the rubbish this week and she said, 'No. Old wedding pictures depress me as much as they do you.' Quite. Say no more. But you can't throw one away, can you? What about the other people in the picture? It takes an hour to go through such a snap. I wonder where Susannah is now. Seven years ago she spent £40 on a pair of knickers from Liberty. And there's our witness, Charles St George. To think he owned such cracking horses as Bruni, Giacometti and

Ginevra and what about the party he gave us at Epsom on the day Shirley Heights won. Of course I'm cutting a lot of short stories short, but you see why I'm stuck in this treacle mire of times past.

There you – or at least I – go again. How did that biography of Edith Piaf get to be on the mantelshelf and why haven't I returned it to John Le Mesurier who lent it me in hospital ages ago? Good old John. I spent two of the nicest days I've ever had with him. One in Devon chez Dan Farson and one in Newmarket at Teddy Lambton's house and yard. John Le Mes, as he's called, introduced me to Tony Hancock and what a momumental piss-up that turned out to be. Hancock and I started out at opening time in the French pub and I saw him off ten hours later. I put him into a taxi – the driver wouldn't have taken him if he hadn't been Hancock – and he collapsed on to the floor and then handed me his card from a supine position saying, 'Phone me if you get into trouble. I think you may have a drinking problem.'

Which reminds me, what a pity John Le Mes and I never got around to writing the Dictionary of Clichés we planned that weekend with Dan Farson. Come to think of it what a pity Dan doesn't come up to town more often. Such a good and jolly companion and what a twit I must have been twenty years ago to borrow his Pembroke College scarf in an effort to impress a bird in the Duke of Wellington that I was an undergraduate. Now there's a pub that's gone right off. Christ almighty. That's where Dennis Shaw told me that Kennedy had been assassinated. But they did very good Scotch eggs in the Wellington. Gilbert Wood used to buy me halves of bitter there when he was painting scenery and when I was an assistant in the cutting rooms at MGM. What the hell was that film called?

God, what a bore that was working in the cutting rooms. *The Guns of Navarone* wasn't too bad though, what with those sessions in the old house at Shepperton Studios. Yes, Gregory Peck took the day off to fly to Rome and back just to see Herb Elliott run in the 5,000 metres. And what was that other race? Oh yes, Chataway *v* Kuts. I watched that in the Swiss pub with George Barker and we won 10/-each. What would that be – 10/-? Just over five pints of bitter I suppose. Pity you couldn't have stuck to bitter isn't it. When on earth was it you – I mean I – first went on the whisky? It must have been 1962 touring *Expresso Bongo* with Mick Tobin as chippy. How I got those flies cues right at the Royal in Newcastle, pissed as a pudding, God alone knows. Married to Jacki then and there's that John Deakin photo of her. When poor old Deakin died in Brighton Francis Bacon went to identify the body and said, 'That's the first time I've seen him with his mouth closed.' Yes, I must return that Piaf book, John Le Mes.

Steamy weather

Ever since Russell Square and Jermyn Street ran out of steam I've despaired of ever getting a Turkish bath again. I much prefer them to saunas, which I find claustrophobic and akin to a punishment box in which you sweat it out metaphorically, so to speak, as well as physically. The Turkish bath is, by comparison, spacious. It's also nicely social. You can walk about and have a chat and all sorts of odd balls loom up in the steam. To my surprise and delight our friendly *Spectator* publican, Dave, introduced me to a steam bath just the other day; it must be one of the very few left in this clapped-out city (name and address withheld for fear of tourist invasion). But what a pleasant afternoon I had and in the best of company. As soon as I'd undressed and left the locker room I was introduced to some very stalwart men who were lolling about and melting in the steam room. 'This is Jeff. I'd like you to meet Freddie. Freddie's one of the most successful bank robbers in the country. This is Jim. Jim's just come out after a seven stretch and here's Tom. He's got a spieler in the Commercial Road.' What a jolly bunch they were and the only one who wasn't smiling was Solly, a seventy-year-old taxi driver, who was staring mournfully at his prick and intoning: 'We were born together. We grew up together. We got married together. Why, oh why, did you have to die before me?'

The surprise of the afternoon was the picnic they produced in the locker room. Ice-cold lager, vodka, cold chicken, grouse or what you would and then back to the steam and in and out of the cold plunge. After that, a fairly ancient man with fingers of steel gave me an excellent massage which really toned up the cupboard I live in. Just as I was about to get off the slab he surprised me by pouring shampoo on my nut and giving my scalp a massage. Then he hosed me down. I haven't felt so good since Emprerey won the Derby. In fact I felt five years younger, which brought me down to about seventy. I think I'll go regularly from now on, and for all that it's a snip for a fiver. It's also quite safe for me to visit Turkish baths now that I've lost my looks. In my pugilistic days, in the days when I could look a clock that was saying eleven o'clock in the face without breaking into a brisk trot to the nearest pub then I had to repel quite a few would-be boarders. Yes, the sign of being over the hill isn't policemen getting younger as far as I'm concerned, it's not being bought drinks by rich queens; the last time someone tried to drown me on the strength of my being a pretty face must be twenty years ago. The journey to the grave is studded with injuries to one's vanity.

Yes, for my money – and that's a joke – the Turkish variety beats the Swedish one hands down. And saunas can be dangerous. A very well-known friend of mine (name withheld, birds still pining, address Heaven) got into the habit of indulging in sexual intercourse in a sauna in a private house. I caught him at it one day and showed him the yellow card, but he would persist. Ten days later he had a heart attack and dropped dead in the street. Sex at 100 degrees and more Fahrenheit just isn't on and it's a pity, considering the climates of their respective countries, that Khomeini, Amin and Gaddafi don't screw themselves to death.

But there'll never be another Jermyn Street. When the jockeys used to use it to take off pounds after the races and after a session in Jules Bar then that was a night on the tiles. And the stories you heard, never mind the tips. But the Russell Square establishment was the best one for a night's kip, which is exactly what I used it for when I was on the bum. At ten shillings a night it was the cheapest hotel in London and I was the cleanest man in London. And, as I said, I was pretty good at getting ten bobs in those days. Next week's steam bath will have to be paid for by the sweat of this old brow.

Language

Last Saturday I went to Newbury for the races and there was a nice little to-do on the train with a ticket inspector. I'd bought a race-train 'special' ticket but jumped aboard an Inter-City when I heard it was going to make a hitherto unscheduled stop at Newbury Racecourse itself. Just before we arrived, this extraordinary ticket collector came into my carriage to do his business. He was real Waffen SS material. About 6ft 6ins, severe-looking with a pencil moustache and wearing an impeccably pressed Germanic BR uniform, he wasn't one to take prisoners, I could see. I was sitting in a first-class compartment and had to give him the excess fare. But the bastard made me pay the entire fare again because he said special race-train tickets couldn't be transferred to other trains. This peeved me somewhat, as did his officious manner. I remarked, with some sarcasm, seeing how he relished the incident, 'I suppose you really enjoy your job.' Drawing himself up to a good 6ft 7ins he replied, 'Yes, sir, I do. And, furthermore, I was created and not born, sir.' I'd be extremely grateful to any reader who can tell me what on earth that might possibly mean.

At the time words failed me, except for the short one which always springs to mind. I barked it out and a sixteen-year-old boy in the corner of the compartment busy taking down railway engine numbers turned scarlet and seemed on the verge of a fit. (However boring swearing may be I'm suspicious of people who are squeamish about it.) I was feeling very irritated by now and was tempted to turn on the boy to tell him that if he spent more time abusing himself and others his spots would clear up in no time. Then at Reading we were joined by a man who was carrying a copy of the *Sun* and was covered in tattoos. By Newbury I was feeling sick. The idiot inspector who drew himself up to his full height every time he opened his mouth, the boy a physical wreck at the mention of an obscene word and a tattooed *Sun* worshipper. What were they trying to tell us? Not for the first time I reflected that *The Desmond Morris Guide to Body Language* is only the half of it. These gestures bear closer examination.

I often wonder about a girl who works on a newspaper I go to, whose every physical movement and gesture is pure posture. You probably know the type. They sit on the floor a lot and, if they're wearing jeans, they wave their legs about.

When they stand and talk their arms point and wave like so many Isadora Duncan contortions. They smoke cigarettes *professionally*. The smoke is inhaled very sharply and the teeth are bared. Then the head turns to give you a profile and the smoke is exhaled slowly and deliberately and the grey jet stream becomes a beautiful blue cloud of smoke. What are they trying to tell us? Well, all that, like compulsive face-pulling, is simply a sign of pure, stark terror. Such women also have their disgusting equivalent of the male tattoo; that is, they wear their sunglasses on top of their heads. This is to indicate that they are racy, with it and a cut above a shop girl.

But it's 'Fat' Tom's body language that fascinates me most. About once a month in the Colony Room Club you can see him sitting upright on his bar stool swigging away, when suddenly but slowly the stool starts to tilt backwards and Tom descibes the perfect arc of 90 degrees and crashes full length on to the floor. What is Tom trying to tell us? It's hard to say. I've examined him closely when he has come to rest on the floor, but I've never been able to get a flicker of recognition out of him.

To come back to the sunglasses on the top of the head, it did ring a bell when I read in *The Human Zoo*: 'Female monkeys in captivity have been seen to offer themselves sexually to a male as a means of obtaining food morsels...' Ah yes, all those dinners in Wheeler's in the good old days.

Downcast

One afternoon last week I lost a £50 note. The same evening I had a carrier bag containing a brand new sweater stolen from the French pub. This morning I received a buff-enveloped rebuke from Barclaycard. I went into the kitchen to read it and as I did so I dropped a piece of toast and marmalade on to the floor and it landed face down. The loss of the £50 note infuriated me and left me with just a quid but the toast landing marmalade-down has really depressed me and I feel I can no longer remain an atheist. There can be no doubt that there is somebody up there and they hold me in the greatest contempt. I shall leave my flat later this morning carrying a white flag. I give up. D'you know, the toast and marmalade has *always* landed face down. It has to be symptomatic of something. Cliché-mongers keep telling me that 'something will turn up' so why can't it be the toast and marmalade? It may all sound frightfully trivial to you but, you see, it's the thin end of the wedge of which a slightly thicker section is having lost at least 12lbs while waiting for a cheque from the *Daily Telegraph*.

There is one consolation, though; I can't stop laughing, albeit inwardly. Most blessings are heavily disguised. Apart from the fact that I'm not allowed to eat marmalade anyway, I vaguely remember having left a chunk of cod fillet in the carrier bag with the sweater and by this time the thief will have come to acknowledge that it is better to give than to receive. And when I think of the men that women have left for me then I can barely repress a chuckle. I remember once being given a severance kiss in favour of a property dealer who turned out to be impotent. There was also a woman in Marylebone who, having recited to me the famous soliloquy 'You Make Me Sick', jumped into her car and drove straight into a wall, blinded no doubt by crocodile tears.

But all that's behind me now and there'll be less marmalade face-down, so to speak, now that I've decided to give up the pursuit of women. Until now I've never been anti-blood sports but at last the chase has begun to sicken me. It's so incredibly undignified for one thing, and it's an elementary fact that if somebody doesn't reciprocate then they're simply the wrong person. What one needs is a load of self-protective arrogance. Only recently – my very last metaphorical marmalade incident I hope – I became pretty interested in a very obvious-looking woman; that's to say a well-packaged one. I offered to make her extremely unhappy, but she preferred one of the ghastliest and ugliest men in Soho, whom she thought to be 'steady' and 'reliable' since he dabbles in publishing, whatever that is. In fact the man's as shallow as a single Scotch but he can wag a wallet as well as his tail. Now I'm very well aware of the fact that the easiest way to drive a woman into a man's arms is to knock him behind his back, so I did the reverse. I told her that the creep was good, kind, talented and a candidate for heaven. This was pretty nasty of me. For the next twenty years she'll be scraping the toast every morning and he'll be dropping it marmalade-side-down. Buttering a man up can occasionally mesmerise a woman but, as I say, the reverse is usually true, and since I'm supposed to be 'difficult' and 'wicked' according to my Soho press agent I can't understand why some nice woman isn't knocking on my door. Some shit has obviously been saying nice things about me. Yes, it's been a lousy week and Puccini hasn't helped much. With him being composer of the week I've spent every morning crying from nine a.m. to ten a.m. When Mimi drops the toast marmalade-side-down it breaks my heart.

All abroad

My French stinks. It seems that when I asked somebody for a light I asked them to set me on fire and when I asked the concierge for an alarm call I apparently asked him to wash me at six a.m. Never mind. Their English stinks too. I got caned at school for reading a novel during a French lesson and the memory of it was pretty sharp in Paris last weekend where I went to see the Trusthouse Forte-sponsored Prix de l'Arc de Triomphe. Personally, I wouldn't have trusted Trusthouse Forte to sponsor a cup of tea but it was a great race and God knows the Aga Khan needs the £168,000 prize money. Anyway, the weekend kicked off with a freebie trip to Boulogne sponsored by P&O Ferries and they and the Boulogne Chamber of Commerce laid on a champagne breakfast on the boat and then your slap-up lunch in the town itself. I don't really get it. Can my mentioning P&O get them any more business? And what of the other hacks in the party? With the exception of my friend and agony auntie Irma Kurtz they were, as hacks tend to be, pretty bloody ghastly. But, what with giving Irma the loan of my ears and being unable to keep my eyes averted from the amazing legs of a very jolly PR lady called Judy Carter, I managed to avoid them. Press trips usually contain 90 per cent bores, although Hazel Evans once pushed me into a moat surrounding a chateau in the Loire valley which was very refreshing.

Now the lunch was really good, and between Irma telling me about the meaning of life and telling me to give up sex because it's overrated I did manage to eat some crab, prawns, langoustine, moules marinière, boeuf bourguignon, coq au vin and ice cream. Oh yes, and a glass of wine as well. Drinking is one hell of a problem in France for me since vodka's too expensive there and it's the only drink that doesn't make the pancreas scream. After lunch I lounged around a few bars sipping pastis and watching the English at play. What on earth is it that turns an Englishman into a Manchester United supporter as soon as he crosses the Channel? I saw one lout actually whistle at a waiter to gain his attention and afterwards

I felt compelled, albeit somewhat pompously, to apologise to the patron for my own race.

After watching the idiots kicking beer cans in the street I retired to Wimereux and the Hôtel du Centre which advertises itself as having an *'ambience sympathique'*. It's funny how the French go on about being sympatico but I suppose we all have our silly fantasies. A good hotel though, and to bed with a veal escalope. Incidentally, although I ate very well in France by my standards, things were slightly spoilt by an odd compulsion to wonder, 'Now, would Bernard Levin eat this?' every time I sat down to munch. I suppose an obscene article he once wrote about food still hasn't been digested by my mind.

The following day I caught the train to Paris and was reminded for the thousandth time how awful British Rail is. Saturday was a scorcher. I walked for miles, got back to my hotel, filled the bidet with cold water and stood in it for ten minutes to cool off the feet. I'd watched the rich at play in and around the Champs Elysées and, by God, they really are pretty revolting. They're so bloody posh and they never stop play-acting at being stars. If the Prince de Galles is the high life then give me the gutter. A man shouldn't have to *wear* his money. One lovely sight though, and that was the food shops in the Rue des Martyrs. But even the French are having an attack of the hamburgers and there was a Wimpy next to my hotel near the Gare du Nord.

Came Sunday and the Arc de Triomphe. I'd seen two before only. In 1970 my first column for the *Sporting Life* concerned the Arc when Sassafras beat Nijinsky by a head. That day I got involved with a couple of Irish trainers and we were still at the paddock bar as the moon came up. A year later I was back to see Mill Reef win. I won £50 on the race and moments after I'd collected it someone walked up to me and said, 'By the way, you've got the sack from the *Life*.' That called for more champagne. This year the French were at their most uncooperative and the men on the gate refused to believe that the Jockey Club had left me a pass. Luckily my old friend Charles St George, who owns Ardross, was nearby and he, of course, marched me in. It seemed something of an omen to me to bump into him first and I was just one of a thousand English people rooting for Ardross.

But what about Longchamp? It lacks the atmosphere of Ascot and it's packed with people who go there to be seen. The office, too, was even more toffee-nosed than I'd remembered and although they did give me a pass they said I couldn't go into the enclosure until after the last race because I wasn't wearing a tie. I was beginning to wish that I was back in the Coach and Horses, and suddenly I was. I walked out of the office and, lo and behold, who should be standing there but 'Bookshop' Billy, 'Big' Tom, Brian 'The Burglar' and 'Irish' Patsy. I could have hugged them. What a sight they were drinking beer in front of the lawn where stands the statue of the first French winner of the Epsom Derby in 1865, Gladiateur, nicknamed 'The Avenger of Waterloo'. We swilled away at the beer and the Soho lads went to back the English-owned-and-trained and Pat Eddery-ridden Sharpo.

He won quite beautifully, and he won about £60,000 and 'un objet d'art' for his owner Monica Sheriffe. Here was ammunition for the Arc and the Soho team stuck it on Ardross for England, and themselves of course. It's history now but the Aga Khan's Akiyda just beat Ardross. Lester rode a great race on Ardross but the horse needs a shade further and, in fact, in fifteen races now Ardross has only lost three times and over the Arc distance of a mile and a half. Charles St George and a mite of patriotic fervour apart – I didn't have a bet – I was a little bit choked that the Aga Khan won. Not a nice man and here's not the place to say why. Still, the prize money didn't go to Daniel Wildenstein either, another prize one.

At the end of the afternoon I was in my usual state which is on my uppers. The Soho team took very good care of me though and we retired to a beautiful hotel called the Harlequin for cocktails. After that a very good and expensive dinner, so I'm told, but wasted on me by then. The next morning it was back to Boulogne again to get the ferry. The buffet car on the train this time was first-rate. An English woman and her ten-year-old daughter gave me dirty looks all the way because I was drinking pastis. How odd it is that some of us still think it's immoral to drink before official opening time in England. It's also odd that the inventors of chips, the English, seem to make them out of cotton wool. My 'desert island' meal, apart from a bible-and-Shakespeare sandwich, would be that old French standby of steak, pommes frites, salad, cheese and claret.

Today, I'm afraid, it's back to steak pie and two veg in the Coach. It's also back to the likes of Brighton, Uttoxeter, Lingfield and Sedgefield – a far cry from Longchamps, but a cosier one. Yes, it's back to earth, finding the rent and that old spot of skating on thin ice. But you wouldn't want that thin ice to give way in Paris. They'd hold you under. By the way, I'm not talking through my champagne, but P&O are better than Sealink and even the people in Greek Street are better than those damn people in the Champs Elysées.

Country Matters

I went to Suffolk last weekend after ten years. I fled it with tears in my eyes and the return match on Sunday brought tears to my eyes for different reasons. God, what creeps! Of course my old cottage has been done up. You could play billiards on the lawn where I spent summer afternoons with my hand up someone's skirt and they've knocked down the garden shed in which I began the novel of the century – the skirt distracted me after page one – but the twits have torn down the honeysuckle. Most of the village bores are still intact though and the next idiot who tells me to 'always plant your potatoes on Good Friday' is going to have his pint of bitter poured over him. As I explained, through gritted teeth, there are no potatoes in Great Portland Street. Although the Peacock Inn has been done up too I felt as though I'd just popped out for a pee when I walked through the door. The same conversations were still in progress if you can call standing and thinking progress.

Sundays are the days when the middle classes dress down. The men wear old army jerseys full of moth holes, green gumboots, torn trousers – a barrister wears an old court-room striped pair – and the stains of motor mower oil are displayed like Pistol's wounds collected on St Crispin's Day. For the ladies, husky coats are *de rigueur*. Conversation embraces the price of property, jam making, jumble sales and was the vicar pissed this morning. The middle bar is two steps down the social ladder and is packed by the sort of people who indulge in roadside picnics, keep budgerigars and use metal teapots. They all share the same brain. The back bar is for the local working men. All of them can tickle trout, catch pheasants with their bare hands, sell you a car for £5, mend your washing machine for the price of a drink and tell you never to put in tulip bulbs on an odd day of the month when it's raining and the missel-thrush is silent. The likes of me are regarded as dangerous and eccentric. Twelve years ago, the local gentry struck me off the cocktail party circuit because I had a piss in the rectory flower bed – a little recycled Tio Pepe never killed a wallflower, but such things live in their memories. My affair with the vicar's daughter has now assumed Profumo-like proportions – mere dalliance in the organ loft – and legend has it that I used to drink *all day* in Sudbury with Maurice Richardson on market days. I should bloody well hope I did. Dear Maurice.

But there were some new faces. Anybody with a few bob these days puts it into a cottage. The men take up weekend lawn mowing as though it's a career and the women are drawn to crafts. If there's anything more disgusting than art then it's crafts. Making corn dollies is not a suitable pastime for an attractive woman and, by the way, the country is still beautifully untouched by feminism. Furthermore I'll thank country women to clear out the pottery clay from under their fingernails before they caress my magnificent body and I'll thank them too for not cooking everything in sunflower seed oil, attracting flies by nude sunbathing and bringing their peanut butter encrusted children into pubs. Yes, it's odd that. Middle-class children are addicted to peanut butter. I suppose it's an easy way to keep them alive and far cheaper than an oxygen tent.

Sadly, my host was cruelly exposed by his small son at the weekend. His friend asked him, 'What does your daddy do?' Jimmy told him, 'He goes to London every day, goes into pubs, cashes cheques and gives the change to Mummy.' There's no answer to that, nor should there be.

Off colour

I've known Aubrey since we were teenagers but I never realised until last week that he's a paranoid hypochondriac.

Like most of us he's worried about pollution, excessive
crop-spraying and the fast-vanishing hedgerow. The general
decline of his neck of the woods and fields has got him
twitching and the thing that bugs him most is the physical
damage that he claims to have suffered in the last year from
motor car and lorry exhaust fumes. Now, what he's done is
to list his ailments on paper and circulate them to neighbours
within a five-mile radius, and if they too can say they've
suffered from any affliction on the list then he wants them
to sign a petition asking the government to ban insecticides
and cars from the said neck of woods and pastures. I shall
allow Aubrey to continue this column now by simply quoting
his 1982 health chart. You're not going to believe it, but I
promise you this is his circular. This is what one man claims
to have suffered from in one little year.

1. Lassitude *(acute* tiredness). 2. Distraction (lack of
concentration). 3. Aching (heavy limbs). 4. Bouts of severe
depression. 5. Backache, shoulder ache. 6. Sudden acute pains
in rib cage, limbs and extremities. 7. Lengthy headaches.
Sudden sharp pains in temples and forehead. 8. Pains on
inside of forearms. 9. Cystitis, difficulty and frequency in
passing water. 10. Drawing sensation towards lower abdomen.
11. Aching backs of hands as with sprain. 12. Popping, aching,
tickling ears. 13. General acute itching. 14. Violent sneezing.
15. Indigestion. Inflated, bloated, acidic. 16. Nausea. 17.
Catarrh (not necessarily related to a cold). 18. Sore gums,
tongue and inside of mouth with ulcers and cold sores. 19.
Sores in nostrils. 20. Sore throats and swollen glands. 21.
Bowel trouble – diarrhoea, motions in small quantities of
soft consistency. 22. Very sharp hot pains of short duration
in rectum. 23. Raw stinging circle around anus. 24. Eye

trouble – stabbing sensation through eyeballs, pulling, drawing feeling. 25. Watery eyes, itching eyes, dry gritty eyes, itching lids, blurred vision, foggy eyes, winking eyelids. 26. Sweating, not related to exercise. 27. Runny nose. 28. Slurred speech. 29. Bad physical coordination. 30. Bleeding from rectum. 31. Irritability. 32. Dizziness. Loss of balance. 33. Continuous clearing of throat. 34. Bad breath and bad taste in mouth. 35. Heavy lump high in centre of chest. 36. Fluttering in chest. 37. Hormone trouble. 38. Erratic pulse.

Phew! Amazing, isn't it. And I thought I was dying a little too soon. But there are some lovely unconscious touches here and only a serious man could be so unintentionally funny. I particularly like 'sweating, not related to exercise' – the buff envelope with the window syndrome? – and I'm not surprised that 'irritability' follows 'bleeding from rectum' although medically speaking I'm sure he doesn't know his arse from his elbow. But he's obviously taken to drink hasn't he? (I haven't seen him for ten years.) The slurred speech, stomach pains, bad coordination and loss of balance all point to it and, speaking as a specialist, I'm rather touched to see that he's tried to go on the wagon. 'General acute itching' is merely a withdrawal sympton. The bit about bad breath leads me to suspect his tipple is white wine. People who drink wine without food smell like drains. The heavy lump and fluttering in the chest is what we call angst. As for the bouts of severe depression and acute tiredness one can only suppose that he's embarked on the *Spectator* Treasure Hunt. Why he doesn't go to a hospital God only knows. Perhaps, in spite of being a hypochondriac, he agrees with my friend Eva. She once asked a man in a pub, 'What do you do?' He said, 'I practise medicine.' She said, 'Practise? Why don't you get it right?'

Too much

There hasn't been a lot to laugh about this past week. After thirty years I'm back to 9st, the featherweight limit, and what's more I now need middle-distance glasses to read the bathroom scales. Is a mere 5ft 9ins middle distance? The looking-glass has lost its fascination for me and now, as the trembling razor scrapes along the hangdog valleys of my face, I'm moved to morbid curiosity. When the doorbell rang this morning I was sure it was the grim reaper, but luckily it was the milkman. What worries this incredible shrinking man though is the fact that I've been working on a magazine feature about food and over the last two weeks I've tucked into as much good grub as you or I could want. On top of that, Messrs West and Wheatcroft kindly fed me in the Gay Hussar yesterday – unfortunate name that nowadays – and when Victor suggested the goose he was staring at my neck. Yes, I feel well and truly plucked. Too late, I fear, has come the news that surgeons at Addenbrookes can now play at pancreas transplants. Of course what they should be working on is the cash transplant. Which reminds me, Taki's in town.

Now what else was I going to moan about? Oh yes, the old gripe about staff hacks on £15,000 and more a year who don't know how lucky they are. Get this. A female reporter on the *Daily Mirror* was asking Jilly Cooper about the fact that she was selling her London home and moving to the country. When Jilly said, 'To paraphrase Doctor Johnson, I'm sick of London but not tired of life', the reporter asked, 'Is this Johnson private or National Health?' It's bloody marvellous, isn't it? Here we are, supported only by belt and braces, struggling to make a large vodka last twenty and not fifteen minutes, stealing hardboiled eggs from the counter of the Coach and Horses when Norman's not looking, reduced to 50p each way accumulators, humiliated into seducing those who'll do it for a Chinese takeaway, burning our candle at one end and our fingers with dog-ends, writing our sexual reminiscences for a soft porn magazine, recycling teabags, cadging Sunday lunches, going in for newspaper competitions, smashing our piggy banks and we have a professional journalist who's never heard of Doctor Johnson but who can bank her salary and live comfortably off her expenses. Pass the hemlock.

You know, I just don't know what goes on in schools today. Last week I saw my daughter. She's nearly thirteen but her reading is slow and her handwriting is laboured. With luck she may suddenly blossom, but I suspect that the priorities at Holland Park Comprehensive School are rolling joints of marijuana and listening to pop. Well, this pop has been asked to get the autograph of one Harrison Ford. Now I don't expect her to ask for Professor A.J. Ayer's autograph but I do hope she's heard of Doctor Johnson by the time she's been deafened by her first disco.

And I'm off to a seat of learning soon. The Cambridge Union want me to do something silly. What I want to know is how the hell they thought to phone me up at the Coach and Horses. There I was, having a quiet drink with a *Daily Mirror* reporter and explaining that Magna Carta was *not* King John's wife and that the Duke of Wellington was *not* a general but a pub in Wardour Street, when this undergraduate homed in on me. You can't give a vodka and history master class without someone getting at you now, and I wouldn't be in the least surprised if God or the devil phoned up next week to ask me to drop dead for some charity or other.

Trial and error

It's been another silly week I'm afraid, and one punctuated with some very strange judgements. On one day, I forget which, a woman who inflicted sixteen cigarette burns on the hand of her baby was sent to prison for six months. On the same day, a man who stole £25,000 from his firm was sent down for four years. And what is £25,000? Pieces of paper. Then there was the Miss World contest which I think may have been judged by blind eunuchs. Miss Trinidad and Tobago, the one with the Cleopatra-style hair, was head and shoulders above her rivals but came nowhere. But why stop at head and shoulders? And why the hell should the result irritate me so much? God knows, but I know how much the contest irritates some women. It shouldn't. If I had the chance of winning £10,000 by walking across a stage wearing swimming trunks I'd jump at it and I'd thank the men's liberation movement to mind their own business.

Another thing that's subsequently irritated me about Miss World is that she's been boasting in the press that she's a virgin. She says she wants to keep herself pure for her marriage. Quite frankly, I do not wish to know such things of this particular nature. I tried to keep myself pure for my first marriage, too, but fell by the wayside when I met Miss Notting Hill Gate 1947. But that's beside the point and a story I'm saving for *Spare Rib*.

Yes, the judges of the Miss World contest say that 'personality' counts for a hell of a lot. By personality they mean saying – preferably with a Venezualan accent – that you like water skiing, want to start a family, be a model and open your own hairdressing shop. Faced with the same interview, covered in goose-pimples and standing in my swimming trunks on the stage of the Albert Hall, I can see that I'd lose valuable points for saying that I'd like to stop a family and open a beach bar in Barbados with an intact and pure Miss Trinidad and Tobago.

The other judgement which I found odd was the one made against me in court. I've fallen behind with some monthly payments and when I explained to the beak that the reason for this is because I've been a trifle skint, he *upped* the instalments. I can't see the logic of it. The man could get a job with the Arts Council, whose judges always give the money to those who've got enough already. Incidentally, and I'm sure I've said it before, have you noticed how much it helps nowadays to be a little bit black if you're after a grant or a world beauty title? Personally, I don't much mind being discriminated against but what I do object to is the ridiculous business of not being allowed to make jokes about black people or Jews. Sorry, Jewish people. Why you should be immune and the Irish and Polish not, I don't know. I should have thought they too have suffered enough over the years.

Anyway, another crazy thing this week was the invitation that came through the post inviting me to a press conference and buffet lunch given by the British Diabetic Association. God knows how they got hold of my name since I'm not a member, but a diabetic buffet lunch? I ask you. Of course I didn't go. My idea of the lunch hour *(hour?)* does not encompass a plate of bran washed down with whatever we're allowed to drink, and I don't even know what we are allowed to drink. And, apart from Jews and blacks, did you know that it's considered bad taste to make jokes about diabetics. There's too much squeamishness in the world.

Which reminds me, I couldn't help but laugh when I read about the poor sod who'd had a heart transplant and who sadly snuffed it this week. His widow complained that immediately after the operation he became a raving sex maniac. I've never heard of such post-operative spin-offs but I have experienced that same sort of sense of urgency in the middle of the night when I've heard my own heart beating. A shortage of breath confirms the diagnosis that I must now rush out to contact some Smirnoff and Miss Trinidad and Tobago before it's too late.

Scrubbing along

With the passing of time, words change their meaning and, most of all, their feeling. Young people today have got the word 'scrubber' all wrong and Miss Zetterling's film has further distorted the meaning of the word. This is not to knock the film, just the title. Originally, scrubber was a Royal Navy word. A seaman who scrubbed the deck of a ship was doing the lowliest job on board. The word then came to be used to describe a woman in port who was easy to pick up; that is, available. It has never meant prostitute and it has never applied to a woman solely living by crime. It has to do with style. It is NOT necessarily derogatory.

As a general rule scrubbers tend to be rather lonely, a little frightened, untidy, kind, promiscuous, fond of men, vulnerable, brave and a bit of a mess. One clue to a scrubber is the way she treats her knickers. They are often worn for two consecutive days and/or left on the bedroom floor until it's launderette day. By Norman Mailer's account Marilyn Monroe was an extremely unhygienic woman in this respect and she was also one hell of a mess. She was, in fact, the Queen of Scrubbers. But that had nothing to do with blonde hair, tits and legs. Mae West was a lady, but Jean Harlow was a scrubber. Madame de Pompadour was a lady, and that lovable, funny, pain-in-the-arse Dorothy Parker was a scrubber. Scrubbers often turn up early for dates with hopeless men whom they try to look after. Sex is emotional currency and a great comfort for the bedsitter girl with ladders in her stockings and mascara on the pillow. She can laugh through her tears though. (Can you imagine Margaret Thatcher crying herself to sleep?) Most scrubbers, like old soldiers, fade away, although they're prone to suicide attempts which go wrong and succeed. They have a very unlucky track record as far as unintentional pregnancies are concerned. Life has them on the ropes but they rarely go down for a count of nine breather.

But, to turn to men, it's to be hoped that if anyone is contemplating a film called Spiv that they get that right too. Spiv was originally an American police acronym for Suspicious Person Itinerant Vagrant. Its wider usage came into being during the austerity years imposed by Stafford Cripps. The Spiv wore gaberdine drape suits with massive shoulder pads, heavily Brylcreemed hair and suede 'brothel creepers'. He bought and sold cars, clothing coupons or anything you found hard to get. Above all, he never had a regular job when work was more of a virtue than the necessity it is now.

He no longer exists. Spiv has taken on a new meaning and here again it's a matter of style and feeling. Today's spiv is a smoothie more than anything. He is to be found in advertising, television, Fleet Street and, by the score, in the House of Commons. Harold Wilson was a spiv, as is David Steel. Andre Previn is a spiv and so are Michael Caine and Michael Parkinson. A friend opines that Melvyn Bragg is one but I'm sure he has occasional moments of self-doubt. Most Soho spivs work at producing television commercials. They gather in the French pub and are compulsive chatters-up of women. (Very boring, that.) Henry V was a spiv but Edward

VII was a gentleman. Napoleon was a spiv and Wellington a gentleman.

Spivs like eating in trattorias and they frequent cocktail bars like Stringfellows and discos like Tramp. I suppose that one of the things I like about my pub, the Coach, is that we have hardly a spiv on the premises. Survivors are thick on the ground. We have idiots, bores, hooligans, scallywags, scoundrels and the passing scrubber, thank God, but we're mercifully understaffed when it comes to spivs. What I have got which is odd is the feeling that in a previous incarnation I was a scrubber. Sometimes I could swear I once sat on Edward VII's knee, my lipstick smudged and my knickers at half mast.

In all sincerity

There are very few sights more revolting and disgusting afforded to the owner of a television set than that of a gaggle of actors and actresses freeloading in a common, vulgar Park Lane hotel collecting awards that look like bronze Henry Moore turds and slapping each other on the back and kissing each other on the cheeks with all the sincerity of a psychopath committing perjury in the Number One court of the Old Bailey. What is even more ghastly is the fact that these people have their words put into their mouths by writers. Thespians, by and large, strike me as humanoid puppets suspended and operated by egomaniacs and entrepreneurs like Peter Hall and National Theatre white elephants like any director with a beard and a house in Hampstead. The body language of the self-congratulatory theatre clique is as thick, treacly and sick-making as the treacle and brimstone of Dotheboys Hall. Barry Norman grows his hair over his ears. Why? As the awards are announced, dinner-jacketed, so-called stars clap and laugh at pedestrian speeches, mini-addresses and embarrassed asides as though they were applauding Sheridan, Fox or Churchill. Watching the box last Monday night – I can't even remember the names of the awards or programme – I was reminded of a typical Francis Bacon aside – not the 1561–1626 Bacon – that the only way to survive life, that short interval 'twixt birth and death, is to regard very, very nearly everything as being totally unimportant. Show business, it seems, is terribly important. But I don't not respect just actors, I think the wordsmiths who make them ejaculate are as bad.

Put it another way. Last week, our lovable editor was in the Duke of York and in a good mood. 'Look here, Jeff,' he said, 'I thought your column last week was pretty okay. Have a drink.' Silence descended as Dave Potton assaulted the vodka optic twice before plonking the ice, squeezing the lime and squirting the soda into the crystal goblet. I walked up to the bar – trotted and bounced up to it more like the stars in fact – and turned to address the pub.

I kissed the barmaids on both cheeks and said, 'Thank you, darlings. It's been a great privilege and an honour to receive this drink. I'd like to say that it's been a team effort and I want to thank, not only my wonderful editor, but also Jennifer Paterson without whose motorscooter peregrinations to the Coach and Horses the column would never have arrived at the typesetters; Gina Lewis whose expert subbing prevented the column from being spiked; Jenny Naipaul for phoning me to remind me it was copy day and last, but not least, Sukie Marlowe for giving me an encouraging wink. I'd also like to thank all those people who made me feel sufficiently inadequate to take refuge in journalism – my mother, my headmaster, four wives, bookmaker and Smirnoff. Finally, I'd

like to add that I'm sorry Richard West is away in Hong Kong
or Huntingdon and I'd like to accept this other vodka on his
behalf. Thank you.'

It was a wonderful evening and I shall always treasure
the drink that is now on my mantelshelf. It makes me feel
so important and it's wonderful to know that we're all truly
wonderful.

Eva

Eva Johansen died last week in a typically extravagant, sad
and infuriating way: drunk in bed with a cigarette and, like
what ever little money she ever had, up in smoke. It's unlike
her to be so inconsiderate. Soon there'll be no one left at
all to drink with. Melancholy is giving way to a sort of dull
anger at being deprived of the pleasure of her company. She
once wrote to me, 'It was good to see you the other day. I'd
forgotten how much our rows meant to me.' And again last
week after I tried to cheer her up, 'Thank you for looking after
me; it's so nice to know that you're there between rows.' But
it was she, in fact, who looked after me. No wonder I feel so
selfish about her death. I too will miss our screaming matches
as well as the blissful days.

In spite of having just the one foot on the ground – she was
a bit of a romancer at times – she set great store on us both
being Gemini and it appealed to her that Marilyn Monroe
and Judy Garland both were too. There's no need to remind
you of what happened to them. But if there was anyone
famous whom Eva put me in mind of it must be Dorothy
Parker. Sometimes her unconscious efforts to imitate that lady
infuriated me and I'd tell her not to try so hard. That would
invariably lead to a slanging match – invariably in a pub – and

to an anxious and inquiring landlord. She'd stop swearing at me, smile and say, 'Oh, it's quite all right. This is a friend of mine and I'm simply trying to explain to him that he's a stupid bastard.' Exit puzzled landlord.

Our longest-standing trivial row, which became eventually our longest-standing joke, was about the breakfast she demanded when she was staying with me in the country. I asked her what she wanted and she said, 'I'd like a slice of cold, rare, roast beef and a glass of Tio Pepe, preferably from the fridge.' I said, 'Why can't you have a fucking egg like anyone else, you flash cow?' and she replied, quite rightly, 'Because I'm not anyone else.' And she wasn't.

She was also very deft at putting a man down when she wanted to, although in the end, they put her down with an almighty thump. I remember a creep of a travelling salesman – she picked up the phrase from one of her heroes, Auberon Waugh, and called the type 'these people' – approached her in our local with a view to picking her up and said, 'Good morning. Nice day.' She gave him a look of utter disdain and said, 'Your place or mine?' Exit frightened rabbit. But if there is anything to astrology and her obsession about Gemini then it is borne out by the two faces that were Eva. Inside the abrasive, tough, hard-drinking woman there was a frightened little girl trying desperately *not* to get out. Well, she got out last week.

I shall miss the asides as well as her company. A very good friend of hers was once foolhardy enough to tell her, 'You know, Eva, if I hadn't met you I think I would have taken up keeping bees.' He was ever after referred to as 'The Bee Keeper' and she said, 'The poor sod wanted to keep bees and he ended up with a hornet's nest.' But let her finish this column with an excerpt from a typical letter she wrote three years ago.

'So I have no flat, no job, no lover, no income and – as far as I can see – no prospects. Even my cat has left me. I keep sitting around expecting fear and all I'm getting is exhilaration ... So here I am exulting in the clean dry air of absolute selfishness, secure in the knowledge that there is nothing more they can do to me. If it weren't so totally out of keeping with everything I've been told, I'd say it could only be described as happiness.'

Out of the mouths

If the age of consent was raised from sixteen to fifty, lunatic asylums would be empty. I came to that conclusion ages ago and long before reading Monday's *Daily Mail* in which some young people agreed to be interviewed and express their idiotic opinions on such trivia as life, love, sex, marriage and divorce. Normally I wouldn't dream of reading the opinions of pipsqueak teenagers but I was killing the longest half of the day, 10.30 – 11 a.m., and someone had left the *Mail* on the table in the patisserie I use as a waiting room. Anyway, what about Donna Wheeler, 18, catering assistant, Leicester? She said, 'First time I had sex, I was sixteen and I hated it. It wasn't the way I imagined it would be. My mum told me that sex was wonderful if it was with the right person and I thought oh, this is going to be fantastic. Well, it wasn't and I felt disgusted with myself.' Quite so, and I must point out to teenage boys that this bears out an old adage of mine. Whenever you meet a pretty teenage girl always make a beeline for the mother. I've found it to be usually very rewarding.

On the touchy subject of abortion the *Mail* concludes that a third of the girls they spoke to disagree with the idea that abortion should be made legally available to all who want it. Looking at the teenagers around me I think it should be made compulsory. If ever I make anyone pregnant again – and I suppose I might in Pakistan, Wales on a Bank Holiday, or during the impending soda-water strike – I shall be only too well aware of the possible dangers. Just imagine having a baby son – called Darren on his mother's insistence – who'd grow up to read the *Sun*, get tattooed, ride a moterbike and drink light ale out of cans while watching breakfast television. Alternatively you might sire a daughter – called Trish by her mother – who'd grow up to work in an advertising agency, wear sunglasses on the top of her head, frequent discos and describe everything as being 'brilliant'. No, the human race has been battling long enough and should declare its innings closed.

On the very beautiful subject of marriage, Alexandra Duce, 19, classics student, Leeds University, says, 'Marriage is outdated. I don't see the need to legalise a relationship with a scrap of paper.' What a terrible thing to say. I suspect a printer's error here and that Ms Duce is at Leeds *United*. Marriage is the opium of the mentally unstable. A truly wonderful thing if a trifle addictive. And as for 'trial' marriages, they interviewed a really crafty one in Marc Chambers-Willis, 16, son of a former nurse, London. He said, 'I'd definitely want to live with the girl I wanted to marry first, so that if at the last moment we knew marriage would be wrong for us, we could back out.' What a cheek! My advice to young Marc Chambers-Willis is that if he wants to have the leg over and then *back out* as he calls it – and he clearly intends just that – then he should never give his right name, it being as memorable as his mother's present occupation. (I must change my occupation on my passport to 'former schoolboy'.)

We now come to divorce, not a pretty subject, and a sixteen-year-old schoolboy, Jason White, knows it all. 'I'm never going to get divorced. When I marry, I'm going to make sure the marriage works.' Well, well. What Master White should be pondering is the far more profound problem of how to make his divorce work. Speaking as a man who's been through three of the wretched redundancies I can tell you and him that it's not easy. Take my last wife. We get on like a house on fire. Last week she took me out to a splendid dinner, she buys me presents, calls me 'old bean' and even phones the Coach and Horses to see whether I've snuffed it or not. But final and damning proof of the failure of our divorce is that she *still* laughs at my jokes. I wouldn't swap her for a wife.

Away from it all

The literature on my bookshelves is gathering dust. There are only two things I read now, quite obsessionally too, and they are travel brochures and cookery books. Byron has been ousted by Elizabeth David, and the *Sporting Life* has been replaced by guides to the Greek Islands, Istanbul and India. Exactly three years ago I managed to get a free trip to Barbados and the following year I earned myself a holiday on the island of Serifos by writing some stultifying soft pornography which would have made a satyr yawn. But it was Barbados that spoilt me. Now, as Charlie addresses me on the price of satsumas in Berwick Street market, as Norman Balon unfolds his philosophy, and as Julia reiterates that she doesn't fancy me, all I can hear is the surf, the thud of a falling coconut, the comforting tread of an approaching waiter accompanied by the reassuring tinkle of ice against glass and, with luck, the soothing and distant screams of

German and Swedish tourists drowning in the foaming undertow.

Norman brings me back to earth for a moment by throwing a menu at me. 'Are you going to eat?' he snarls. 'We've got steak pie, chicken and mushroom pie, savoury mince and toad in the hole. Hurry up. Someone wants your fucking table.' But I drift away again. Sitting beneath the palms, sheltered from the throb of the sun, I can hear the fizz of frying prawns, the dying hiss of a lobster and the rattle of a cocktail shaker and, with luck, the scream of a German tourist treading on a sea urchin. Norman, damn him, breaks the spell again. 'Here you are, large vodka, put your own fucking ice in and give me a pound.' Insensitive to his charm I drift off to Serifos to watch the fishing boats come back across that clear, sparkling blue. The waiter brings me another ouzo and in the back of the taverna the soft chunks of spicy lamb are nearly ready. Just as it's about to be served, someone shouts across the bar, 'Ere, Jeff. Broadsword won the first. Two to one.' I'm disgusted. If Doctor bloody Johnson had ever walked down a gangplank in Bridgetown and spent a morning catching his clap there, or if he'd ever had an afternoon nap in a citrus grove, then we wouldn't have had that daft utterance about London and not getting tired of it (a man, like him, who has an opinion on *everything* can be a bore).

But here we are in the grey, damp gloom of Greek Street, caught up in the exhausting career of doing absolutely nothing and hanging on by our fingertips in intensive care on a Smirnoff drip. But there are, of course, holidays I wouldn't swap for this weather and waste of life. Last Sunday, on Cliff Michelmore's holiday spot on television, we were treated to a rundown on Rimini and guided through it by a woman who'd holidayed there. The idea of sharing a beach with a bigger crowd than the one that gathers at Wembley on Cup Final day, living on pizza, plonk and pasta and whiling away the evenings in discos nearly made me throw up. It looked worse than the first holiday I ever had after leaving school.

That was in 1949. Two of us plus two girls rented a caravan of all things at Newhaven of all places. The caravan itself was infested with earwigs, in the evenings we were continually dive-bombed by maybugs, on an outing to Brighton one day I got hit over the head by a billiard cue – the handle end is weighted, you know – in a sleazy billiard hall and, finally, the calor gas stove blew up in the face of my partner causing her a sudden lack of interest in the proximity of my perfectly formed body. Shock, I suppose. But in those days I used to find it almost impossible to be in the dumps on hot, sunshine-filled days. Even being skint was just about bearable. If you took up your sunbathing position on the pavement outside the French pub, sooner or later someone in funds would cool you down with a beer.

Further back, I remember school holidays being pretty ghastly. I spent every day dreading the return to school and the anxiety made me feel quite ill. Anyway, there was very little to do in Holland Park in the Forties apart from trying to destroy it. I was fond of throwing stones through people's windows, popping thunderflashes through their letterboxes and burning things down from my mum's summer house to half of an unkempt Ladbroke Gardens. They saved the resident barrage balloon. Thank God I've nearly grown up and now take my holidays a bit more seriously. Next month I hope to be writing to you from India. I can hardly wait for the diarrhoea and the vodka drought. Meanwhile, I wish Norman would leave me to my Caribbean and Mediterranean dreams.

Fresh start

Breakfast television is something of a boon to a man who wakes up, stares at the ceiling and wonders what the hell he did last night and what he's going to do today. To sit in bed with my first cup of steaming Earl Grey to find Anna Ford discussing female circumcision was a wonderful experience. I've done some incredible and strange things in my bed but I can't remember any of them having resulted in laughter before. Tears, yes (in the summer of 1979 I seriously considered buying a rubber sheet). Usually I wake up with Patricia Hughes, two eyes that feel like fried eggs and a mouth like an ashtray, but since Anna has graced my bedroom, I can't wait to wake up and the bags under my eyes seem to me to indicate that I'm giggling in my sleep. It's early stages yet but my one worry about Frosty and Anna's programme is that it's going to have a feminine bias. Why wasn't mine host Norman hauled into the studio to discuss male circumcision? Charity begins at home and I'm far more concerned about what goes on in Golders Green than the happenings in the Sudan.

What I'd very much like to see is a slot for men called 'Where were you last night?' They could bring in almost any man off the street and have him grilled by Irma Kurtz and then slapped on the wrist by Anna Raeburn. I'd also like to see my own slot in which I'd concoct a hangover drink and breakfast cure (kedgeree, a crème-de-menthe-based cocktail and a cheque in the post, for example), and a man could swap punches with the likes of the 'Peace' women who beat up Heseltine, and quite rightly too. There are quite a lot of men too – talking of peace – who aren't hell-bent on a nuclear holocaust, but they never get a look-in with the media. But it's nice to see a female gardener for a change and one with the obligatory Hampshire accent.

The riddle is how they get Hazel Evans to the studio on time since she's never got to the Coach on time. And the same goes for Irma who has often soothed this agonised uncle over a jar.

Yes, I've my own gardener and aunt and all I need now is someone to tell me whether or not it's raining outside. Much as I like the Commander I find him a trifle flamboyant and I'd like to see a no-nonsense Charlie do the weather spot occasionally. It would simply be, 'It's pissing down in Scotland and there'll be a force 7 skirtlifter from the West.' But although I said I was worried about the female bias I do think that women should be allowed a shot at the weather: 'It's a perfectly wonderful day and there's no need for you to be cooped up in the pub all day.' There's also room for a woman doctor who could demonstrate home vasectomies to housewives and a Closed University for truants.

But if we are to be faced by women on breakfast television can we please have some ordinary, middle-aged boilers? It's ridiculous that you have to be what the public in general consider to be glamorous to read the wretched news. Personally, Angela Rippon's eyes remind me of Tony Zale's eyes. He was middleweight champion of the world in 1946 and after, and if looks could kill – never mind the left hook. I'm not squeamish, not even at eight a.m. and I'd even watch one of my ex-wives read the news, but I suppose we're lumbered with these well-packaged jobs for ever.

Breakfast apart, I accidentally caught the evening job documentary about how much harm alcohol does to people. Who on earth do they get to research such stuff? School leavers? What nonsense. Practically everybody I know should have been dead years ago. But alcohol and television go well together. At weekends particularly, now, television is so bad you have to be drunk to watch it, even if it does mean having to keep one eye closed to see just the one set. But I've hardly had a drink since this morning nonsense began. I get enough kicks from Anna and Dave to last me the day.

Jogging along

When the lease of this body I live in expires I hope to be buried in Canada. It was there, a few days ago, that a gravedigger was sacked for being too cheerful. Apparently he whistled and hummed while acting as a pall-bearer at a cemetery. Another time he held up a skull to his colleagues, while they were shifting remains from one grave to another, wearing a large grin on his face. I like it. I know I shall go to the grave kicking and screaming but there's no need for anybody else to join in the hysteria. Mind you, what these people actually whistle is quite important. I'd prefer to go out to 'Goodnight Ladies' than 'I Know That My Redeemer Liveth', because I know no such thing. Anyway, the vicar of Chaddleworth once told me that I was beyond redemption. A pretty shitty thing for a vicar to say, by the way, but he had been at the Bells. (Appropriately, the slogan on their labels is 'Afore Ye Go' and I'd like to suggest to the Smirnoff people that they adopt 'Just the One' as their slogan.)

Yes, what with all the recent digs, I've been more than usually preoccupied with death. The other night I had one of the worst attacks of angst I've ever suffered. I was utterly exhausted but I didn't dare close my eyes so convinced was I that if I did then I'd never wake up again. But, as you can see, I did, and to the good news of the jolly gravedigger. The bad news was an article about how to achieve longevity, jogging, health food, taking care of one's body and all the rest of that area of nonsense. I do wish people would stop telling me what I 'ought' to do. It's so bloody Germanic.

Anyway, we elected a new member to the low life hall of fame last week – the jazz man who died aged 100. Just before he snuffed it, on the actual birthday itself, he uttered the immortal words, 'If I'd known I was going to live this long I would have taken better care of myself.' Marvellous stuff. He'd smoked from the age of six and all his life he'd refused to drink water. Now that's what I call a marathon and it puts this smoker-since-fourteen and Perrier addict firmly in my place. Quite obviously our hero must have carefully avoided free-range cornflakes and any form of exercise for 100 years. As I've said before just what the hell do these health freaks want to get fit *for*? Cranks is a damned good name for a health food chain and, by God, don't the customers therein look absolutely ghastly? Joggers too, like militant feminists, tend to look pretty unattractive and a three-mile canter isn't going to turn a toad into a prince. I can suddenly visualise Cyril Connolly filling up with muesli, donning shorts and then running round the park, and it's ridiculous. I think jogging might be rather like listening to pop music on earphones all day in so far as both occupations relieve their mindless followers of the burden of actually having to *think*.

There are far less strenuous ways of avoiding constructive thought, such as reading the *Sun*, masturbating or listening to Norman Balon on the subject of the Middle East. Jogging, eating bran and most forms of abstinence are about a futile effort to avoid death. I remember Maurice Richardson once telling me, 'I don't read the obituaries any more. Death has lost its charm for me.' If only he'd lived to read about the Canadian gravedigger. Perhaps the reaper isn't so grim. I'd like to think that one day our man in Toronto – if he gets another job – will hold up my petrified pancreas to his mates, positively wreathed in smiles. I had intended to leave my body to the hepatic experts of the Royal Free Hospital, not to further science but to relieve Norman of the burden of a whip round in the Coach for the funeral expenses. But now it has to be a single to Canada, a perch in a cosy bar and then a wait. Life is a waiting room anyway. Sometimes I think I can hear the station announcer: 'Owing to an unforeseen fault – a strong constitution – and a refusal to take the timetable seriously, death will not arrive until tomorrow.' And, as far as waiting rooms go, it's not too bad. There are plenty of cigarette machines, plenty of steaks, ice cream, chocolate cakes, booze and you don't *have* to eat the nut cutlets or jog up and down the platform. Yes, tomorrow will do.

Taxing

If there are as many as 1,760 readers of this wretched column with current accounts in the black I'd be obliged if they'd sponsor me to run a mile at the rate of £1 per yard. It would almost exactly pay the bill I've just received from the Inland Revenue; £176 would just about kill me but £1,760 is a joke and utterly beyond me. As an estimate on the part of these tax officials it proves that their heads are even more deeply submerged in the sand than mine. Never mind, I've still got three days before they take me to court or start distraint proceedings or both. Of course, running a mile would kill me but that too would cancel the bill. What I also need, and it may be too late, is an accountant and one who can grasp just how much it takes in the way of expenses to lead and write about the low life. It's cold outside and if you're not on the firm or on the staff then you're in the shit. Only workaholic writers like Benny Green survive, and they can work and write so much because, luckily for them, they have the extraordinary idea that what they churn out is good. If a man's pleased with himself he can make money.

Right, having got that whinge out of the way I shall proceed to break down my day in the hope that someone at the Inland Revenue will appreciate just how much it costs to do absolutely nothing without expenses. Morning tea, Kleenex, cigarettes, phone call to apologise for night before £2. Copy of the *Times* and hair of the dog £1.40. Taxi to the Coach and Horses (unable to walk, too down at heel) £1.60. Three large vodkas by myself to face oncoming day £3. Drinks for information, gossip, dirty jokes, tall stories and autobiographical reminiscences from Charlie, Conan, Jeremy and No Knickers Joyce £6. Two more large vodkas by myself to keep going £2. Chicken in lemon sauce, beef with spring onions and ginger, mixed vegetables in Jubilee Dragon to sooth infuriated pancreas £6.50. Iodine, sticking plaster and bandages for wounds inflicted by Chinese waiters £1.75. Drinks and fruit machine in afternoon club £6. Returned favourite 3.30 Kempton Park £5. Refresher course of vodkas in Coach at 5.30 £7. Taxi home £1.60. Money for old rope for suicide attempt £3.50. Long-distance phone calls to friends in middle of night to moan, whine and complain £4.75.

Now something out of that lot has to be tax deductible. But take a day out of Soho. In an hour's time I'm off to Bristol University to speak to the students. God knows why. I've got nothing to say, but it may sell a *Spectator* or two. Anyway, apart from the fare being £24 return, I shall need four large ones for Dutch courage and at BR prices that's about £7.20. Then, drinks for students and drinks for my wounded pride on the way home and you can see that it's pretty easy when you suffer from fiscal haemophilia. The thing is, if you work from nine to five in an office, then you can't spend money.

Now, apart from tax, I'm being sued by a company for £500. More folly. For years and years alchemists the world over tried to make gold and they only turned to that daft pursuit after having spent 3,000 years trying to get blood out of stones. You'd think history would teach someone something. But no. If things get much worse I might have to buy a bugle and start practising the Last Post.

Oddly enough, I did have an idea about how to make some money the other day if only I could get it off the ground. I should have thought American tourists, for example, might be getting heartily sick of seeing the Tower of London and the Abbey etc. In conjunction with some hideous place like the Hilton why not, I thought, organise a low-life sightseeing tour of this stinking metropolis? At £100 each a day a coach load would gross £5,000. For that they could get thrown out of the Swiss Tavern, visit a betting shop, have a typically English meal thrown at them by Norman, meet a bailiff, get taken to Wormwood Scrubs by a tipstaff, and wake up the following morning skint on a park bench before going to court. If I can get this one going I reckon I could earn £30,000 a week. Very nearly as much as Benny Green and Frederick Forsyth put together.

Indisposed

At last, after years of trying, I've finally landed the Spring Double. Pneumonia *and* pleurisy. I wonder how much Ladbroke's would have laid me against getting the two? Anyway, I'm back in St Stephen's Hospital where I was first shown the yellow card in December 1965. But this is the first time I've ever been in a hospital for something that wasn't self-inflicted and that makes it seem somehow a little unfair. They didn't *conscript* kamikaze pilots.

The ward I'm in is called Ellen Terry and down the corridor there's a ward called Alfred Tennyson. I tried to get moved to Benny Green or Larry Adler but they're completely filled with industrial accidents: people who've fallen into typewriters etc. There are six of us in Ellen Terry. Mr Rice opposite has a dodgy lung and he also has diarrhoea which he reports to me on in graphic detail every thirty minutes or so. I think I hate him. Next to him there lies a sheer hulk, poor Mr Collander, whose bladder is up the spout. Then there's Mr Handley, a costermonger from Fulham, who is rather delightful really and who has cancer of the lung. He quite rightly got a little crotchety with a young doctor last week who told him to give up smoking. As he said, 'A little late for that fucking advice, isn't it?' My chest man and registrar is all right though, even if he has developed the habit of draining my right lung via a needle inserted into it under my shoulder blade. Sadly, his students who play games with me preparatory to taking their finals all suffer from halitosis. A couple of them couldn't diagnose a decapitation but I gather they'll qualify.

What has been fascinating though, here in the bowels of Ellen Terry for the past three weeks, is the behaviour of the 'domestics'. Nearly all these ladies are West Indian, and by Christ what a mistake people make in thinking black is black and all the same. Africans are far more benign as a rule. But my *bête noire* is Granadian and we fell out a fortnight ago when I asked her to include a paper cup in the rubbish she was clearing away from the top of my locker. She erupted more rawly than the psoriasis in the next bed. 'I clean away shit,' she told me, 'and I clean away wine. I clear up tissues and wash glasses, but I don't touch paper cups.' Then, grabbing a handful of her own flesh, she went on, 'And this skin is black. Pure black. It's black, West Indian skin and what's more I know who my father is and I know who my mother is.' Never have I known such sudden paranoia. That evening Miss Barbados declared war too. She gave me a bowl of soup but wouldn't give me a spoon. 'I serve soup,' she said, 'but I never have anything to do with spoons.' 'Particularly white men's spoons,' she muttered under her breath.

But open warfare has existed since I became addicted to tea twenty days ago. Not a drink or a cigarette for twenty days and something had to give. (Are addicts addicted to addiction?) I must have continuous tea now. I chain-drink the stuff but I'm not allowed in the kitchen to boil the water for my teabags and the West Indians watch me like hawks. I run dangerous gauntlets to boil water. Yes, it's quite a serious place is the Ellen Terry Ward and you don't have to behave that eccentrically to get into their bad books or get classified as I have by Sister as being a 'difficult patient'. Only the other night as they were doing their final round with the drugs trolley I asked the staff nurse in charge of the amazing vehicle, 'Do you have anything to make love last?' *Eine kleine Nacht* aside, but that nurse has been off me ever since. This is a very serious place and if my friend Mr Handley doesn't start taking his impending death a little more seriously he could be in for some cold treatment. Meanwhile, the cockles of my heart have been wonderfully warmed by the amazingly kind and touching get well cards and letters I've received from readers of this column since I've been in Ellen Terry. What a nice lot you sound. And now for two weeks' convalescence. My man with the long needles has told me to do absolutely nothing when I get home. That shouldn't be too difficult.

Big guns

In the past, I've always resolved to while away those endless hours of boredom while held prisoner in a hospital bed by reading those books I've never got around to but which I've stupidly felt *obliged* to read. *The Mill on the Floss* and yet another attempt at *Ulysses*, for example. But it doesn't work. Reading can be hard work and too much for a sick man. You have to be pretty fit to read Bernard Levin on Soviet dissidents, but to get through *The Mill on the Floss*, Proust or even the more recent and slender but overrated *French Lieutenant's Woman* while stuffed with more tubes than the London Underground system, you need to be a marathon man capable of beating Jack Dempsey after twenty-six miles. What I did get stuck into though was a load of hospital C.S. Forresters. The 'Hornblower' books. I liked them when I first read them and they stand up well. Excellent, lightish, stirring stuff. Anyway, I've always been a fan of Nelson and his colleagues and recent events in Europe have in no way diminished my wish to blow a few Frenchmen and their ships clean out of the water.

But there I was in St Stephen's, no seventy-four-gun ship of the line, but a mere sloop shipping water, short of provisions and out of powder. Ever since I've been back here in port licking my wounds I keep looking at the captain's log book for that last day of memorable action in St Stephen's. Cape St Vincent palls beside it. Anyway, three days ago, I awoke at three a.m. and lay there tossing in my hammock until six a.m. I was desperate for my fix of tea and by 6.15 a.m. when the West Indian enemy still hadn't hove in sight with the tea trolley, I made my own way with my teabag and limped to the kitchen. All seemed quiet and deserted. I put the teabag in the cup, boiled the kettle and then, too late, I heard it – the rustle of a dress. It could have been the crack of a mainsail. My inbuilt lookouts, utterly exhausted, were asleep. I turned round and, clapping my reading glasses to my good eye, I beheld the awesome sight of Fernanda, the gorgon of Granada, bearing down on me, her top gallants straining in front of the wind. There was no time to bequeath my dear Susan to the nation or to run up a patriotic signal. This mere sloop, as redundant as a dinghy at Trafalgar, was suddenly about to be engaged by the 136-gun, Santissima Trinidad, the biggest warship afloat. Vainly I swung the wheel hard to port but her first shot knocked the cup out of my hand and sent boiling water everywhere. 'You not supposed to be here,' she screamed. 'Dis my kitchen. Get de fuck out.' Now she was wrestling the kettle away from my grasp and, weak, panting and undermanned as it were, the last thing I could afford was a Rastafarian boarding party. I backed away and dropped anchor by the fridge. She stood by the sink riding the swell, a master gunner wearing gold-rimmed bifocals and peering down the barrel to judge another broadside.

There are, thank God, and always have been, moments of inspiration that have changed the course of history and as my right hand suddenly felt the comforting lump of a half pound of butter I knew she was but a Rupert to my Cromwell. I had offered my kingdom for a horse and got Shergar. The butter hit her on the left shoulder with such force she spun round and dropped the kettle. Making full sail and all speed she sailed past me, screaming, to take refuge in Alfred Tennyson ward. I could hear her in the distance as I refilled the kettle. 'De man in Ellen Terry, Mister Bernard, he fucking mad. Try to kill me. He cut my arm wid butter. Crazy man.' It was a momentous victory. Britannia rules the kitchen.

Of course, there were diplomatic peace talks as I lay in the cockpit panting, trembling and almost vomiting after the strain, the loss of temper and what you might call the exercise. A friendly Jamaican envoy, the night sister from Alfred Tennyson, brought me more tea and soothed my fevered brow as the church bells rang out the length and breadth of England. At midday I came home. Whether I can take two more weeks in bed, even at home, I'm not sure. I still can't read a major opus and when I dipped into Carola Oman's *Nelson* last night it made me restless and I lay here fretfully, longing for action again and my own seventy-four-gun command in a really big hospital like the Bellevue in New York. I'd give them a teabag party that would make the Boston one look sick. But it's all brought one thing home. My body wants no more of the low life. It's in a dreadful state and it wants mollycoddling.

By the way, there have been more lovely cards and notes from readers, whom I thank from the bottom of my pacemaker. To them I shall reveal in my will where I've hidden the teabags.

Saturday fever

It seems to me that the League Against Cruel Sports only opens its mouth to change step. One expects a load of horse manure during Grand National week but if these people were really concerned about cruel sports you'd think they'd be venting their concern on such cruelties as getting married, having a family, eating in Trusthouse Forte establishments, the licensing laws and editors who can do without me. One horse, Duncreggan, did get killed, having received the kiss of death the day before when I drew him in the *Spectator* sweep, but if he'd got killed at Southwell or Plumpton on a Monday afternoon you wouldn't have heard a dicky bird.

And oddly enough, talking of getting killed, I nearly died laughing on the morning of the National when I read in the

'Notebook' (9 April) that our old friend Geoffrey Wheatcroft spends his Saturday mornings doing a little work in the Reading Room of the British Museum when he's stuck in London. Pull the other one. I know for a fact that when he says he's off to a recital in Smith Square he is in fact off to the Savile Club to play snooker. But don't think I'm getting at Geoffrey. I remember well just how important this sort of thing was before I had my own library, record collection and games room. Mind you, I was lucky enough to have been steeped in culture and scholarship from the word go, so it's all water off a duck's back to me and hardly worth mentioning; suffice it to say that my mother left me in a Fortnum's carrier bag on the steps of the London Library when I was an hour old. That was a Saturday morning in 1932 and I believe my mother had been browsing in Hatchards when she gave birth to me in the poetry department. At the same time, my father was preparing for the event just up the road, browsing in Cogswell & Harrison for a pair of twelve-bores.

Yes, Saturday mornings have become one hell of a problem. Geoffrey went on to say that after the literary grind he goes on to shop in Soho and then to do some drinking in El Vino. Luckily for me I was brought up by my foster parents – my foster father was the chief librarian of the Bodleian – to make my own pasta, so I've never had to join that precious throng of BBC Talks Producers who walk up and down Old Compton Street on Saturday mornings clutching sprigs of fennel and would-be bedside lamps in the shape of chianti bottles. Not that you see much of that sort of thing nowadays. What's screwed up Saturday in London, deadened it if you like, is that nearly everyone now has a weekend cottage, or invitation to one. If you haven't been invited to an 'in' county for the weekend by a Tarquin, Rupert, Cassandra or Candida you can count yourself dead or dead drunk in El Vino. This is, of course, a large helping of sour grape juice on my part. There's nothing I like more on a Saturday morning than sitting on Jasper and Letitia's sofa sipping a stingy Bloody Mary, scratching myself and my last two 10p pieces together and listening to them saying that things have got so bad they can barely pay the gardener, the bill for the logs, Eton and the second Range Rover, and that they're very much afraid that lunch is lamb and not beef.

But to go back to the League Against Cruel Sports for a moment, it's on these weekend occasions that they're conspicuous by their absence. Letitia and Jasper always have six children – they're either practising Catholics or they conceive in post-Badminton Horse Trial euphoria – called Sebastian, Benjie, Magnus, Samantha, Arabella and Sabrina. At weekends, starting on Saturday morning when Geoffrey is pretending to read Pascal in the original but in fact making out a Soho shopping list, these children completely take over the house. Darling Bashy knocks your vodka out of your hand, Benjie stands on your balls, and Magnus sticks his finger in your eye. Letitia, vaguely spotting all this, stirs herself and says, 'Oh *do* come along, darlings, I'm sure Jeff doesn't want you doing that.' These children should of course be put down like Duncreggan or put out to grass until they're twenty-one. They throw jam at you at teatime, cheat at Monopoly, cry when they lose, have epileptic fits at bed time and they know at a glance that the clothes you stand up in are the only ones you've got or very nearly.

On reflection, Geoffrey Wheatcroft has it right. Saturday mornings can be well obliterated in the British Museum and, as he admits, there's no need to tarry after opening time when Pascal gives way to *Man on the Spot*, *Augur* and *The Scout*. But I have, and always have had, my doubts about a Saturday drink in El Vino. Imbibing with hacks and solicitors is another thing the League Against Cruel Sports should look into. Meanwhile it's back to bed for me for another week where Saturday is much like any other day.

Comeback

The comeback trail, as that unprepossessing would-be, Joe Bugner, could testify, is one hell of a slog, pitted with potholes and boredom. I thought I'd retired and that the days of tightrope walking and hustling were over. There I was, lying on my bed, sipping tea and watching the Embassy World Snooker Championship on television when my manager phoned up out of the blue. His old, familiar and horrible voice had my adrenalin pumping in seconds. 'What's the matter, have you given up or something?' 'No, Norman,' I said. 'In fact I'm feeling much better.' 'Well then, if you're not bleedin' dying why don't you look into the Coach? I mean, don't fucking give up, eh?' It was like hearing the bells for 'seconds out' again.

I dropped my insulin into the wastepaper basket, opened a packet of digestive biscuits – the ones with plain chocolate on one side – and stared at the old-fashioned tumbler full of swizzle sticks that was gathering dust with other souvenirs like my typewriter on the desk. I got up and looked at myself closely in the mirror. Was I too old to drink again? Had the head, legs and pockets gone? Norman had said, 'You can always drink Perrier, you know', before he'd rung off, but the sound of his voice had me suddenly longing for those ten- and twelve-round bouts again. To hell with starting at the bottom again. The lure of the main event was as strong as ever. There I was, sitting on my stool in the corner. Norman

bent over me flapping a tea cloth in my face and pressing a
£20 note to my jacket pocket and whispering urgently, 'You'll
need twenty more stitches there later but you've got him now.'
I eyed my opponent, a particularly successful friend, but he
looked depressingly strong. True, I'd outfumbled him for
eight rounds, but he was still there. Norman pushed me off
my stool and out again and for one second, a split second, I
dropped my guard and smiled. I never even heard the bell for
last orders. I heard my voice feebly asking, 'Where am I?' and
someone answered, 'It's all right, champ, you're in the Colony
Room Club.' You win some, you lose some.

I shook myself out of the daydream and took another close
look at the old face. My eyes were quite white for the first
time in eight weeks and the telltale angry red denoting liver
damage had vanished from the palms of my hands. I was
ready to spar if not fight. I got my kit out of the wardrobe –
the old jeans and jersey that brought me luck – put them on
and then stepped out into the roar of Great Portland Street.
I bobbed and weaved my way down to Piccadilly avoiding
the Stags Head, George and Woodcock – something told
me I wasn't quite ready – and walked into the tea room of
Fortnums.

Within fifteen minutes, after a pot of tea and a scone, I
realised I'd walked into a hornet's nest. Those crazy sessions
in the Coach and all over Soho paled beside Fortnums. This
was where the champions hung out. The hardest bunch of
nuts I've ever found myself in the midst of. At the next table
there sat six Iranian students sipping lemon tea and counting
travellers' cheques. In a far corner the ex-film star, Terence
Stamp, sat pretending to learn some lines and at the next table
a varnished, lacquered, dyed blonde sat yawning opposite her
seventy-year-old meal, clothes, rent and holiday ticket. I was

joined by an American tourist who ordered a peach melba and who then said, 'Sure is one hell of a place, your London.'

I threw in the towel and the waitress took nearly ten minutes to bring me the bill. For the same money I could have had a harmless vodka in the cosy comfort of the Coach with the added bonus of Norman propelling me from my corner at the sight of a new punter like a man saying 'bone' to a dog. Make no mistake, the Fortnums mob are like tempered steel. There's no Charlie there to press your head against the cool porcelain of the lavatory pan when you've been beaten. No Conan to tell you how to dodge the tipstaff or Tom to tell you how to open a buff envelope. And I thought it was tough at the bottom. And what of the manageress of Fortnums? A Grenadier compared to Norman's Catering Corps NCO.

The comeback proper started in earnest yesterday. I had a glass of cider before lunch and went to my local instead of the corner shop for cigarettes, to drench myself in the atmosphere again. It stinks but it's the stink I know.

Finders keepers

There's something slightly obscene about the American obsession with litigation, but then, with a handful of exceptions like Lincoln, W.C. Fields, Flash Gordon and Rocky Graziano, they always have had their values all wrong. The latest nutcase is a thirty-year-old unemployed docker called Joey Coyle I read about in Tuesday's *Standard*. He found $1.2 million (about £756,000) in the street in Los Angeles and is suing the owner of the money because he says it has ruined his life by giving him a taste of how the other half lives. Mr Coyle went on a little spending spree, and when the police found him two weeks later when he was down to his last $105,000, a paltry

£64,000, which he had stuffed in his boots. To cap it all an insane jury accepted his plea of temporary insanity and found him not guilty. I'd very much like to know just how he knocked out the odd £692,000 in two weeks and I'd very much like to have a lawyer with the gall to stand up in court and say, 'My client has suffered severe psychological disruption and mental instability. If the security company (who lost the money) had been more careful my client would not have been damaged.'

Speaking as a middle-man I have had mouth-watering tastes and sick-making tastes of how both other halves live and I can't say that either have ruined my life; such a hefty sum is a punch that a one-time docker should be able to ride in comfort. A man who'd spent his entire life living at one extreme or another I could feel sorry for, but Mr Coyle, at some time pretty comfortably employed if our lads in Wapping and Liverpool have been anything to go by, should be able to regard a million-dollar windfall as a mere loan from the Almighty and proof that every time it rains it rains dollars from heaven. It's nothing to go mad over.

But take the very disturbing opposite end of the fiscal spectrum and consider just how awful and brain-damaging it could be for the Duke of Westminster or Lord Howard de Walden to find a fiver in the street. 'Duke found wandering in Grosvenor Street, mumbling incoherently and talking gibberish. Police say the Duke went missing yesterday and was found with 5p in his shoe. In a statement last night the Duchess said, "Buffy must have been absolutely shattered to find such a small sum. We're trying to retrace his footsteps and we'd very much like to contact the man who saw him buy a half of bitter and a cheese roll in the Antelope." Inspector Smith of the Chelsea police who is leading the investigation said that they are working on the theory that the fiver was dropped by a dropout. A tramp is believed to be helping them with their inquiries. The Westminster family motto is "Spend, spend, spend".'

One can only hope that Mr Coyle gave most of the £692,000 away as well as buying himself a headache and AIDS. But forgetting him for a moment, if you need further proof that Americans are mad – all right, naive – then what about a ridiculous book just published by two of their doctors called *How to Control Your Drinking*. This is claimed to be a self-help book which shows that an alcoholic doesn't have to abstain for ever. In my opinion the barman in *Lost Weekend* had it right when he told Ray Milland, 'One's too many and a hundred's not enough.' But Messrs Miller and Munoz don't agree, and in this ridiculous book they list alternatives to getting drunk when getting drunk is what you want. They advocate relaxation when the thirst hits you and they recommend 'Waiting in line (American for queueing). Riding a bus. Doing housework. Playing ping-pong. Talking to a very angry person. Taking care of an emergency.'

Playing ping-pong? I ask you. As for an emergency, could there be a bigger one than queueing up in the Coach with a glass of Perrier in one hand waiting to play ping-pong with Norman just as he's been told by his mother that she's leaving all her money to me? Could this really help keep one moderately sober? But relaxation isn't enough. According to Miller and Munoz you have to be assertive as well as relaxed to drink moderately and control it. And they give the readers a list of assertive remarks to trot out when you're screaming for the Smirnoff. 'I don't like being called honey.' 'I really enjoyed that dessert.' 'I am very angry with you.' Only if I'd met Mr Coyle when he found his million dollars, and he'd taken me out to dinner and then refused to lend me any money could I justifiably say anything like that.

Dear Diary

I was deeply disappointed that Hitler's diaries turned out to be fakes but I wasn't in the least surprised. He was far too unstable, I thought, to keep a diary and anyway the madness and evil of his day-to-day existence was always going to ensure that he wouldn't be forgotten. He's always held a morbid fascination for me and even now, when I see a photograph of him, I feel a sort of unbelieving and bewildered horror such as I experience when I'm drinking coffee in Maison Valerie and find myself surrounded by women dressed from jumble sales and reading the *Guardian*. But anyway, when I told you the other day that I'd been sorting out old papers, letters and snapshots, I forgot to tell you that I found two diaries: one for 1975 and the other for 1978. Sadly, the *Sunday Times* are unlikely to offer me a single, lousy penny for them – they like to keep their diaries benign and bland – but I do think I ought to now own up to a few entries before they're unearthed in thirty years' time in the cellar of the Coach and Horses and have doubts cast on their authenticity. As I said, Hitler was far too unstable to keep a diary; to address such a book, day in and day out, the author needs both feet firmly on the ground plus the sincere intention of plodding towards the grave with a sober, realistic tread devoid of fantasy, anger, paranoia and self-pity, simply recording the beauty and wonder of the daily round.

With that in mind I find it rather strange that my entry for Friday 4 April 1975 should read: 'I find it almost impossible to believe that anyone can be as unhappy as I am. Can misery cause insanity? Saved by a 32/1 double at Sandown Park.' Happily, I must have come back down to earth a week later, when I see I wrote: 'Met a very nice girl called Valerie at a party in Hampshire. She asked me what sign I was and when

I said Gemini she said, "So was my father. I killed him in a
car crash and when they took him to hospital they found a
dozen french letters in his pocket." I cheered her up by telling
her that he must have had a lot of love to give around. Driven
back to London with John Le Mesurier by a man whose hobby
is flying a Spitfire.'

Well, whoever it was who said – and I think it was me – life
is ghastly and boring and the good days are the exception and
not the rule, got it right. I doubt very much whether Hitler
ever spent his birthday, 20 April, like: 'Went to launderette
and sat there wondering where on earth Miss Right is.' On
the other hand you wouldn't be bowled over with surprise
if he'd written as I did for 22 April: 'Had tea with Caroline
who told me that she's "very serious" about a major in
the Household Cavalry.' But when you can't get any lower
you have to surface, and by 1978, three years later to the
week, the launderette had closed, Caroline had vanished into
Knightsbridge Barracks and Barbara had appeared. 'Barbara
came over for lunch and then we had a row in bed. She kept
on talking about her shopping expeditions while I was feeling
terrible about being skint. Eventually it was all right and she
drove me to the Chelsea Arts Club. In a very tense foursome,
partnered by a dentist, I potted the last four colours to win a
good game. After, in the ladies bar, talked about insanity to Bill
Redgrave and Freddie Deane.'

There must have been many days even in Hitler's life
when he wouldn't have bothered to record, 'Eva came over
for yoghurt tea and then drove me to the Chelsea Arts Club
where, partnered by a dentist, I shot four people.' Yes, life
is dull but there are odd, underlying mysteries in the most
pedestrian of diary jottings. More from mine. 'Went to *Sunday
Times* and spoke incoherently to Magnus Linklater about trip

to Chantilly. Tea with Barbara who gave me book of love poems. Then delivered piece on Les Blair to Bob Smythe at the *Radio Times*. He mentioned Joan of Arc and I said she was such a bitch, if she was alive now she'd be a sub on the *Radio Times*.' A very silly day, by the sound of it, and matched only by a never-to-be-published entry made by Hitler: 'Went to Nuremberg and spoke incoherently to Keitel about trip to Moscow. Tea with Eva who gave me Shirley Conran's book on gardening. Delivered *Mein Kampf* to Frank Giles at the *Sunday Times*. Got advance on expenses. He mentioned Chamberlain who is, I believe, a sub on the *Sun*.'

Lucky devils

My comeback was unintentional and it's been a little disappointing so far. You could say it was forced on me. I called into my ex-wife's office to have the weekly cup of tea with her. She was out but back in ten minutes, so I thought I'd kill the time by having just 'the one' in a revolting pub next door in Berwick market called the Blue Posts. Who should walk in but Norman Balon. I felt I'd been caught *in flagrante*. Not since Mavis's husband came home unexpectedly twenty years ago and found me sitting next to her, stark naked on a chaise-longue, have I felt such an utter shit. Out of bed at last and in the Blue Posts and not the Coach and Horses. Norman, of course, was doing his daily Soho round being bloody inquisitive and trying to assess how much more or less other pubs in the area were taking. So I had to go back to him and, unlike a lot of wives, he took me. Half an hour later I was in the Coach and having 'the one' as though I'd never left it.

One of the things I loathed most about school, the army and regular employment was the feeling that I was missing something and that in the pubs, clubs, cafés, dives and racecourse bars there was some sort of magic in progress that I wasn't able to conjure with. How must a bank clerk feel when he sees the clock moving towards opening time or the first race? So there I was in the Coach, back in the fold, and seeing for myself what I'd been missing. I must say Norman was charming. Some poor bastard, an absolute stranger who'd walked in for a quiet, small beer, was told: 'Get off that fucking stool and give it to Jeff here. He's sick.' No, nothing had changed. It was Friday and fish was on the menu and a few people were 'unwinding' after a hard week's slog in the office making personal telephone calls, stealing stationery and working out their expenses. A couple of pornographers were moaning about excessive police raids, someone said it hadn't been the same without me (better?), another person shook me by the hand, and many others said how well I was looking, although I know just how I look.

What did surprise me was everyone's astonishment that I was shortly off to Spain *alone*. Alone has very nearly become a dirty word. It's taken me about forty-nine years to get to not minding being alone, but it doesn't do to mention the fact publicly. Out of sheer, dreadful sentiment my heart used to bleed at such sights as a man or woman eating alone in a restaurant – on a Sunday particularly – but I think people are disturbed by someone being alone because they presume that he or she is automatically on the verge of suicide, living in squalor surrounded by dirty shirts and unwashed dishes and as friendless as a Getty. I've also been told that a man who lives alone forgets his manners since he's not always jumping up to open doors for ladies etc, but such a man should have at least one set of spare keys.

Anyway, if one person asked me, 'Haven't you got a girl you can take to Spain with you?', fifty did. Except for Norman, of course, who said I'd save money. No, I've had my share of holidays for two, and rubbing Ambre Solaire into someone's back while they read Harold Robbins and then suggest going somewhere miles away from a bar for a 'nice walk' isn't my idea of a healing fortnight. It's also a very dodgy business having a row with someone on holiday. You can't actually hide when you're sulking, and anyway you can only sulk until the next lousy meal brings you together again. A certain amount of sexual athleticism is also expected on holiday even when it's ninety-five in the shade and the cheap brandy is bubbling around in your gut. Then there's that dreadful foursome. Madam takes her head out of her paperback, spots another couple and in no time at all you're together having a drink as though it's Christmas. They tell you they come from Sidcup, Spokane or Perth and that last year they went to Majorca but they're not going to go back there ever again and that they're in a marvellous hotel that's only £10 a day. Then you pair off. He tells you that he's in computers and when you tell him you're a hack he says he can't say he's ever heard of you but you must meet some 'jolly interesting people'. Back at the hotel, between bouts of diarrhoea, Madam is not talking but pretending to read. Her shoulders are peeling and suddenly it's don't touch me time. A cockroach crawls out of your sponge bag and it occurs to you that by London time the Coach has just opened. You can almost hear them saying, 'Gosh, I bet they're having a marvellous time. Lucky devils.' What you do hear is, 'I hope you're not going to get drunk and be rude to that nice couple again.' Not for the next fortnight though.

Well mauled

William Harrison 'Jack' Dempsey, the 'Manassa Mauler' has taken the final count as *Ring Magazine* would, and will, say. He

was born on 24 June 1895 and was exceptionally well bred
for the business of fighting, his ancestry being Irish-Scottish-
Cherokee. He weighed 187lbs and he was 6ft ¾in tall. Before
Muhammad Ali, who tipped the scales at anything between
186lbs and 230lbs, all the class heavyweights were Dempsey's
size and with the exception of the exceptional Ali they must
have thrown three punches to the likes of Larry Holmes's one.
But one from the likes of Dempsey or Louis could suffice.
Some nut of a scientist in New York once fixed a mechanical
device in the heavy bag at Stillman's Gymnasium and came
up with the thought-provoking fact that a left hook from Joe
Louis was the equivalent of a 90lb weight being dropped on
your head from a height of 6ft. Not many hung around long
enough to dispute the possibility, and Dempsey certainly hit as
hard. Dempsey had, for the benefit of record freaks, a total of
eighty fights of which he won forty-nine by the short route and
he lost seven. Two of them of course, to Gene Tunney. And
there's the crunch for me. Dempsey's death has me thinking of
Tunney yet again and that's not to detract from the old mauler.

Years ago, there was an amusement arcade in the Charing
Cross Road where for a couple of pence you could – and I did
hundreds of times – see an old hand-wound flicker movie of
Tunney beating Dempsey. I'm not here to revive memories of
the famous 'long count' or to speculate as to whether Tunney
could have survived after nine seconds but I do remember
very well how extraordinarily vunerable Dempsey was to
Tunney's overhand right crosses. That's why, I suppose, I have
never been able to rate Dempsey in the top four. Comparisons
may be odious but they kill the time of day. Tunney beat him
decisively twice. Ali would have boxed his head off. Louis
would have stopped him and Marciano was unstoppable. For
all of that Dempsey was a great fighter who had a sort of

uneducated ferocity that brought a glamour to the ring that died when Ali packed it in. In February 1926, Dempsey boxed twelve exhibition bouts in the space of one week, winning them all and eight of them by knockouts.

Even the names of his opponents have a ring about them that provokes the deepest nostalgia. Where are they now? Fireman Jim Flynn, Ed 'Gunboat' Smith, One-Round Garrison, Battling Levinsky and the Boston Bearcat. It makes you want to weep to look at Joe Bugner. Watching Dempsey chase Jess Willard around the ring when he won the world title is a remarkable reminder that the brother of the 'noble art' is that exciting animal the fighter. Pitted against each other Dempsey and Tunney were a pretty uncivilised spectacle that I find irresistible. Tunney psyched him, though, as well as outpointing him. Before the first fight the referee told Tunney, 'I don't want any squawks from the loser when this fight is over.' Tunney answered, 'Go over and tell that to Dempsey. He'll be more interested in what the loser has to say than I.'

But one of the more endearing human qualities is bravery. Guts come in all shapes and sizes. The little Lord Nelson had a hundred miles of them as did Edith Cavell, and Jack Dempsey wasn't the hero of thousands of young men in their day because of his patent leather shoes or flashing smile. (You have to be very well-loved to smile like Errol Flynn or Dempsey.) There's something about boxers, though. I'm biased, having had a shot at it, but I soon realised in my Jack Solomon's Gymnasium days that they're the 'nicest' of sportsmen. When and if you can box and fight like 'Sugar' Ray Robinson you don't actually find it quite as necessary to be *nasty* to people. Temperament is part and parcel of it all, and John McEnroe, for example, will always be an arsehole as far as I'm concerned. No, it's all frightfully proper and upstanding even when the adrenalin is gushing. I like a piffling but touching quote from Tunney's autobiography, *A Man Must Fight*, concerning his last encounter. 'Jack greeted me as I entered the Ring: "How are you, Gene?" "Quite well, Jack, and you?" I replied.'

Let mayhem commence. I seem to have been waffling more about Tunney than Dempsey and what I meant to say was that Dempsey was a great fighter and one of the great sportsmen of this century. In the ghastly event of their being such a thing as a repeat known as an afterlife I imagine the aforementioned quote being reversed. 'Gene greeted me as I entered heaven. "How are you, Jack?" "Quite well, Gene, and you?"' He was *all* very well.

Train in Spain

It's widely claimed that it was W.C. Fields who uttered the immortal words 'Never give a sucker an even break', but it isn't so. God murmured them during an afternoon nap on the seventh day. A few million years later the Arabs coined the proverb, 'One minute, life is in your hand. The next minute, it's up your arse.' And three weeks ago I was kept awake all night by two nightingales who were singing in an orange tree outside the bedroom window of my Spanish villa. Well, it's not *my* villa actually, but you'd think a man could remove the nightingales before he lent you a few nights in the gardens of Spain. Keats, Granados, de Falla? Don't make me laugh.

But to start at the beginning, they said, 'Don't fly all the way. See Spain. Get the train from Madrid and see the countryside.' What they didn't say was, 'If you go by train the journey will take thirteen hours and you'll be surrounded by Moroccan shepherds shitting on the floor.' Now I know that last bit may sound a little like a drunk with denture problems trying to sing a carol, but it's quite true. They're really amazing, are these people. Take me to the Race Relations Board if you like, but I'm here to tell you that the Arabs are quite ghastly. I don't mind them shoplifting in Marks and Spencer with £5,000 in their pockets – money *should* be reserved for self-indulgences – and I don't mind them squatting on the pavement outside my front door munching melons, but, when they've watched their flocks and then sold them I wish they'd go home by car. Anyway, I'd taken my right lung to Spain for an airing and that journey took another year off its life.

But I recovered over the next two days and, by a private pool in the sun that overlooked cork tree forests that went down to the shimmering sea, I gazed at the blue mountains of Africa beyond, full, no doubt, of shepherds shitting by their flocks. It was a heavenly sight; but God, omnipresent and not wanting to be outdone by his own work, had put a couple of vultures overhead in that heaven purely for my benefit. If it's not nightingales then it's vultures. Why I'd been picked on like this was my main preoccupation for the next few days as I loafed among the bars of Tarifa. It also occurred to me that if Norman put morsels of octopus, chorizo and salads on the bar in the Coach and Horses and if he also sold quadruple vodkas for 45p to the accompaniment of strumming guitars and clacking castanets then he wouldn't be a half bad bloke.

It was by the pool – put there by Him because I can't swim – one afternoon that I met Helen, the resident English widowperson. A delightful and friendly lady, she had merely two faults that I could see and hear: she said 'Well, this is it' in reply to everything I said, and she was accompanied everywhere by a dog called Roy. As Alan Rawsthorne once told me, 'Never trust a dog with an unsuitable name.' How right he was. Roy was right up Keats', Grandados's and de

Falla's streets and he took up barking when the nightingales came off the night shift. But she was potty about dogs was Helen and there was a stray one nearby that she fed every day. She'd park her car precariously on the mountain road every morning, get out and whistle and then feed left-over french bread rolls to this thing that would come wagging out of the rocks. I mean, you just don't feed french bread to a dog. You might as well offer a cat a sandwich. Anyway, that was the routine every morning and after that she'd drive us to the market in Tarifa, or along the coast to a hotel owned by Nazi war criminals, where I'd have cocktails while she took Roy to the beach to bark at the bare breasts of tourists. I don't think anyone liked Roy very much.

So there I was getting a healthy tan in the middle of a scenic, culinary and alcoholic idyll when He Who Must Be Loved played his last card of the holiday. I was sitting by the pool one afternoon wondering if any of the local oranges would end up on Charlie's stall in Berwick Street when I suddenly got this God-awful pain in my chest. I guessed it might cost about £500 a week to be ill in Spain and anyway I want to be scattered in England and not fed to vultures or Roy. The only way I could get back to London was via Malaga and the only way I could get to Malaga was by taxi. Would you believe 160 kilometres in a taxi? It made my wallet break out in a sweat. Then the additional airfare to Madrid on top of that. Still, better than Moroccan shepherd smells. When I did get back I felt better. All a bit of a cock-up, but that's life, or, as Helen would say, this is it.

Drip feed

I wasn't feeling very well last week. My man who dealt with my chest complaint implied that I might have lung cancer and the thought didn't concentrate the mind, as Doctor Johnson said, but dulled it and made the approach to this wretched typewriter something of an obstacle course. But last Monday, during a visit to Brampton Chest Hospital, a specialist told me that I had nothing 'sinister'. I drew a great breath of relief which made me cough for five minutes. Now this specialist struck me as being something of a shrewd nut. He guessed that I had the odd cigarette and cocktail, and how can you tell that looking at a bronzed Greek god across a desk in a consulting room, God only knows. What did fascinate me was the sight of my heart on the X-ray screen. It's there all right and it looks a lot bigger than it feels. Furthermore, it is not broken as I'd thought it was in an emotional accident I had in 1972 when Juliet told me for the last time, 'You make me sick.'

But what a bloody miracle this body is. If you fed into a cow or a horse what some of us consume in one day, what on earth would happen? I'd very much like to wake up one morning with a cow of the Friesian variety and walk her down to Soho to the Coach and Horses, stopping on the way to buy twenty Players, ply her with vodkas until closing time, whip her off to an Indian restaurant, take her up to the Colony Room Club till 5.30 and then to the Yorkminster, Swiss Tavern, Three Greyhounds, get beaten up by Chinese waiters at midnight, have a row with a taxi driver, set the bed on fire, put it out with tears and then wake up on the floor. Could you then milk the said cow? I doubt it.

During one of my animal visits to the great Fred Winter's yard I said to him, 'Good God, Fred, your horses look magnificent. Beautifully fit.' 'Of course they do, you twit,' he said. 'They don't sit up all night drinking gin and tonic and playing cards.' Anyway, although the past four months have been a bore and then a fright for me, I shall never be converted to jogging, wheat germ, deep-breathing exercises, free-range women or press-ups. It's put-downs and not press-ups that keep a man on his toes. But, as I say, this body never ceases to amaze me. It's very rebellious. It won't lie down. Now that the right lung is mere scar tissue it comes up with another card. The legs and feet are aching and it's got to be circulatory problems. The eyes are deteriorating all the time and what is in good nick doesn't get put to the test as often as it did in the old days or would wish to now. And one of the problems of losing weight is that you get a bony arse and the only thing I can sit on in comfort is a bar stool.

But the crunch is, I suppose, the brain. It's never had more than two or three tracks but they are now in need of repair and like British Rail I shall devote future Sundays to repairing them with Perrier water, the Oxford Dictionary, sackcloth, and ashes. The old nonsense about dying brain cells isn't nonsense. I'm starting a book (I shall bore you with excerpts in the near future) and the difficulty is not being able to remember anything before last Tuesday except for the odd bet, lady, fight and unpaid bill. The fact that my hands tremble indicates no more than a sensitive nature but the fact that my head trembles too has initiated my making another appointment at St Stephen's.

Talking of St Stephen's I must mention the Registrar, Dr McNab, who nursed me through my pneumonic and pleuristic days. I have always held that 99 per cent of the medical profession were, and are, idiots: the playing God with the white coat and talking to you with the sing-song voice as though you were a twelve-year-old halfwit. But this man, like the specialist at the Brompton Chest pad, has restored faith. Not often is it that you meet a man you can immediately trust. Very few spring to mind. I can now add Doctor McNab and

Collins to the list comprising the first Duke of Wellington, Mr Micawber, Rocky Graziano, Fred Winter, my brothers, my ex-wife Ashley and the breakfast television weather forecaster on BBC. I used to think that you could go into the jungle with my old doctor in Suffolk but he died of drink having told me for five years to abstain.

Yesterday I met a fantastic-looking young woman who looks like a gem but with luck might not be as hard as one. What's extraordinary is that she's a qualified nurse. This is what I've been seeking for years: a beautiful nurse. Matrons I've had basinfuls of but with luck – she loves me, she loves me not – I could end up with my own private drip feed.

Just the one

Last Tuesday was as nasty a day as I can remember. I had a bronchoscopy at the Brompton Chest Hospital and it made my eyes water, I can tell you. I was woken up by apprehension at five a.m. – the sickening sort I used to feel waiting for the 10.15 from Newbury wondering if they'd taken the buffet car off – and wandered slowly all the way to the hospital pausing at a bench in Hyde Park to smoke some cigarettes, indulge in some self-pity, and attempt an estimate of the number of my days. Wiping the tears from my red, white and blue eyes I strode purposefully on, thinking *England expects* and *once more into the breach*. I got to the hospital two hours early and sat on the steps smoking more cigarettes.

While I waited in the ward for my pre-med injection a couple of nurses and a young doctor told me so many times that I had nothing to worry about that I knew I had. Above their reassuring smiles their eyes were screaming at the thought of themselves having a bronchoscopy. So they wheeled me off and the pre-med had relieved me of very, very little anxiety. Now this is what happens and doctors need read no further. You're put in a semi-reclining position and the man squirts some anaesthetic jelly up each nostril which really does make your eyes water. Then he sprays your throat with something to dry it up a little, and then it's sprayed with anaesthetic which induced more coughing. Then it's crunchtime. The amazing, reptilian tube with its light at the end is inserted into your hooter. My man had a little difficulty getting through and around the top and a Welsh nurse patted me and said, 'It'll be all right. You've such a small nose, you see. But pretty it is too.' I attempted some facetious jocularity to the effect that small noses didn't mean small everything but, too late, the snake was in my throat. My man, its charmer, now began to take great interest and he repeatedly said to his colleague 'Come and have a look at this', as they stared intently through the other end. Quite obviously there are more navigational problems getting into the lung than I realised. But they were two good men and they told me what was happening all the time. I got one fright. Before getting to the voice box, the one that produced such old immortals as 'I'll Have Just the One', he said, 'I think you've got thrush.' Jesus, that's all I need, I thought, having just discovered Miss Right again. But it was a false alarm.

Then a rather alarming thing happened. He attached a syringe on his end of the line and squirted anaesthetic down. My end didn't like it and tried to reject it. I thought I'd throw up and choke. This he did three times in rapid succession. Then he had trouble in getting into the lung itself – small again, no doubt, in the nurse's opinion – and probably difficult to enter owing to the pub ashtray that's been lodged there for some time. Once in the lung the snake spewed more anaesthetic and I retched and coughed and shook.

The lads were fascinated though and really enjoying themselves. 'See this.' 'What about that?' 'Look at this.' One of them even held my hand, seeing my discomfort. I was rather touched in spite of being busy coughing. Well, they spent what seemed an age looking around the old bellow. More anaesthetic squirts and then something like a thin wire was put down to 'brush' the lung and get a sample of whatever it is that lives on that dreadful, stalagmite-encrusted surface. Then a bit more looking around and chatting and then it was suddenly whipped out of me.

'There we are, all over. It seems to me that you've got a perfectly average lung with maybe some scarring.' Of course, I demanded my money back. What a bloody horrible experience. Then it was almost like handshaking time. 'Well done.' 'You were very good, dear. Behaved véry well you did.' 'Yes, jolly good.' It was rather like being debriefed in an old Ealing film. Perhaps it was the pre-med and all the anaesthetic. I felt like saying, 'I'd like to claim one Me 109 and a possible, sir.' 'Jolly good show, chaps.'

Back in my empty ward I dozed. After three hours or so I thought I'd try a cigarette. Leaning out of the window to avoid detection and still weaker than I realised, I nearly fell out. Now that's a thought. I've never been in traction or an orthopaedic hospital. I might give it a whirl next year.

Settled

Richard Burton overtook me last week but I can assure you that this is only a temporary setback. I have eight years in hand, am cruising into the final furlong hard held and am certain to pip him on the line. All I'm worried about is marrying a Booby. You see I met this strange man last week

– he's a racing correspondent – who calls his wife Booby. I asked him why and he told me that the dictionary definition of booby is 'Flightless bird. Ridiculously easy to catch'. Well, I don't like things to be *that* easy. I've worked hard for my four wives – one of them is a *Spare Rib* reader – and I don't eat windfalls. Burton would marry anything as long as it could walk and breathe.

I did, as it happens, meet a possible fifth Mrs Bernard last week but it turns out that she's got the most extraordinary ideas about what's called 'settling down'. This is a very curious phrase used only by women. I have seen feathered birds settling down and I have seen dust settling down and I have even seen bookmakers settling *up* but just quite what women mean by settling down is another matter. I suspect it means that life is no laughing matter. You could have fooled me. But what puzzles me is what on earth did my four wives think they were getting when they married me? It really is a mystery. I mean, you can see a train when it's coming can't you? My fourth wife, who was and is a scrumptious angel, actually said to me, when she called it a day, 'I thought you'd change and settle down.' I wonder if Elizabeth Taylor entertained the same notions about Mr Burton when they first met. Change? Settle down?

What they don't understand is that it takes money to change and settle down. Lawnmowers aren't cheap, you know. Semi-detacheds in Chislehurst don't exactly fall off trees. (Try saying 'semi-detacheds in Chislehurst' after six large ones.) Settling down means giving up eating Wheelers oysters on borrowed money and taking up shepherd's pie. It also means betraying spirits and sycophantising light ale and real ale. Of course, it would be churlish to accuse all women of having settling down syndrome. It's 66/1 against Nell Gwyn ever having told Charles II that she hoped he might change and settle down. (Incidentally, you may not know but Nell Gwyn was found drowned in a shallow stream in Chelsea. Pissed as a pudding, no doubt.) It's also doubtful that Emma Hamilton had these daft notions. Lady Byron on the other hand was a tremendous change-and-settle-down woman and what a ghastly bitch she was.

Now, there are certain conditions in and under which I could change and settle down. I could do it in Antibes with the Queen Mother and I could do it with Cyd Charisse in Barbados. It would entail tremendous sacrifices – I'd miss my hangovers – and I wouldn't be able to look myself in the mirror after having mowed a lawn or washed a car on a Sunday afternoon after helping with the washing-up and changing the odd nappy, but there's no doubt about it, there are ladies I'd give up talking to bailiffs for.

What I'm not quite sure about is whether it's the change or the settling down that's the hardest part. I think I have settled down in so far as I'm pretty set in my ways. I have come to terms with the fact that my dinner is in the oven and always will be. I have also learned to accept the fact that you only get out of life what you put into it. The sagacious prick who informed me of that piece of information would have had his teeth knocked out if I hadn't been in an alcoholic and diabetic coma at the time, but he meant well. And, bless my soul, don't the ladies mean well when they ask you to change and settle down. Never trust people who mean well. Hitler probably meant well and Cromwell certainly hoped we'd change and settle down.

Anyway, I was tremendously flattered when this girl yesterday said to me, 'When I first saw you in the pub I thought to myself, what's that handsome man doing surrounded by rogues?' Apart from her suspect eyesight she's answered her own question, if you see what I mean. Surrounded by rogues. Say no more. But, for her, I'd try to change and settle down. 'Darling, I've asked a few rogues to Sunday lunch. "No knickers" Joyce says she'll weed the border. Maltese Laurie's going to mow the lawn and Charlie says he'll carve the joint. We could play bridge in the evening and perhaps we might splash out on a bottle of sherry.' 'Oh, Jeffrey, you're an absolute poppet. I'm so glad you've changed and settled down. You don't miss Soho and all those awful people, do you, darling?' 'Of course not, my angel. Take your knickers off. Oops. Sorry. Forgot. We're married and settled down in Chislehurst.'

Privileged

The idea of becoming a writer first came to mind in 1937 when my nanny was pushing me in a superbly upholstered pram across St James's Park on our way to Westminster Abbey for the coronation of King George VI. I was lying there in my ermine nappy sucking on a bottle of Jersey cream – the less fortunate babies of the working and middle classes were sustained on Cow & Gate powdered milk, so Mama told me – contemplating my inheritance when it suddenly occurred to me that when I learned to read and write then I'd write. The idea stuck with me for the next ten years right through my preparatory schooldays in Switzerland and I remember vividly, when I was being flown home after having been expelled for climbing Mont Blanc during prep with another boy called Richard West, that the idea came to me to write a novel based loosely on my sexual experiences up to the age of twelve.

My next memory of this burning ambition to assault my father's typewriter is of the morning of my 13th birthday.

It was a pleasant summer's morning – they started in May in those days – and Jenkins had just handed me a glass of Buck's Fizz. I had wandered past the fountains, on the lower lawns when I bumped into McGregor, the head gardener. As I plucked an orchid for the buttonhole of my MCC blazer I turned to the grovelling man and said, 'I'm going to be a writer. What d'you think of that?' 'Ee master, tha'll never be a wreeter,' he said. 'Tha moost soofer to wreet.' In spite of his ridiculous accent I continued to listen. 'Tha's too preeveliged,' he continued. 'Why, there's lads oop North who'll wreet reet enough but they's born to it.'

He went on to tell me a remarkable story of three boys of roughly my own age called Alan Brien, Keith Waterhouse and Michael Parkinson. Words, McGregor said, flew from their fingers. Brien, he told me, had pulled coal wagons 3,000 ft beneath Durham's pastures when the pit ponies were too exhausted, Waterhouse lived by stealing cigarette cards and selling them to antique dealers from London, and Parkinson earned money for charities by walking to school with no shoes on his feet and only a jam butty to sustain him. Of course, it came as no surprise to me that a mere gardener could impart such information. Rumour had it, below stairs, that McGregor had himself once written a book about a Nottinghamshire coal miner before going to Mexico to have a nervous breakdown with a wretched Hun woman. The fact that in his dotage and obscure retirement he spent most of the time masturbating in the greenhouse endeared him to me somehow. But that is by the by. A mere aside.

I pondered his words as I wandered back to Groomstail. Was it going to be an insuperable hurdle the fact that I wasn't having a deprived childhood? Would it prevent me from writing the novel of the century or getting a staff job on the *Sunday Times*? I determined to consult my confidant Gervase, a young footman my father had found loitering in Hyde Park one night. At that time I spent many hours with Gervase when he was off duty, drinking White Ladies in his room with him while I watched him powder his wigs. Ah, what wasted hours! To think at those very moments Benny Green was in Hackney Marshes Public Library memorising the Encyclopaedia Britannica. But, 'tis bootless to exclaim. Soon after, at the start of my first term at Eton, I begged Mama to let me walk barefoot to Windsor with a jam sandwich in my pocket but she put her delicate foot down and I was whisked off to Windsor in the Hispana Suiza.

My days at Eton were quite miserable. I had to fag for the school bully, a boy called Colin Welland. He stole my gold fountain pen – surprisingly left for me by McGregor in his will shortly after he was found dead of herpes in the greenhouse – and wrote six television plays with it, although Logie Baird was still perfecting his invention above Bianchi's. The only consolation at Eton was the time I spent punting down the river with Richard West, whom I had bumped into again. We'd drift downstream drinking vodka and White Shield Worthington chasers dreaming of getting staff jobs on national newspapers.

The rest is history. Brien became one of the greatest conversationalists in England since Sheridan, Waterhouse became a great columnist in spite of putting his editor's wife's chihuahua in the fridge at a party when he was drunk one night, and Parkinson became such a wonderful human being he actually disappeared up his own arse and was never heard of again. Poor West went mad and the last I heard he was in Zimbabwe writing a history of the Arts Council. As for me, I spend my days pondering what *might* have been.

Once a year I put some flowers on McGregor's grave when I
revisit Groomstail, and sometimes I bump into Gervase who's
running an afternoon drinking club in Mayfair. For the most
part I wish to God I'd suffered a bit more. I'm sure I could
have written that book.

Life history

When you get to be fifty you find yourself talking and thinking
as much about death and money as you used to about sex. The
nearness of one and the shortage of the other fill me with a
sense of urgency, but urgency about what I'm not quite sure.
I suppose it's a feeling of wanting to *cram* it all in; 'it' being
just about everything. I used to leap out of bed at six a.m.
and get on with the trivialities, now I wake at six a.m. and
lie there smoking and thinking of these matters until it's time
for an analgesic Smirnoff. (That time gets fractionally earlier
which is worrying. Why is it perfectly okay abroad?) Anyway,
today's heavy-heartedness was provoked by good news I had
last week. I'm going to start writing a column again for the
Sporting Life after an absence of twelve years. It won't make
me rich but it will be great fun. It seems that my passing out
when I was guest speaker at the National Hunt dinner in 1971
has been forgiven. Incidentally, what was odd about that was
that no one minded at all except for my boss and trainer, Bill
Marshall, who always said to people, 'If you want a really
good after-dinner speaker get Jeff. He's not boring because
he doesn't say anything.' But, as I say, the heavy heart within
is weighty because of the memories of those days on the *Life*
between Nijinsky's narrow defeat in the Arc to Mill Reef's
victory in the Arc exactly one year later. In fact, just as we
were swilling champagne after Mill Reef's victory it was none

other than the champion trainer today, Henry Cecil, who told me I'd got the sack from the *Sporting Life*. He'd heard it on the grapevine.

But those 365-odd days were heady, great fun and eventually disastrous for me. To my astonishment the column took off like a rocket and became immensely popular. I wrote a lot about loss and I suppose the average reader could identify with that. There was a ghastly little picture of me at the top of the column so complete and utter strangers recognised me at the races. They'd send me over bottles of bubbly in the Members Bar and trainers who befriended me and showed me the ropes, like Bill Marshall and Eddie Reavey, poured whisky down me like I was a drain. Of course I loved it. To be famous on any circuit in this life is fun and we all want to be loved, don't we. Typical was Ireland. I went to see a trainer called Con Collins one morning and he was on the blower. A maid brought me a tray on which was a bottle of gin, a bottle of whisky and a bottle of brandy. She said, 'Mister Collins will be with you in five minutes. If you need any more to drink ring the bell.' *Any more*! That was just after the first lot had been out, about nine a.m.

At Newbury one day I won a fair bit on the first race and then started laying favourites to bookmakers and won a little bundle. Risky but beautifully adrenalin-filled days. And the race trains I loved. The restaurant cars filled with bookmakers, spivs, villains, mug punters and scallywags of all kinds playing cards, telling amazing anecdotes about the Turf and drinking as though there was no tomorrow. In those days I think I'm right in saying that the only train in England to sell champagne was the race train to York. We drank the buffet dry by Doncaster. Well, of course, it couldn't last. The whisky was killing me and the bouts of pancreatitis became more frequent.

As I said, the end came at the National Hunt dinner at some dreadful hotel in Kensington. It was suggested that I be the guest speaker and they should have known better. I was extremely nervous, never having spoken publicly before, and I went to the *Life* offices at six a.m. to try and write something, couldn't and thought a jar in a Smithfield pub might get the typewriter going. I was accompanied by one of life's and the *Life*'s real eccentrics, a greyhound correspondent called Albert Bright. He used to come out with some very odd remarks and I remember him once saying, apropos of nothing, 'Yes, Jeff, I had my first fuck when I was firewatching on the roof of the *Greyhound Express* during an air raid in 1941.' Anyway we got smashed in Smithfield and then continued in the Stab – the *Daily Mirror* pub – at opening time. Still no speech. From there I went to the Colony Room Club and so it continued all day. I got to the hotel, fell asleep in the lobby and was taken upstairs and put to bed by the waiters. Here endeth the first lesson.

The next morning I flew to Paris for the Arc de Triomphe and Henry told me I'd been fired. The fact that I could never behave as I did in that year ever again doesn't diminish the depression at the memory of it all. Even at the end the lily demanded gilding. The whisky nudged me into a nervous breakdown and I ended up in a nuthouse. When I came to, there was an Irish psychiatrist sitting on my bed. Peace and saved at last, I thought. Then he opened his mouth and said, 'What d'you think will win the 2.30?' You just can't win, can you.

Loopy

What people will do to be loved! Dear God. There's a dog in the house I've been week-ending in which got me thinking about it. She eats your shoes and clothes and then, tail wagging, presents you with the remnants as though she's done you a colossal favour. Her eyes plead for reward. That's okay. What isn't is the appalling man I met who balances a wine glass on his head at closing time. He also describes a circle through the air with a glass of beer, the idea being that centrifugal force will prevent a drop of it being spilt. On the occasion I saw this odd plea for love and attention most of the beer went over me. Strangely enough I feel sad that this clown is a member of a dying breed. They're brave enough after all, and I wouldn't fancy having been Will Somers and trying to make Henry VIII laugh all day. But back to the man who balances wine glasses on his head in the hope of a pat on the back.

He's middle-aged, balding, suntanned, well-dressed, cuckolded and deserted, well-spoken, pickled in whisky and wine and he could have been a tea planter in a Somerset Maugham story or maybe a lounge lizard on a pre-war Cunarder. As it is, I see him utterly alone, shuffling downstairs in his slippers in the morning to make a cup of tea with trembling hands and wondering for the millionth time how and why it all went wrong. After the circus-dog-like tricks with the beer – and the wine glass – balancing I finally lost patience with him at an otherwise perfectly lovely garden party. He suddenly leant forward in his deck chair, the white wine sweat pouring down his face, looked at me earnestly and asked, 'Jeff, what do you think life means?' I said, 'You're a prick.' What do I think life means indeed! What a bloody stupid question, even from a drunk. Undeterred he went on to tell me, 'You see, I'm a philosopher.'

That went a long way towards explaining why he was dangerously serious and he went on to tell me how his wife had left him. Apparently she got very depressed and only allowed him the leg over once a month (once a year should have been more like it). He suggested she attend a crazy fortnight's seminar on philosophy somewhere, which she did, and when she came back she packed her bags and told him, 'I'm going off to do my own thing.' What a wonderful, meaningless phrase – 'do my own thing'. And serves him right. If I had a wife I wouldn't let her within a hundred miles of a philosopher. Anyway, after the party we went to the pub for more tricks and pleas for attention and at closing time he informed me that 'Life is a dream.' I was sorely tempted to give him a clout over the ear to show him that it isn't but the bell for last orders sounded which also proved it.

The next day he called round to where I was staying and asked my weekend companion if she'd like to go up in an aeroplane for a joyride. Yes, a philosophical pilot too. 'We can loop the loop,' he said. She was as excited as a twelve-year-old boy would be at the prospect of meeting Ian Botham but she asked me did I mind. Well, I did bloody mind but I looked at her lovely face and thought she might just as well get killed in an aeroplane crash as meet Mr Right and bring up four children in Penge or Purley. It also occurred to me that hiring an aeroplane for an hour to loop the loop must be just about the most expensive way man has yet devised to look up a girl's skirt. The loop the loop in Wheelers – bisque to you – is only £1.50 and I've had some good results with it. But they came back in one piece each, she exhilarated and he deeply philosophical, either because it was before opening time or maybe because he'd caught a sight of God up there above Felixstowe. (What a dreadful thing to show a girl. Felixstowe!)

Since then I've tried to be perfectly honest with myself, not delude myself and work out just what it is I do to try and get love and attention. I know I'm not loved for smoking and coughing in bed for an hour every morning so it must be something after opening time. A survey reported in last Tuesday's *Times* said that women like men to be kind and humorous. A survey in next Tuesday's *Times* will doubtless inform us that Queen Anne is dead. That must be it. I did once offer a woman my barstool and it ended disastrously in marriage. I must have told her a joke too on the way to the registry office. But looping the loop is beyond my means and nerves and, anyway, I'm more interested in removing skirts than looking up them. Frankly, I wouldn't have thought aerobatics to be either kind or humorous, but the paths to a girl's heart are not as the crow flies. I shall now retire to the Coach and Horses to balance a glass of vodka, lime, ice and soda on my head and ponder on just whose skirt Icarus was planning to look up.

In a pickle

I read that a member of the General Medical Council has called on his colleagues for quicker identification and treatment for alcoholic doctors. The article, in the *Times*, was headed 'Alcoholic Doctor Tells How He Fought Back'. There are two things that interest me here: first the business of identifying an alcoholic, and secondly the matter of fighting back. How on earth they can have trouble in not identifying an alcoholic immediately, heaven alone knows. I can spot one a mile away. But could they spot my friend Keith I wonder? They must be blind as bats. Anyway, Keith woke up one day sitting in pitch darkness. He groped around for a while and realised slowly that he was in a cinema. Further groping got him to an exit door and he eventually got out on to the street.

He didn't know what town he was in but made his way to a
pub where, with great embarrassment, he asked the barman
where he was. 'Dover', he was told. Then it all came back to
him. 'Christ Almighty,' he said. 'I got married yesterday.' I can
put the General Medical Council in touch with several Keiths,
but I suppose only the 3,000 out of 81,000 alcoholic doctors in
this country would be able to identify them quickly.

But we must help the medical profession and give them
some clues. A man I know once went to a literary booze-up
and walked over to a glass-fronted bookcase to see what sort
of stuff his host had to read. To his amazement there were
no books in the case, only John Raymond standing there in
a stupor. I myself once woke up in Cowes of all places and I
have even woken up in a drawer at the bottom of a wardrobe.
That was fairly frightening. Trying to open a drawer from the
inside. It's quite tricky. Then we have our hero on the *Mirror*.
I've mentioned him before but, for the benefit of doctors, he
is worth recalling. He broke into a pickle factory one night
with his girlfriend with the purpose of laying her and fell into
a vat of chutney. Then we have the doctors themselves. There
were two of them, patients like myself in 1972 in Max Glatt's
ward in St Bernard's Hospital. One of them was addicted to
barbiturates. He didn't interest me, no drug addicts do, but I
asked the alcoholic doctor how did he first know he was an
alcoholic and he told me, 'When I sprayed vaginal deodorant
on a man's face.'

But the business of the doctor telling how he 'fought back'
gets me. I fought back too. I fought back from two and a half
years of the most boring, depressing desolation of sobriety you
can imagine. I wouldn't go on the wagon again for all the tea
in China. For two and a half years I felt apart from the human
race. The day I cracked in 1976 I called round to my friend

Eva and we cracked a bottle of Scotch. Then we went round to the Dover Castle – always full of doctors – and we met up eventually with Frank Norman and drank more Scotch. After all those years a bottle of the stuff is damn nigh a killer. Of course it is poison. Frank took me to the Connaught for breakfast the next day and I thought I was going to die. The fact that I'm here now and that Eva and Frank are dead seems unfair.

To go back to the doctors: they apparently consider heavy drinking to be more than four pints of beer a day, or four doubles or a bottle of wine a day. I should have thought that to be the national average lunchtime consumption. But just listen to this. 'I do not remember ever making a mistake, but one of the worst aspects of alcoholism is that you black out. One day I had to ring up the surgery to make sure I had done one of my visits the night before.'

Well, surprise, surprise. What I want to know is, if he blacked out how the hell does he *know* he never ever made a mistake? The wrong leg off? I know I've had the wrong leg *over* because I too have had to ring up the surgery to find out where and if I had done one of my visits the night before. I just don't understand how doctors can be so naive. Well, I do. It's the old business of all the time at school and then in hospital of not seeing anything much of life itself. The Middlesex ought to send their students along to the Coach. They'd find ample opportunity to practise spotting and identifying alcoholics. They're the ones smiling.

Home truths

Most days page three of the *Daily Telegraph* is a haven of sense and sensibility. There's usually something there to remind one that the world is not entirely mad or without some sort of entertainment value. Still, as Frankie Howerd used to say, I suppose one shouldn't mock the afflicted. The trouble is, if you can't mock the afflicted, and obviously this includes one's self, then who the hell can you mock? Anyway, this week's touching tale concerned a woman of sixty-one who battered her seventy-nine-year-old lover to death with a champagne bottle during a sex session at his flat in the South of France. What a way to go. Knowing my luck it would be a bottle of light ale over the nut in a Camden Town bedsitter. Worse still, it might be a bottle of Perrier over the bonce in a Salvation Army hostel. We must learn to be grateful for small mercies. Anyway, apparently the old man took a new lover, forced his sixty-one-year-old lady into oral sex and she did her nut. Or, to put it more accurately, his nut.

Now, one of the first things to horrify and amuse me about this tragic business is the fact that I've been banking on the supposed fact that once you get to fifty or, say, sixty these aggravations melt away. If I really thought that I'd be crazy for all that nonsense in five years' time I think I'd despair. There's something a little undignified about the behaviour of this couple although the late Mr Hubbers did have the style to keep bubbly by the side of his bed. (Was it vintage I wonder?) I'm an Earl Grey man myself and I wouldn't trust a woman or myself with a bottle in my bed. To be fair to the sixty-one-year-old Cheltenham-Ladies-College-educated Pamela Megginson though, she might well have thought it was only a *half* bottle of champagne. Even so there's something deeply depressing about domestic violence. To this day the slamming of a door fills me with gloom evoking as it does memories of childhood scenes.

And last week at Ascot races of all places I heard of more trouble in the home. I got chatting to a lovely waitress over a lunch hosted by Evelyn de Rothschild and one thing led to another and she asked me if I'd ever been married. 'Not much,' I said. 'You should see my body. It's covered in scars.' 'Really?' she said. 'Well, no not really, but I once was stabbed.' 'That's funny,' she said, uncorking yet another bottle of wine, 'I stabbed my husband six months ago.' 'Oh, do tell,' I said, examining the nose of the wine. 'Well, he left me for another woman but he came back three days later when he discovered she couldn't cook. So there I was in the kitchen mashing potatoes and him lying there soaking in the bath and I suddenly thought what a bloody cheek and what the hell am I doing cooking for him so I grabbed a kitchen knife, went into the bathroom and stabbed him.' All I could thing of was what a mess it must have made of the bathwater.

The other thing the champagne bottle case reminded me of was a story about the late Ali Khan I once heard at the races. Apparently he kept a champagne ice bucket by the side of his bed into which he'd plunge his hand to prevent premature ejaculation. Mind you, I don't think an ice bucket over the head would exactly kill you, but caution should be exercised as to what to take into a bedroom. There was the business of the editor and the electric fire a few years back. This man on his wedding night was making love to his bride and got his foot caught in the bars of the electric fire which was at the end of the bed. I don't know that position. Anyway, you can imagine the agony. He went absolutely crazy and started to scream the place down. She, silly cow, came to the conclusion that she was the greatest lover in the world until he started hopping around the bedroom with his smouldering foot. It's nice to know a thing like that about a man when you're asking for a job. (Hacks can send me a stamped, addressed envelope for his name.)

There is an aspect of the champagne case though that does raise a smile of cynicism. I quote Ms Megginson. 'The irony is that I lost control so completely that I destroyed any claim to his estate.' Well, Mr Hubbers might well have been a right bastard, but is it irony, or perhaps agony? He was very good with the handouts until he found another mistress and in the beginning he 'showered' her with expensive gifts and paid her bills at Fortnum & Mason, Simpsons and Selfridges. And some stupid bird on LBC the other morning said women weren't mercenary. But, in the final analysis, I think Pamela Megginson's heart is in the right place. After all, the bottle was empty.

Rum do

Barbados was very much as I left it three years ago: 80 degrees in the shade, humming birds for breakfast companions, the surf whispering along the beaches, too many sickly rum punches – if you could bother to wait twenty minutes for them – and a bit too much Caribbean music. But all quite beautiful. The sun raises the spirits, as do fresh limes, and when the dust settles after ten minutes of tropical rain the exotic flora and fauna of the island seem to vibrate life itself and plunge one into a world of wondrous scents. I even heard a Mozart piano concerto in a hooker's hang-out in Bridgetown one morning but I expect that was a mistake. Anyway, in case anyone should think I have deserted the low life, I should point out that the past ten days were what's called a freebie, courtesy of a PR firm called Infopress and Caribbean Airways. But nothing, of course, is really free and I laundered my way through £200-worth of cocktails, gazing at sunsets, wondering at how odd it was to be doing so with garnishee orders out on me back in London. A double life is the only one.

Our party comprised four women representing the *Sunday Telegraph*, the *Sun*, *Honey* and *Family Circle*, and proud of it too. We male hacks numbered five, all of whom were appropriately appendaged with feet of clay. Now, in these situations – film locations are similar – geographical changes affect some men strangely. Just as I used naively to deceive myself into thinking that books could be written in the country, most men think that most women can be laid on foreign soil. At least it becomes something of a compulsion to attempt the deed. For my part I detach myself, stand back and watch. No one on the *Sun* could look any better in paradise than they could in Shepherds Bush anyway. So, to our first drama.

One night a very nice bloke indeed arranged a cocktail party in his rooms. Shock, horror, he got drunk. In a fleeting moment of paranoia he told the assembled hacks to fuck off. They did and one of the ladies burst into tears as, of course, any Grub Street lady would do on hearing such appalling language. The next morning at breakfast (orange juice, melon, corned beef hash, poached eggs and more humming birds) our man apologised to the first of the ladies to appear and his apology was greeted by silence. Now, apart from the fact that an apology wasn't really necessary, the high-mindedness of a pipsqueak from *Family Circle* was something I couldn't quite take. It rankled all day. By the evening, when it was my turn to get drunk, I expressed my feelings with more unfamiliar four-letter words that Fleet Street hackettes never hear. I also said that I found it odd that ladies earning three times as much as I did couldn't buy a round of drinks, that their assumption – in common with most women – was that all and sundry fancied them something rotten, while I personally thought they were a bunch of slags. I was told later that this sparkling discourse was conducted fortissimo. (Oscar Wilde could have learnt a thing or two at my knee when it comes to calling a woman an old cow.)

What does amuse me in retrospect though is the fact that – so I was later told – our host from the Barbados Tourist Board remained quite cool and made the understatement of the year when he murmured, 'I suspect a little tension. A possible clash of personalities.' All that really happened was that one of the ladies threatened to slap my face and I warned her that in the event I would be obliged to break her arm.

But it was a jolly good trip and I must advise the Barbados Tourist Board, Infopress and Caribbean Airways that since my return I have plugged Barbados to everyone within listening range, particularly all of my friends who can afford a £1,000-a-week holiday. And, as the same sun sinks in the west over Great Portland Street and not the steel calm of the Caribbean, I find myself wondering did God ever seriously intend that men and women should get on with each other? Do two humming birds make a summer? Is it worth being black to be born in Barbados? Will Bajan Sunshine win the Cesarewitch, as I hope? What on earth can the Tourist Board think of English hacks now? All these imponderables I shall take to my friend, mentor and bank manager, Norman Balon, in whom we trust. The awful alternative, I suppose, would be to take out subscriptions to the *Sun*, *Honey* and *Family Circle*. The world is not yet ready for that, my dear Watson.

Foot fault

Here we are again. This time the Middlesex. St Stephen's has lost its appeal for me and the King George V ward here, not to be confused with the George Cinq, has more ambience than the Grenadian-battleaxe-staffed Sir Alfred Tennyson ward in

Fulham. Here, tea is served by Malaysian charmers and I'd no more dream of throwing a half pound of butter at them than I would fly or break into a swear. Yes, it's been a ridiculous week. From sublime Barbados to the Middlesex via Bow Street Magistrates Court where I appeared for chastising the staff and one rubber plant in the Raj of India restaurant in Old Compton Street. Fined £10 with £15 damages and suffered one twisted knee getting into a squad car. After I limped out of court I was reminded of a particularly sore left foot. A pebble or a piece of coral on the beach the week before. Nothing much, but the next day my foot was raw, swollen, weeping and painful. Mindful of the diabetic's proneness to gangrene I popped into the clinic where they took one look and then bundled me into bed. I have been occasionally legless but I do like to have *both* feet on the ground.

Not much changes, least of all the medical profession. I was tucked up, put on an antibiotic drip, X-rayed and God knows what. I lay there waiting for the inevitable first skirmish with the administering enemy. I hadn't long to wait. A young houseman, looking at my records, said, 'You drink and smoke a horrendous amount. Why do you drink?' I thought of saying, 'If you have to ask, then you don't know.' But I replied, 'To stop myself jogging.' I shook my head sadly at him and he got the message. What a silly question. How do these people qualify? Later that evening I was in considerable pain. The infection had swollen the glands in my groin and I asked a female late-duty doctor for some analgesic. She said okay and went off. Forty-five minutes later she returned with two aspirin. I couldn't believe it. She'd be a real wow at the Royal Marsden.

Today my right forearm looks like the treble 20 on a dart board. Never have I had so many needles stuck into me that missed. But what has amused me until now has been the way that nurses, when they inject or draw blood, always state the obvious. There they are with poised syringe about to plunge and they say, 'Just a little prick.' Half an hour ago when that happened it suddenly occurred to me that that dear nurse might have been referring to me.

Sadly, the patients never ever change. Are they provided by some sort of agency? Is anyone worth talking to ever hospitalised? I fear not. So very awful are the regulars in the day room that I've had to take up smoking in the lavatory again after all these years. *Sun* readers to a man, they stare vacantly at Hungarian children's cartoons all afternoon on the box, occasionally coughing and farting. And to think that is going to be the curtain-down scene for most of us. And, talking of curtains-down, it occurred to me that the last supper menu, quite literally, will be brown Windsor soup and minced beef with cabbage and boiled potatoes. But no expense is spared when it comes to food. Even the ice cream is sent up in the hot wagon. It would be a crime to cut back or destroy any of this and the dreadful Norman Fowler's ears should be burning. If they fell off I doubt whether any of the doctors or nurses here would care a jot. They're rightly upset. Perhaps I'm biased, but these people keep coming to my rescue. Yes, they hate Fowler and I fear we may have to learn how to come to our own rescues.

P.S. Fleet street colleagues seem to have their wires crossed. When I mentioned last week the harridans who accompanied me to Barbados I did not mean to include the delightful lady from the *Sunday Telegraph*. She was fun and got her shout. As in *Macbeth* there were only three witches in Barbados.

Last resort

We were idly wondering what on earth Watneys will do to the French pub when Gaston Barlemont retires. Piped accordion muzak à la Maigret? Barmaids with red, white and blue aprons and caps? Fitted carpets? God save us. In no time at all there will be nowhere to go, and what's more I read in the *Telegraph* that the sun will snuff out in 5,000 million years' time. I give Soho about another five years and I have a very uncomfortable feeling that I might survive it. The trouble is that there aren't many worthwhile villages left in London. I used to have a fondness for Marylebone High Street when I lived there but it's far too bland and benign. Chelsea seems to consist of nothing but shops which sell jeans, people too young to talk to and failed faces too embarrassing to look into. I haven't got the socialist wardrobe obligatory for drinking in Hampstead – woollen tie, corduroy trousers and tweed jacket – and the fact that I was born in the wretched place, had my first experience of sex on the Heath and my first liver biopsy in the Royal Free doesn't justify loitering in the Flask watching people pay homage to John Hurt, who was a nice chap before he became a naked civil elephant man.

Fleet Street you can keep. I've had enough dealings with solicitors not to want to drink with them in El Vino and, weighed down as I am by a quantity of chips on the shoulder and an innate bitterness, nor do I want to talk shop with hacks who earn £20,000 a year for putting in an appearance to write 300 words a week. There was a time, would you believe, when Notting Hill Gate swung a little. I had a fight with Roy Campbell in a pub there on my 18th birthday and nearly every day was a party day when the Roberts, Colquhoun and

McBryde, had a studio in Bedford Gardens. George Barker also livened things up and John Minton subsidised the drinks to a certain extent. Later, in the Sixties, the vision of Sally Vincent must have depressed the female populace of Notting Hill.

The place I can see making something of a comeback is north of Soho – its old annexe, Charlotte Street. Unpolluted by sex shops, dirty bookshops and strip clubs it still has a certain charm. The fact that the denizens of the Duke of York, the Wheatsheaf, the Black Horse and the Fitzroy are mostly dead doesn't mean it couldn't be repopulated. I can also see Islington gaining in popularity, although there are far too many people living there with tenuous connections and pretensions to the 'arts'. A lot of people in Islington have been hinting at potential talent for at least fifty years. Most of them end up as rip-off antique dealers feigning an understanding of culture which in reality is materialised by a discussion about nuclear disarmament at a wine and cheese party and by their revolting children.

In spite of being a Londoner, the City remains a mystery to me. But there must be some good men there. Britain is Great Britain because the majority of the people who run the stock exchange, like those who hold the reins in the House of Commons, are permanently drunk. So I presume there must be a few good dives there although I only know Sweetings and a revolting pub opposite Liverpool Street Station packed with lager-swilling travelling salesmen. Women do seem scarce in the City though. I suppose they must be manning the typewriters most of the time. Women are very important to a village, and if saying so gives offence it is only because I am unlucky enough to be a male heterosexual. This has caused a lot of interference to the smooth running of my life.

Nevertheless I like to see the odd sex object over the rim of my glass. And that's one reason for not drinking in the village of Mayfair or in the Grays Inn Road, where only very important people from the *Times* and *Guardian* drink.

No, when Soho dies it might even mean moving out of London altogether. But where to? I could never live in a village proper again because of the necessity of driving. Brighton, Bristol and Cambridge have occurred to me as possibilities and although I gather from my colleague Michael Heath that Brighton is almost 100 per cent homosexual it does have a school of journalism which might be useful and possibly lead to a job on the *Sun*. We can all dream.

Meanwhile I sit by the bedside of dying Soho holding her hand but wondering wouldn't it be kinder to switch off the life-support system. When the likes of my brothers, Tom Baker and Conan Nicholas, who gave the world cat racing, stop frequenting Soho then it will be time to charter that bus which is going to drive us over Beachy Head. Book your seat now. There's only room for fifty-two.

Dessert island

The business of being shipwrecked on a desert island is something that has intrigued me ever since Roy Plomley started his radio programme *Desert Island Discs*. I've thought of the people I'd like to take, and those I'd hate to, and I seem to remember vaguely having written about them in this column. What came to mind the other day was desert-island food and it's a tricky business choosing twenty-one meals assuming you're going to eat breakfast, lunch and dinner every day. At first, what sprang to mind was cordon bleu, haute cuisine, provençale and all the sort of stuff that the likes of Bernard

Levin drool over. But this excludes some of the great dishes of the world that have gone unrecorded by fatty Carrier and the great Elizabeth David. Consider the bacon sandwich washed down by a pot of 1983 Lyons Orange Label tea sipped from a bone china cup (mugs are for cocoa only). I prefer my bacon in the white sandwich loaf bread that's supposed to be so bad for you – wholemeal bread detracts from the bacon flavour – and there should be just a hint of brown sauce. And what about that prince of leftovers, bubble and squeak? As a child, my favourite meal was Sunday supper. Cold lamb left over from lunch with pickles and bubble and squeak fried gently to a golden brown on the outside.

I could not eat à la Gavroche or L'Etoile twice a day every day. I could eat Chinese and Indonesian food nearly every day. Indian once a week and certainly a paella, just about my favourite dish, once a week. A funny thing about paella is that I've never had a really good one in Spain. I've had plenty of rice concoctions that were the consistency of porridge, but I suspect that you have to go to a three-star job in Madrid to get the real McCoy. Taste apart, it's great fun to make a paella if you've got a couple of hours to spare and I have most days. It isn't, by the way, necessary to cook everything in a paella together. Ingredients can blend just as effectively just before serving. I suppose you might call shepherd's pie a sort of English equivalent of paella and it's an obligatory weekly desert-island dish although it has fallen into disrepute in recent years thanks to the ever declining standards of British pub food. I once stood in for a chef in a pub off St Martin's Lane who'd fallen ill and my friend and guvnor asked me to make a large shepherd's pie. I used steak tartare mince for the foundation and a bottle of 1949 Châteauneuf-du-Pape to bolster the gravy. It was quite stupendous, sold like hot cakes and the guvnor lost about £6 on the dish. The next day I devoted my time in the kitchen to preparing that old classic, the Beethoven's Fifth of food, bangers and mash. Again the guvnor and I nearly fell out. I took a taxi to Jermyn Street to Paxton's for the sausages and he raised both eyebrows when I put egg yolks and cream into the mash. Mashed potatoes must be whipped and not just pulped.

Ill health forces me to eschew most puddings but I do like apple pie and fresh fruit salad. What I would want plenty of on this wretched island is ice cream. Where this could be flown in from, God alone knows. I know of only three places in London: Marine Ices, the one next to Goodge Street tube station and the new one whose name I've also forgotten in Battersea. A word of warning here about ice cream. Never eat the popular brands. I once worked nights as a packer in the most famous establishment and I saw them add left-over fat from their sausages to the ice cream. I also once saw a lunatic urinate into a vat of ice cream.

Another gastronomic must would have to be the weekly injection of fish and chips. Although it's necessary to travel to France to get properly cooked chips, efforts are being made here in some brasseries. For the most part English chips are too fat and soft and remind me of fried cotton wool. Even Wheelers haven't got the hang of them. What amuses me in that restaurant are the faces of people when they see me anointing my fish and chips with tomato ketchup. I gather from their toffee noses that ketchup is frightfully infra dig. And speaking of fish I would like kedgeree once a week for breakfast.

I think what I might miss on this island is the hassle, rudeness and aggression I seem to experience in Indian and Chinese restaurants. But I'm sure Man Friday could be trained to get hysterical when I try to pay by cheque having lost my cheque card. He could bang my plates – palm leaves – down in front of me and then sneer at my tip. On second thoughts I think I will get a friend with an expense account to take me to the Connaught as soon as possible.

Rover's return

I took myself away from the well-beaten track last week and dilly-dallied in Chelsea for a couple of days. It's well known that the Kings Road died some years ago when it was taken over by jeans shops and so-called trendy young people obsessed by pop music, but the cancer is spreading. There isn't a pub or restaurant in the entire street worth going to, with the possible exception of the Man in the Moon, which is physically a very pretty pub. Further north the Fulham Road isn't quite so bad. At least it's populated in the main by middle-aged people whose world-weariness is such a refreshing change from the youth who think that entertainment consists of throwing bread rolls at each other over dinner.

But the Fulham brigade, centred mainly in the Queen's Elm, Finches and the Chelsea Arts Club, are an extraordinary bunch, all of them caught in a sartorial time warp. Most of the men are greying, wear roll-neck jerseys, jeans and desert boots and you know damn well they sculpt or paint and have just missed the boat in both departments. The more solvent ones probably have teaching jobs, studios and common-law wives they first beheld in a life class. Fulham must be the last outlet for manufacturers of corduroy. The place is also chock-a-block with women painters and I think they're very brave considering that what women are far and away the best at is writing novels. They are so good at it in fact that I find it slightly uncanny. Alice Thomas Ellis says it's like playing with dolls' houses. You move people from room to room and wonder what you're going to do next with them. Another strange inhabitant of the Fulham Road is the man who supports Chelsea or Fulham football club and who you'd think would have more intelligence than to do so. There's an awful sort of snobbery about football, and local thespians and television persons suffer from it the most.

But, when all's said and done, the strip 'twixt the Arts Club, Queen's Elm and Finches is still one of the better villages of London. I have some pleasant memories of it anyway. The 'Master', as we used to call the poet George Barker, kindly gave me my first experience of amphetamine in the Queen's Elm when I was eighteen and I once worked behind the bar there for the guvnor, Sean Treacy, who very understandingly one evening gave me five minutes off to hit one of his more boring customers. The Anglesea down the road has fallen off disastrously, being full as it is of Hooray Henrys, but you can catch a glimpse from it sometimes of Miss Ava Gardner walking her dog. I did live there once, albeit under the enormous thumb of a paranoically jealous woman who thought I'd been to bed with someone even when I popped out for five minutes to buy some cigarettes – five minutes! I ask you – but I'd quite like to return to the area had I £1 million to buy a flat. As it is, the disgusting Soho is a mere twelve minutes walk away and Soho is going to become even more disgusting soon. A sure sign of Gaston Berlemont's imminent retirement from the French pub is that he called in the £20 I owed him last week. I think we can all guess just how Watneys will refurbish the place.

Which reminds me. The Queen's Elm, the French pub and the Coach and Horses were the only pubs I came across during the festive season which did *not* have any Christmas

decorations. A very good sign indeed. The *printed* card wishing
all its customers a happy Christmas, either in shop window or
pub, is a shabby hypocrisy, as is the ill-disguised advertisement
on scaffolding announcing that McAlpines apologise for any
inconvenience to the public. Bollocks. But, as I say, the
contemplation of London villages has become something of
a permanent fantasy. Charlotte Street has a lot to recommend
it, good shops and activity, but with sufficient loot I could settle
for spending the rest of my life in a hotel, preferably Browns or
the Ritz. I'm very fond of room service and in the Park Lane
Hilton you can get more than a chicken sandwich and a drink
sent up to your room. In the Shelbourne Hotel in Dublin the
staff have real wit and cunning. I'd just moved in there one
day and was having a clean up in the bathroom – stop me
if you've heard this – when a little bell hop knocked on the
door and squeaked, 'Mister Bernard, I've a message for you.'
I shouted out, 'Slip it under the door.' 'I can't, sir,' he said, 'it's
on a salver.'

Eye contact

I keep getting bombarded with unsolicited mail. More often
than not it's publicity rubbish from Channel 4 which should
be going to Richard Ingrams, the humorist and television
personality. This morning I received an invitation to a preview
of something called *Pictures of Women – Sexuality*. The blurb
goes on to say, 'Women today are limited and defined by
sexuality in ways that men are not. Starting from this premise,
a production team called Pictures of Women has fashioned
six programmes asking why this situation has arisen and looks,
from a woman's point of view, at its effects on a wide range of
contemporary social issues.' Etc, etc, Blah, blah. 'The series

examines the nature of sexual attraction, pornography, sex in advertising, prostitution, sexual harassment at work and the continuing limits to sexual equality.' Then, at the foot of the page, 'Refreshments will be served after the screening.' *After?* I ask you. Not only after but the wretched preview itself starts at 11.30 a.m., by which time I will have already been hard at work in the Coach and Horses for half an hour. What's more, you'd need a skinful to sit through this sort of film.

But what's really been getting up my nose for the past five or six years is the revolting way women take sex and themselves so bloody seriously. The fact that so very few of them do so is little consolation to me since, being a hack, I'm permanently surrounded by those very few or, at least, a large proportion of them. I used to have a soft, and occasionally hard, spot for Germaine Greer, but just see how fame destroys people. It's awful. With a Booker Prize she'd be certifiable. But I wonder, does the business of taking sex so seriously have anything to do with the fact that so few women can bear to own up simply to liking it very much? And just what is the problem concerning prostitution? The expense. If any reader knows of a call girl who accepts Barclaycard I'd be grateful to be informed of her name and address. (My new Barclaycard arrived this morning. The old one was cut in half by a shop assistant in the Victoria Wine Shop in Berwick Street in front of six other customers. That was far more serious than sex.) What I do think is utterly rotten is the business of 'No Knickers' Joyce, who told me that one of her customers paid her by cheque and then stopped it. Not cricket.

But the business of sexual harassment in the office is, I think, slightly exaggerated. I have, would you believe, been on the other end of it. Fifteen years ago, at the *Daily Mirror*, there was a secretary who couldn't type for crying over me. It got on my tits as well as the boss's but I suppose tits is a sexist word in spite of the fact that men have them – of a sort – too. But I'm all for sexual equality. When I was in Moscow I can't tell you what pleasure it gave me to watch women shovelling concrete on building sites. I don't like watching them write very much, they have such a facility for it, but I do like to see them work. Sadly, I know only three equal women, Irma Kurtz, Sally Vincent and Hazel Evans, all of whom generously stand their round. Oh yes, and my landlady and Liz Elliot at *Private Eye*. As for pornography the worst thing I can say about it which women will be totally unaware of is that it's ruined Soho. My heart bleeds for the low life café society that's been taken over by dirty bookshops and strip clubs.

But you note that this film examines the nature of sexual attraction. What is there to examine? Speaking as one whose life has been totally ruined by falling in love with the packaging and not the woman I find it pretty hard to believe that women don't want to be sexually attractive. Of course, I'm in the wrong business and owning a typewriter as opposed to a cosmetic or high-heeled-ankle-strap-shoe factory is a pretty grim financial alternative. And speaking of sexual attraction, the most extraordinary thing has happened to me. I've become totally besotted by the woman who works in the optician's shop I go to – I keep losing my glasses. It's really quite pathetic. I keep going into the shop on the slightest pretext. It's horribly like being sixteen again. She's not what you'd call a knockout but I fancy her almost to the point of obsession and I'd very much like to be paid by Channel 4 for talking about the problem on television. Last week I went into the shop three times to have my glasses tightened and when she puts them on my head she has to stand very close to me. I fear this could lead to six months in Wandsworth. What I do know is enough about women to be sure that she spends an age every morning making herself attractive to the likes of idiots like me. But I can't go on and on having my eyes tested just to be near her. I would be extremely grateful to any female reader of this column who could tell me of an effective and new verbal opening gambit. I fear she can read an awful history book in my eyes.

Bedfellows

I must be mellowing a little. I can no longer dislike doctors as I used to. Perhaps, at last, I'm too old for them to play God in a white coat to. But for the rest, the Bosch and Brueghel patients, the boils and burst veins, the dentures in glasses, the stumps that twitch remembering old legs, the hideous humiliation of the sick – all is grotesque. Patients are, for the most part, pretty disgusting and sickness reveals the man of straw and not so much of the nobility I've read about for years.

To my left lies Major Saunders, clinging on to the 'Major' nearly forty years after the event. He has circulatory problems and his purple toes are gnarled and twisted and you could probably pick them off his feet like plums from a tree. Without a batman and wife he is lost. A frightened man – I've watched him at meal times and I think he's actually frightened of meat. Opposite the Major there lies Mr Lawrence, a post office worker minus one gall bladder. Yesterday the tetchy Major asked Mr Lawrence where he lived, and when he was told in St John's Wood, near Lord's, the Major said, 'Oh. Are you a member?' I am surrounded by spite. The fourth man who makes up our quartet is Mr Wright who has had a very nasty operation indeed. Sadly it has left him anally fixated. Every day he buttonholes someone to recount to them the

story of his greatest and most satisfactory movement ever.
The memory of that one moment is all he has left. If only
the medical wards weren't full I wouldn't have to endure these
surgical cases.

But the amputees are both jolly men even though, as they're
fond of telling me, they do happen to be grim warnings to
any diabetic. Mr Thompson has one leg and Mr Davies none.
Thompson says his gangrene was the result of fifty cigarettes a
day which closed up his veins. A doctor overhearing this said,
'It's no use telling Mr Bernard. What he closes up with fifty
cigarettes he then opens with vodka.' Being alive is a constant
source of irritation to the medical profession. Or, at the very
least, an okay liver-function test proves that the patient isn't
getting his just deserts.

But worse than this quartet are the ladies along the corridor.
There is an ancient Glaswegian pug dog, and a tart with a
rose-coloured silk dressing gown, dyed red hair and colossal
sunglasses and they spend all day on the landing by the lifts –
the only place we are allowed to smoke – talking to a Greek
toad, poor woman, who is waiting for her husband to die.
They try to converse in mime, sign language or just by talking
very slowly as though that will itself open up the mysteries of
language. The tart constantly asks, 'What is Greek for cancer?'
and is told 'Athens. Very good. Very pretty.' 'And how is your
husband today?' 'Athens. Very good.' Then she starts crying
again.

What we have got here though are some fine tea ladies and
bottle washers. The days of those old naval actions against the
dreaded Santisima Trinidad at St Stephen's are over, thank
God. Here we are looked after by ladies from Manila and
Singapore. Mere junks bobbing harmlessly up and down at
their moorings in the kitchen. You wouldn't put the Middlesex

into the Hospital Good Food Guide, but it must go into the Hospital Good Physician and Surgeon Guide. My houseman, a spectacular Indian woman, is seething with self-confidence and that's always good in a doctor. The only other people here with the same measure of it are the duo with one leg between them. But then it's *fait accompli* and I suppose they haven't much alternative but to be brave. The Major could learn from them. He's at this moment toying with some macaroni cheese which won't bite him back. How *did* we win the war?

Shop-soiled

As you may well imagine, the farmer's wife who is about to inherit £3 million has been on my mind this past week and I'm very pleased to hear that she does *not* intend to change her way of life. Quite right. She did after all have to fly home from a skiing holiday to consult her solicitors; it's not as though she had to walk back from Butlin's Holiday Camp at Skegness to consult them. So why change? The farm must be worth a few bob too, what with land fetching – I'm guessing – something in the region of £1,000 an acre. So why change all that? What she might like to change is her husband, mind you, and a windfall like this could well keep him on his toes for a while. Poor bastard. I feel sorry for him. What a colossal cosh to be under. In fact, if I was him I'd leave her. He'll only have to lower his copy of *Farmer's Weekly* at the breakfast table to give her a dog-like look of affection, his tail so to speak wagging the while, and she'll snap, 'Who the hell d'you think you're looking at, you poxy little creep?'

Anyway, obviously I've done a little fantasising, and not for the first time, on the question of what I'd do with serious loot. And what it comes down to is, quite simply, I'd spend it.

I wouldn't change. It's far too late for that and I wouldn't go mad because I've tried that too and I didn't like it a lot. What would change, I'm afraid, are my friends and acquaintances. I'd hate to see their embarrassment. And women in general? Would they only then suddenly see what's been standing, longing and trembling for mere crumbs, in front of them for the past thirty years? You can bet on it and I'd adore to be loved for my money. Especially over Sunday lunch in the Tour d'Argent.

But these silly dreams don't last long, thank heavens, because I'm fairly contented, and what banished the £3 million from my mind was something I thought of wandering down the Kings Road on my way to the Queen's Elm for the third time in one week. (Where are you Tom Baker?) What I saw opposite the Town Hall was an establishment called the Reject Shop. Now it struck me, like a punch between the eyes, that if you – I mean me of course – stood in the window for a while you might actually get bought by someone quite nice. I mean obviously some people – my ex-wife for example – would walk past and sneer, but you never know your luck. The idea really tickles my fancy. I see myself in a sleazy afternoon club in the Shepherds Market area being introduced by my tarty, blonde purchaser – her bust trying to burst out of her angora jersey, a drop of gin slowly sliding down her chin, her handbag open and full of cosmetic chaos – to her jaded lounge-lizard friends. 'Got him in the Reject Shop in Chelsea. Not bad for twenty quid. Couldn't get it up, mind you, when I first took him home, but it's amazing how he comes to life when you pour a couple of vodkas into him. Have another, dear.'

I can think of many people who could and should be put in the window of the Reject Shop. Edward Heath limped to mind when I first thought about it but what would you want to buy him *for*? Taki's friends would, I think, make a pretty interesting display but, come to think of it, I *am* in a bloody reject shop and have been for years. I suppose a sort of refusal to be gift-wrapped might have been my downfall. But if you've got a few bob and like a dog around the house then I can introduce you to several possibilities. There are dogs here that will sit up on their hind legs and beg, fetch you your *Sporting Life*, lick your boots and stay loyal for a day at a time. Someone I don't want to see in my reject shop is the smocked and pitchfork-holding farmer who'll be gone with the wind after the wife's windfall.

Fireworks

I went out last Sunday to celebrate the anniversary of Byron's birthday – excuses, excuses – and someone transferred me from the Queen's Elm to the Chelsea Arts Club for lunch. All very jolly. But you may imagine my amazement, while I was being signed into the club, to see that the doorman was reading Henry James. I once had an account with Coutts in the Strand and the commissionaire used to stand in the doorway doing the *Times* crossword. I sense a revolution coming. Years ago, in 1952 to be exact, I was threatened with a beating up in Hanley Deep pit when I took my 'snapping' down to the coal face wrapped up in the *Times*. An angry collier asked me was I 'a fuckin' Tory?' and I inadvertently made matters worse by saying no and that I only got the *Times* for the crossword and the cricket and racing. (What the hell I still get it for God knows.) I'm an addict I suppose. But the sight of Henry James, even in paperback, is not conducive to a pissy luncheon. I find reading Henry James akin to self-flagellation. Somewhere, I suppose, there strolls a traffic warden reading Proust between accepting bribes from Rolls Royce owners. If these people really want a laugh to alleviate the boredom of their menial tasks I suggest they turn to S.J. Perelman or the ace of black jokers, Alice Thomas Ellis.

But the biggest laugh I had last week was the one I found in the pages of the *Standard* which concerned the lady who had an affair with a tramp. It seems that a rich German bird, Gabrielle Burchard, met an eccentric tramp, Godfrey Taunton, felt sorry for him and then fell in love with him. When he gave her the elbow she found him asleep one night in Holland Park, poured petrol over him and set him ablaze. Of course, our tramp is a former public schoolboy. It gets better. In a statement to the police she said, 'I wanted to keep him. I was getting more interested in him and took him home. He just sat and sewed patches for hours. I went to bed. When I woke he was kneeling by the bed. He said, "Wake up, it is breakfast time." I noticed something on my mattress. It was a dried rose from the dustbin.' Then she went on to say that the patchman told her he hadn't had sex for years and that then they went through the ordeal five or six times.

Well, the whole affair makes me feel tremendously grateful to the handful of ladies I've spurned. I've received abusive and obscene letters, been hit and had drinks thrown in my face, but not yet been set on fire in the physical sense. I would guess that the rose from the dustbin was the final straw. Even I once bought the entire stock of a flower shop for my ex-wife when I was wooing her. Admittedly it was 4.30 p.m. and they'd nearly sold out, but you have to make an effort. Mind you, there's no gainsaying that five or six leg-overs for a dustbin rose is very good value indeed and any man who can shoot a line as witty as 'wake up, it's breakfast time' deserves what he can get even if it does end in a blazing row.

Anyway, it all ties in with an old friend I met in the Queen's Elm before the Henry James lunch in the club. You wouldn't have guessed that I've played Cupid, but I have. Years ago, my vaguely look-alike mate walked into the Elm and a woman jumped up and screamed at him, 'You shit,' and flung a drink in his face. He said words to the effect, 'What's all that about?' and she said, 'You're that bastard Jeff Bernard.' He explained that he wasn't and she apologised. Then they got talking, fell in love and they've been happily married ever since, their union being blessed with two children. I still live in hope of some woman leaping to her feet, hurling vodka in my face and screaming, 'You're that shit Paul Newman', but I fear it may never come to pass. There was another drink-throwing episode in the Queen's Elm years ago too when I brought two people together. A married couple were having a gritted-toothed row and the wife suddenly threw a pint of bitter in his face. He ducked and I derived the full benefit of it in my face and down my suit. They laughed so much they made it up and got together again. Whether they're still together I don't know. As the patchwork tramp will tell you, where there's smoke there's fire.

Master class

In recent years I seem to have had the somewhat dubious good fortune to attract the occasional gerontophile. It is my friends and acquaintances who consider it to be my good fortune while it is I who consider it a dubious and inevitably disastrous form of coarse angling. What they overlook while they're smirking and saying 'I don't know what she sees in a geriatric old twit like you. She's only twenty-four. She'll kill you', is the ghastly role I end up playing which is that of the teacher. Yes, believe it or not, but for about two months of the year every year I end up being the guru of Great Portland Street. Unhampered as I am by a deep and heavy intellect – I can no longer understand Germaine Greer – I find myself continually plucking and rescuing young ladies from the suburbs and provinces, giving them a glimpse of my Aladdin's Cave, turning their heads with the sights and sounds therein and then being rejected for someone younger when they've had their fill of this old fool's fancies.

The times I've cooked splendid meals for young ladies, introduced them afterwards to Mozart and other friends in the sitting room, lent them books in hard covers, taken them out to meet the lions of Fleet Street, Newmarket and Shaftesbury Avenue, stroked them in every way, converted them from bran to grain products, switched their allegiance from the Beatles to Beethoven, from rock to romance, given them every sort and kind of kiss of life only to see them disappear down a rabbit hole with an advertising executive in a sports car are legion. Last year, there was the twenty-four-year-old nurse. Now I'm well aware that at my age it's a lifeboat and not a dreamboat that I need but I must admit I found her initial interest in me quite irresistible. In no time at all I had her eating expertly with chopsticks, caught her in the bath one morning humming the Waldstein, introduced her to Ascot, Richard West, Lester Piggott, french dressing, taxis and Stolichnaya and there's very little else you can do for a girl apart from make her unhappy and, of course, I got around to that. I ended up snapping. I don't mean cracking up emotionally. I mean snapping like, 'And what the fuck do you know about David Hockney, you stupid bitch.' And that was bad. You shouldn't frighten people, if for no other reason than that they never forget or forgive fear. And perfect fear driveth out all love.

Only once, and quite recently, has the boot been on the other foot and I've played the pupil. I had a fascinating dalliance with a girl who was studying philosophy at London University. She had such a profound effect on me that I didn't actually give up smoking, but I managed to do without the post-coital cigarette for a while (the ones that are obligatory in all BBC television plays). I used to lie there staring at the stains on the ceiling, my left hand cupped around her right breast, while she told me about Leibniz, Kierkegaard, Schopenhauer and Wittgenstein. This was a lot better than the boredom of having actually to plough through the wretched books, and it put me in mind of the delightful affair years ago in Suffolk when I used to snuggle up to the vicar's daughter's warm bum as she told me about Martin Luther. I think I preferred both experiences to that of my most recent tutorial I gave under the duvet to a drama student on the subject of why Lester Piggott is worth 7 lbs, or nearly three lengths, more than any other jockey in the world at Epsom.

Yes, this new drama student, a leggy filly with bags of scope for future development, is an interesting enrolment at the Great Portland Street Academy for Young Women. What I'm trying to figure out though is just why anyone has to go to school to study drama. I study it every day from the moment I get up, check up in the mirror as to my existence and then open the mail. This isn't going to last long either. It's difficult to teach a young bitch new tricks. She's a nail-biting nutter. The word neurotic, like the word 'nice', is overused and misused but I know what *I* mean by it. Neurotic girls are sexually tractable but prone to overact at the end of act three. (The 1983 nurse actually had the gall to come into the Coach and Horses the other day to take a curtain call.) No, I can't take any more of these private master classes. This summer I'm negotiating to rent somewhere like Dartington Hall where I and some of my friends can give a summer school. Young women wishing to enrol for the week's course should report to me with £500 in cash, a toothbrush, seven pairs of clean knickers, seven boxes of Kleenex and an open if not actually blank mind. There will be several lectures and some well-known old classics including Geoffrey Wheatcroft's 'Legless in Gaza', Cosmo Landesman's 'Premature Ejaculation: A Blessing in Disguise', my own humble offering, 'Getting the Most out of your Nervous Breakdown' and an interesting talk by Richard West, illustrated with lantern slides, on how Albert Schweitzer discovered the missionary position. There will be a licensed bar, a little night music and all confidences will be respectfully betrayed. On the last night there will be a ball. Jill Tweedie will decide whose when the time comes.

Rubber plants

It's been another rather silly week in the back garden of Soho. On Monday I met a black bird with thrush and, as I predicted in last week's column, the drama student didn't last long. Lingering over a pot of Earl Grey at the end of an afternoon seminar – included in the service charge – she casually dismissed King Lear as being an old man with woman troubles. I was so irritated I asked her to remove her toothbrush from my bathroom beer mug and make other arrangements for her future unhappiness. Such people come here in taxis but leave in buses and it serves them right. Well, later that evening – back at the drawing board so to speak – in Kettners and sipping Cointreau, the poor man's pre-frontal lobotomy, these tired old eyes came to rest on this delightful-looking black bird who omitted to tell me that she had thrush until I had actually signed her into the Great Portland Street Academy. I've put her on a crash course of natural yoghurt which rather messily has to be applied to the parts as well as swallowed and I've sworn her to celibacy until the start of the flat racing season which opens at Doncaster on 22 March, exactly one day after J.S. Bach's birthday. You could now call her a bird in the bush and I fear I have none in the hand. The next morning I perked up a bit when the telephone rang and I heard the soft voice of my Dublin bookmaker. He told me that Capture Him, held in the highest esteem by his trainer Vincent O'Brien, must be backed when he comes to England in the spring and possibly for the 2,000 Guineas, but that's by the by and I only mention it since the information comes from the same source that gave us Bajan Sunshine for last year's Cesarewitch.

At lunchtime, Charlie took me to a rather superior fish and chip shop where they gave us some tepid white wine in teacups after hours. They meant well, but it was quite disgusting. Wheelers have got it right. If you make it cold enough you can drink Chateau filth without noticing it. Anyway, the plonk went to my head and I ordered a suit I can't pay for on my way home. Which reminds me. The Inland Revenue finally got me to court last Friday and they're going to tap my income at source for the next thirteen months. I think I slipped up badly. I made the wretched collector an offer which he accepted with such alacrity that I knew immediately I'd gone over the top. Can you imagine writing something like sixty columns for practically nothing? So, if I sound a little churlish here until next year's Grand National you'll know it has nothing to do with thrush or drama students. I managed to needle the collector though. What these people don't like or understand after you've been pleading poverty in the dock is one's hailing a taxi outside the court instead of jumping on a bus. That's why they're tax collectors who'll never know the invigorating joys of treading water in the deep end without a life belt.

But something will turn up and a bit did on Thursday. An extremely shrewd television producer called round in the morning and asked me if I'd like to go on the box and talk about the low life, how I got into it and why I like it. Now, for three minutes that would be something of a doddle but this man says it's for twenty-eight minutes straight into a camera. Twenty-eight bloody minutes! If the film doesn't end up in the cutting room dustbin I want you to watch it – I'll tell you the date when I know it – to see how a person can destroy themselves with their own vanity. It's something I've always wanted to do and it will probably turn out to be as farcical as my courtroom appearances. Every time I go to court I expect to see the famous titter go around the court. I think I'm going to be as witty as Oscar Wilde and have everyone in stitches with the judge spluttering 'Not guilty' at the end of the proceedings. What happens is a bit of grovelling and an inane and insincere apology followed by several stiff drinks in the nearest pub. Not the happy hour, but the remorse hour.

Just before I went into hospital – and this is a sordid story that warrants no detail – I collected a criminal record for kicking someone's car parked annoyingly on the pavement. A CID plain-clothes man arrested me in the Coach on a charge of criminal damage and took me to Vine Street where I was fingerprinted and photographed. But this is extraordinary. As we walked past the Swiss pub on our way to the nick the arresting detective said, 'You screwed the landlord's daughter here in 1976, didn't you?' Well, I was amazed. How anyone could have known what went on that Christmas Day after lunch on the saloon bar floor after the guvnor went upstairs for a nap I'll never know. But I liked the magistrate at Bow Street when I went up for the car kicking. He looked at my record and saw I'd been nicked last October for going over the top in the Raj of India restaurant and said, 'The last time it was rubber plants, Mr Bernard. Now it's cars. What next?' Well, you tell me, I thought. Probably a collector of taxes, possibly a drama student, maybe a black bird with the treble up of thrush, herpes and AIDS. All I know is that when I leave this flat it gets bloody dangerous. No wonder vultures are nesting on the roof of the Coach and Horses.

Bygones

Many years ago, round about 1950, I sparred three rounds one morning in Jack Solomon's gymnasium with Al Phillips, The Aldgate Tiger, when he was European and Empire featherweight champion. He knocked seven kinds of shit out of me and then patted me on my numbed head and said, 'Don't step out of your class, son.' Why on earth I should remember that last week as I came off the wagon and opened a bottle of Schadenfreude 1976, heaven alone knows. Until that moment of weakness, when I stretched out my hand for the corkscrew, I'd been reflecting on the sad business of Derek Jameson losing his libel battle against the BBC and about £75,000 into the bargain. Now, I must point out to you that I've never been one to bear grudges. I can barely remember the last time someone did me down and while it's true that Mr Jameson sacked me from the *Daily Express* when he took over in 1976 and sent me sprawling back into the gutter so to speak, I derive no satisfaction from his courtoom demise. Far from it. I take my hat off to any man with his background who can drag himself up by his own bootlaces, overcome almost every hurdle put in his way by a vindictive Mother Nature, and become editor of a national newspaper. It's true that when he did give me the tintack he did it in a very brusque – almost rude – way, but I'm sure that's just his manner and is the result of his retiring and shy way. An endearing disguise you might call it for a man bewildered at having so much so soon. But to reach for the stars and actually get the *Star* is something that goes to no man undeserved. After all, you only get out of life what you put into it.

What's awful is that I've also remembered I owe Mr Jameson an apology. He sat next to me and opposite Germaine Greer at a *Private Eye* lunch one day and Germaine and I were thoughtless enough to embark on a long and detailed discussion about oral sex. A pretty tactless thing to talk about in front of a man with working-class origins when you consider that oral sex is only indulged in by the middle and upper classes and therefore regarded as something of a treat by the workers. The good news is that Mr Jameson says he's actually got the £75,000. Paying it out is going to leave him pretty short but having it at all just goes to prove once again that the wiseacre who coined the phrase 'You only get out of life what you put into it' ranks with Edison, Marconi and Bell as a man who knew how to put it across. But you can't keep a good man down and I'm sure Mr Jameson will land on his feet, as he deserves to.

Life is far too short to bear malice, I always say. You play the cards you're dealt, as I did once with Richard Harris at Shepperton Studios. The fact that I lost every penny I had – he wouldn't play house rules – and that he wouldn't even give me the fare home matters not a fig and is now so blurred in my memory it is hardly worth mentioning.

But to go back to Mr Jameson for a minute before he recedes completely in my mind, what is worthy about him is the fact that he brought his action against the BBC on behalf of Fleet Street and not for his own gain. You've got to hand it to a man whose motives stem from a heart in the right place. Take Colin, one of my oldest friends. Years ago, I came to London for a weekend from Suffolk and had a sudden two-day affair with a girl friend of some long standing. Colin immediately telephoned my wife and told her, 'I think you ought to know, Jeff's been going to bed with Helen.' 'Why are you telling me this, Colin?' asked my wife. 'Because I consider it my duty as a friend,' he said. There again I was in an awkward situation as I was later to be when Mr Jameson gave me the old heave-ho, but it hardly ever crosses my mind nowadays and I can't think why I should suddenly remember it. Anyway Colin asked me to lend him £50 the other day. It's a funny old life, isn't it?

Incidentally, I believe it was the man who said that you only get out of life what you put into it who also coined the phrase 'Let bygones be bygones' and I go along with that. I mean if I were to meet the sergeant who hit me over the head with a shovel when I was banged up in the guardhouse at Catterick in 1951 I'm sure we'd have a drink and a chat about old times. 'Hello, sarge. What are you having?' I'd say, trying to place his face. No, it would be an awful world if we couldn't forget and forgive. The Count of Monte Cristo and Dr Grimesby Roylott give me a pain. Do you remember when Roylott tells Sherlock Holmes, 'I am a dangerous man to fall foul of!' Revenge and threats – such a waste of time and energy. Anyway, good luck to what's his name. Oh yes, Jameson. I'd nearly forgotten.

Wrong track

This was in the *Sporting Life* of all papers last Friday: 'Three hundred youngsters commit suicide every year – many of them out of shame because they are not getting any sexual experiences, the Samaritans reported yesterday.' It made me wonder if the Samaritans have any figures for the amount of middle-aged people who are contemplating suicide out of shame because they are having too many sexual experiences with the *wrong* people. It also made me wonder just who the hell are the *right* people. As for the aforementioned youngsters I didn't give them much thought, although it must be a sad business for their friends and relatives. After all, although I can remember long and fairly painful bouts of celibacy at around the age of eighteen, when girls only fancied you if you were about forty, like being broke it's no reason – or a very bad one – for killing yourself. Admittedly I did have a flash of melancholy at Cheltenham on Gold Cup day when a girl in one of the bars told me that she could just about fancy me if I was twenty years younger but it passed with the arrival of the next round. Yes, I thought twenty years a bit cruel but then it's always some consolation, if you need it, to look at the young twerps who are twenty years and more younger under whom these girls bestow their favours. And is it in fact a favour?

Anyway, at the time of reading that small but sad news item, I was travelling on the Orient Express to Cheltenham sipping champagne, and that's not a situation conducive to considering suicide or the young or both. The Pullman car I was travelling in, 'Cygnus', had been part of Churchill's funeral train in 1965. What a way to go. The free champagne was rather good but how come it's called free when the day return comes to £140? They served canapes on the way down and a three-course dinner on the way back the main course of which was cold on a very cold day. Steak and kidney pudding would have been more in order but who can complain when the ticket is a kind and generous present?

By Paddington my train of thought had me contemplating those suicidal youngsters again and wondering just how many of them would complain if they did have those sexual experiences they were ashamed of missing. How long would they have had to postpone their suicides to discover that we're most of us rather disappointing to each other? Of course, it's no good trying to tell them that a dog can be disappointed in 'his day' and it would be completely pointless to try to explain to them the enormous sense of relief I felt last week when I decided to close down the Great Portland Street Academy for Young Women and cancel our Summer School. The trouble is that the three hundred who ride annually into the valley of shame just don't know what they're missing and what you're missing isn't always altogether a good thing. Reading yet another boring piece about the menopause, this time in last Sunday's *Observer*, I looked at the four photographs of women supposedly suffering or about to suffer that state and to think that they could have male teenagers reaching for the barbiturates and gas taps was and is truly depressing. There are more career-minded, fitness-freaked, liberal ladies like Jane Fonda in Fleet Street than you can shake a stick at. Every trattoria in London has a Joan Collins in it. I cringe to think that's what I wanted when I was what the Samaritans call a 'youngster'.

What I fear I have missed is a sexual experience with the manageress of my local launderette. She's as solid as the figurehead of a tea clipper. She has a nicotine stain which runs from her upper lip to the bridge of her nose from the permanent fag stuck in her foul mouth. She coughs so you can hear her coming. She doesn't bother with make-up like Joan Collins. She's gone to seed completely and finds it cosy. She'd like to shoot those who don't 'fit in'. She's bad-tempered, she sulks and she's lazy. She sometimes mentions her husband and her lip curls at the thought of him. She even sneers at my best shirts, shakes her head and taps her foot at my approach. In

short, she is devoid of any sort of nonsense. She could make
lemmings turn back. At the sight of her, suicidally inclined
youngsters would split the heavens with a rendering of
'Jerusalem'. She may be the woman I've been looking for for
years, and all the time I thought it was Veronica Lake, Anne
Sheridan and Ava Gardner.

Back-scratching

Up until this week the large vodkas in Wiltshire have been as
few and far between as Bernard Levin's full stops. Only the
most appalling withdrawal symptoms have forced me to turn
over an old leaf, but at least I'm sleeping again at night. Could
you believe an itch so bad as to drive you almost to tears? I
had it once before in the Middlesex Hospital when the nurses
bathed me from head to foot in calamine lotion and then, when
that didn't work, held me under too hot and too cold showers.
That didn't do a lot either and eventually they filled me up
with tranquillisers. You'd think that these people would carry
vodka for medicinal purposes, which is just what I've now had
to resort to although I'm a gregarious drinker. Speaking of
which, the Flat Racing season is with us again thank God and
I've never seen as many people fall off the wagon as they did
last Saturday in the Members' Enclosure at Salisbury. It's good
to see the old faces again and it's amazing how well they wear
considering the battering they get from April till November.
Apart from the activity in the Members Bar it was backing
my first loser of the season that stopped my back itching. By
the third race it had sweat running down it, but the afternoon
ended well enough when my man in Crompton, Gavin Hunter,
tipped me his 7/1 winner. But Salisbury Racecourse is to be
recommended anyway, being as it is a damned sight more

friendly and attractive than a London betting shop. Now, it really is high time they did something to tart up betting shops. With three million people out of work you couldn't really say that a comfortable shop would discourage the workers from going about their business. What you should be able to get in the ideal betting shop, apart from a nasty fright, is a drink, a snack, a cheque cashed, every single race televised on a new channel and a free taxi ride home if you lose.

But, as I say, civilised racing is back with us until November and don't the most extraordinary things progress from that contest at two p.m.? After Salisbury last Saturday, I went to Lambourn for a splendid dinner and then finally put paid to the dreadful back itch with several Sunday lunchtime cocktails in the Swan at Great Shelford. Nothing to it really. A jolly nice day with lunch at the Lords, with the *Sunday Express* literary editor, and then home on the rattler sharing a carriage with a *Spare Rib* reader who threatened me with violence. God knows what I've written to offend her, and God only knows how she recognised me. Anyway – and this is what is meant by strange things happening as the result of a day at the races – I woke up the following morning wearing a pair of ladies' knickers. Any transvestite tendencies I may have unconsciously harboured over the years have been well suppressed and I really can't think how this could have happened. As I have already reported, to the *Sporting Life*, the removal of ladies' knickers in the Lambourn area has to be power-assisted, and where it doesn't have to be power-assisted it's no surprise and nothing to be grateful for. Nevertheless I awoke in the old Great Portland Street Academy for Young Ladies on Monday morning, beheld myself in the mirror, and thought I was looking fairly attractive. But before I asked myself out for lunch I suddenly saw who I was. (And she wasn't going to pay the bill.)

I fear it's going to continue in a like vein for quite a while. We have Newbury this weekend and the promised appearance of El Gran Senor. The owner, Robert Sangster, one of the few men I've ever met with money who is not as tight as a drum, I'd like to see win although he doesn't actually need the prize money. It's his trainer, Vincent O'Brien, who bugs me a little. A man who was too nervous to talk to Colonel Mad in the old days is simply too nervous for anything. And, talking of not winning medals, Dave, the guvnor of the *Spectator* pub, the Duke of York, tells me that new *Spectator* employees have been seen buying their *own* drinks with money plucked from *purses*. This is rock bottom and such men should be shot or working for the *Sun* where I'm told they're paid by the purseful. At least you don't meet them at the races during the balmy months.

Rambling

The Easter weekend in Wiltshire was rather special. It was warm and sunny enough to have tea in the garden every morning shortly after nine a.m. and only Eve and the serpent were missing. Healthy-looking rabbits played in the field beyond the apple tree, cock pheasants strutted along the top of an old kitchen garden wall looking like part of a Chinese print, and two beehives I'd thought extinct erupted lazily all day long. There was a sweet smell from the bonfire I'd made of dead ivy and brambles, and jays and magpies fought over some old bread I'd put out on a tree stump. In the afternoons I sat there with my long, iced drink feeling like a pissed badger who'd gatecrashed a Beatrix Potter party. But it was quite beautiful. I could almost hear everything growing. That, of course, is nonsense. I'm getting carried away. I could hear sweet fuck all and to rectify the situation I went inside and put on *Le Sacre du*

Printemps so that I could hear it through the window. It seemed appropriate and I'd been thinking of Miss Rite, as usual, anyway. Then I remembered with some irritation a remark of Stravinsky's that he made some time ago to the effect that there should be no such things as gramophone records and that people should listen only to live performances of music. He should have been locked up in a bedsitter or sat down in a garden seventy miles from the Festival Hall for a few months.

Another source of irritation was and is the love affair Radio 3 are having with Richard Strauss. To escape from him later I switched over to Radio 4 and bumped into *Desert Island Discs*. The guest was Lucy something, the woman who'd intentionally stranded herself on a tropical island with a man she'd had to marry for the purpose. At one point Roy Plomley asked her what she was doing now – now that she'd finished her book about the experience. She said – with a show-jumping accent – that she'd got 'the writing bug'. I couldn't believe my ears. The *writing bug*? I waited with bated vodka for her to tell us where and how she'd got it, but she was far too crafty for that. It's certainly just about the only virus that's eluded me, but give the Lucys of this world a pen and paper and they're infected immediately. (I remember when John Pilger first caught the writing bug. Years ago he reported from Little Rock that 'night came down like a red velvet curtain'. I'd like to know what he'd been drinking.)

Anyway, I can't get Lucy out of my mind. Not only did she get stranded on her sandy strip without the help of an Arts Council grant, but she says she stopped having sex with her old man shortly after they hit the beach. First, I think that all right-minded people will join with me in proposing that the Arts Council commission a ship on the Greenpeace type of line for writers who want to write books about being stranded on desert islands. Secondly, I think we should be told what her

husband did for sex after the nights started coming down. I
have managed without sex since I got stranded in Wiltshire on
Good Friday, but I do have television.

And now, as I sit listening to my first cuckoo in my little Eden
awaiting a long overdue invitation from Roy Plomley to go on
his programme, I wonder more about his last two questions –
what luxury would you take and what two books apart from
the Bible and Shakespeare? – than I do about the music. What
people choose for their luxury on *Desert Island Discs* has often
puzzled me. Champagne, for example, is surely an essential
and not a luxury. Marie Antoinette wasn't uncaring, she simply
had her priorities right – although she did in fact suggest
croissant not cake. I suppose a telephone is useless enough to
be considered a luxury but I think I'd have to choose a large
supply of morphine. As for the Bible or Shakespeare they're
the last two books I'd take. I find the Bible is one of the most
depressing books I've come across and there are far too many
words and phrases in Shakespeare that I don't understand. It's
a toss up between *The Wind in the Willows*, *The Complete Sherlock
Holmes* and *The Count of Monte Cristo*. *Monte Cristo* is the greatest
of plots and revenge is indeed sweet. *Treasure Island* runs it
close but the good guys are a bit wet and I could only like Jim
Hawkins if I thought he went into a rapid decline after cashing
in his loot or went in search of Long John Silver. And was the
Hispaniola fitted out with the aid of an Arts Council grant?
Such imponderables afflict me in the solitude of this garden. It
is time to return to the reality of the Coach and Horses.

Game try

I think I very nearly died last Sunday. I was sitting in the
garden watching the filthy pheasants mating – they really

Dad designing at the Boston
Opera House, 1912.

My mother, Fedora,
about 1925.

My brother Oliver. Photographed by
John Deakin c. 1952.

With my oldest friend, Pete Arthy, in the Mandrake Club in 1949.
Delinquent days.

One of John Deakin's best pictures brother Bruce, Terry Jones, and
me outside the Mandrake Club about 1954.

The rot sets in. Watching racing on TV, 1960.

A little bit drunk. Francis Bacon and me in the Colony Room Club.

Jack Ellis, my second wife, who was acting at the Old Vic when I was a stage hand there. Photographed by John Deakin, 1960.

Jill, my third wife and the mother of my daughter, Isabel.

With my daughter Isabel in 1975.

With Susan Ashley, my fourth, last and most angry wife.

Mirror Group Newspapers Limited

Holborn Circus London EC1P 1DQ
Switchboard: 01-353 0246
Direct Line: 01-822 3 **544**

Telegrams: Mirror London EC1
Telex: 27286

11 July 1975

Mr Jeffrey Bernard
39 Nottingham Place
W.1.

Dear Mr Bernard,

I read with interest your letter asking for information
as to your behaviour and whereabouts between the years
1960-1974.

On a certain evening in September 1969, you rang my
mother to inform her that you were going to murder her
only son.

If you would like further information, I can put you
in touch with many people who have enjoyed similar bizarre
experiences in your company.

Yours sincerely,

MICHAEL J MOLLOY

Registered Office: Holborn Circus London EC1
A Company registered in England (No 168 660)
and a subsidiary of Reed International Limited

Studying the racing page with John Hurt, the naked civil elephant man, in the Coach and Horses.

Terry Jones, Jeremy Madden-Simpson, myself and Conan Nicholas of cat-racing fame.

Enjoying a joke with Norman.

Nursing a hangover
in Red Square.

ought to call it a day now that it's May – and I suddenly was sick and had the most awful pain in my chest. It was probably heart attack number one. Minutes after that a beekeeper arrived to add some boxes to the hives outside to extend them and make room for more honey. I happen to be frightened of most things that sting, apart from women and editors, and when I told the beekeeper he said to stay well clear of the hives during thundery weather. It puts them in something of a tizz. Anyway, all that didn't do much to improve the pain in the chest.

No sooner had the beekeeper gone than a young woman knocked on the door and asked me, 'Are you the gamekeeper?' Now do I look like a gamekeeper, I ask you? Is a gamekeeper to be found in a garden at eleven a.m. nursing a heart and a large vodka? And does a gamekeeper wear jeans and a blazer? But she looked rather nourishing so I asked her in and implied that although I was not a gamekeeper I was willing to learn and had in the past four weeks introduced many pheasants to each other. But she wasn't in the mood for playing, so I went back into the garden to soak up some more sun and more elevenses. Then I saw an extraordinary thing. A rabbit and a weasel having a fight. The weasal won inside the distance, biting the rabbit in the neck. I don't trust a rabbit that I haven't killed myself, so I didn't stew it and threw it over the fence into the field. Within five minutes it was being pecked by rooks.

Mother Nature is working overtime in Wiltshire and she's taken a job in your actual Salisbury itself. When I went into the New Inn on Friday just for the one between Marks & Spencer and the delicatessen, who should walk in but a load of old Fleet Street faces. Now, as it happens, I'm not crazy about journalists, but it was delightful to see the likes of Paul Curran, John Akass and Ed Vine. It was the first time I've seen men in

Salisbury who didn't flinch in front of the bar. And why should they? It was estimated in the Coach and Horses last Monday that John Pilger earns something in the region of £40,000 a year, which is enough for a round of drinks. Anyway, the aforementioned hacks brought a tone of civility to a pub where a man had been talking to me for thirty minutes about the weather.

What is vitally important about the weather is the dependency on it of the state of the going. Saturday sees the 2,000 Guineas and any drops of rain between now (Tuesday) and then will lessen the chances of Keen which I've had the biggest bet on that I've struck for years. That in itself should stop it from winning, but I can't forget the way Lester was looking nonchalantly over his shoulder for non-existent dangers fully a furlong from home when he won last time. When Lester does that it's something akin to seeing Ian Botham walk down the wicket before the ball has left the bowler's arm. To give you a further warning I have inflicted a penalty on the French filly L'Orangerie for the 1,000 Guineas. But a friend of mine who owns a few garages tells me that he's had £8,000 to £15,000 on El Gran Senor for the 2,000 Guineas. I think it's quite crazy since I don't think that 15/8 is particularly good value in a Classic race. What's more he's had £2,000 to win on Mahogany for the 1,000 Guineas. Both horses are considered to be unbeatable by their stables, and so was Sonny Liston when the then Cassius Clay dumped him on his arse at 8/1.

But I do think that there should be Arts Council grants for those of us punters who need a bottle of Dutch courage before they can write out a cheque for more than they can afford to put on a horse. In the unlikely event of Keen winning – God knows the owner, Lord Howard de Walden, needs the prize money – this column should be datelined Istanbul next week. Maybe Bombay, since they're still racing there. But, come what may, I shall be at Epsom on 6 June to see Rainbow Quest win the Derby, and then probably Barbados after Siberian Express has won at Ascot. If all fails I suppose I could get a job as a gamekeeper since I appear to look the part.

Ups and downs

Out of doors it has been a somewhat high life recently, and here in my flat it has been very low indeed. Last Saturday at Newmarket, 2,000 Guineas day, I was rubbing shoulders with millionaires and Charles Benson at a superb pre-race and buffet lunch and the day before in London I had lunch with Alice Thomas Ellis. The latter occasion was a slice of high life that not even Taki would aspire to. But in the early morning, and as soon as the sun has gone down, it has been very low indeed. I see the signs of a nasty descent. When you aim a dirty tissue at a wastepaper basket and it misses and you can't be bothered to pick it up, look out. When you go two days without shaving, feel too lazy to wash up, water the plants, empty the ashtrays, go to the launderette, iron a shirt or pay the milkman and just lie there on your bed nursing a stomach slightly distended with gastritis and wondering just why it is that the world does *not* owe you a living, a good woman, the urge to work and a less haunted face then it's time to pull yourself together, if you happen to have the blueprint for 'together'.

Now why is it that people like Robert Sangster never miss the wastepaper basket? Possibly because they haven't got anything to throw away. And, Charles St George's Newmarket lunch apart, I have to own up to sinking so low as to have

lived on frozen food for the past two days. A Birds Eye cod
steak in mushroom sauce doesn't exactly inspire one to rape a
typewriter and on the Bank Holiday Monday I watched no less
than four consecutive films on television. I'd very much like to
reverse the location and time of day of these highs and lows. I
feel I ought to spring-clean, empty the dustbins, spend a bomb
at Sketchley's, pluck up the courage to see what or who is under
the bed and attend to them, and then, and only then, go out
for lunch at Claridges and fall asleep with my face in the soup,
burn holes in the tablecloth and reveal the holes in my socks
as the waiters eject me. Those of you who aren't addicted to
extreme positions or situations probably don't understand, and
good for you. Stay in your happy medium as long as you can.

The late lamented painter Robert McBryde summed it up.
I saw him one morning actually ironing a shirt with a table-
spoon he kept holding over a gas-stove flame. He was a real
stickler. Then, of course, he'd go out and by evening most
likely he would have spewed up a litre of wine over that shirt.
I suppose the secret of a well-kept, orderly life is to care *all* the
time. McBryde was awfully good in the morning. I was very
good all the time on the wagon between 1972 and 1975, even
taking books off the shelf to dust them, would you believe. In
fact I became so caring that it was only a sudden bottle of
whisky that stopped me blowing my brains out. (And please
don't tell me I would have to be a sniper to do that.)

But talking vaguely of a sort of squalor, I made a fairly
rare visit to the old Colony Room Club the other day to meet
Cosmo Landesman who interviewed me for *Time Out*. I fear I
gave too much away and if you're listening out there, Cosmo,
please don't be too unkind. On second thoughts, sex, alcohol
and horseracing haven't really destroyed me, they've simply
impeded the progress to Haslemere where, as some readers

may remember, I always intended to settle down with a wife, two children – one of each sort, of course – a lawnmower, Ford Escort and steady job. Let's drop it unless you really need the money. Anyway, I stand for everything *Time Out* readers despise. Instead, since you're not a man of extremes, why don't you write to our editor here and suggest a column in between Taki and me? You could call it 'Still life'.

Quails' eggs

Remaining and regular readers may remember that some time ago I mentioned the strange case of the Coutts Bank doorman whom I came across one morning when I entered the Strand branch some years ago on a begging mission. The fact that I had an account there was in no way flash. It was simply that IPC banked there and I was working at the time for the *Daily Mirror*. Anyway, I walked in one morning only to find the commissionaire doing the *Times* crossword puzzle. This was something of a psychological setback. I recorded the fact in the back of my mind but never mentioned it again until recently when I paid a call to the Chelsea Arts Club to find the doorman reading Henry James. That provoked a tiny correspondence and again put me in my place. Until then and this last week I'd always felt it slightly comforting to spend the time of day with my inferiors, since doing so always makes it so easy to be nice, but last week I got the literary soporific punch – as Gene Tunney called his when he whacked Hemingway for showing off – when I walked into Maxim's on Panton Street to find a remarkable doorman called Duncan reading Nietzsche, no less.

Now, as you may recall my telling you, I once got duffed up by a fellow coal miner in Hanley Deep pit in 1953 for taking my lunch (snapping) down the pit wrapped up in the *Times*, but never did I read Proust in my dressing room before a fight in my boxing days and never did I get discovered reading Sir Thomas Browne between dishes when I was washing up in Lyons Corner House in Tottenham Court Road many years ago. I have to admit to a mild flirtation with Byron on a building site, but Nietzsche in a cloakroom takes the biscuit.

But, anyway, Maxim's I can recommend. I kicked off with poached haddock garnished with quails' eggs, followed on with roast duck and red beans, and finished with a fruit salad that comprised West Indian and oriental fruits. It is a nicely done up restaurant – art nouveau – and my companion, unlike the food writer's companion, picked up the bill which I had the good manners not to look at and which came to £35. On the way out I had a word with Duncan the doorman – I made a somewhat jocular remark about Nietzsche – and he told me that he usually reads his books in the original German. He further informed me that he knew who I was and that he has a subscription to the *Spectator*. I have seen a buffet car attendant on a train reading *New Society* and I have seen a derelict on a park bench using the *New Statesman* as a napkin but I doubt very much whether these people had your actual subscription. I can only surmise that there must be money in being a doorman and that the plunge from navvying into journalism was a grave error on my part.

Anyway, after Maxim's the day deteriorated. I went to the Coach and Horses and had a few drinks with my friend Graham Mason. After what we in the business call 'the one', Graham suddenly assaulted my right knuckle with his face and I am writing to you with great difficulty at this moment since my fourth and fifth metacarpals were then broken by his belligerent forehead. The hand that once attempted an ineffectual tattoo on Sandy Saddler's face when he was featherweight champion

of the world is now out of action. And this is not the first time
Graham has hurt me. He once refused to give me our mutual
doctor's telephone number when I'd run out of insulin in the
Swiss Tavern and he once turned off my drip when he came
to visit me in hospital. Could he be trying to give me some sort
of hint? The broken hand does of course mean that I can't
write out a cheque to William Hill for the money their man
on the rails lent me at Newmarket and if this typewriter wasn't
electric I'd be in the Coach drinking with my left hand. I shall
have to learn to kick like Taki. And the awful 'High life' man
has had me thrown out of his cottage, which has screwed up
the forthcoming summer. His facetious remarks concerning my
having left enough vodka on the premises to keep a Cossack
regiment happy were taken at face value by his landlady and
she now considers me to be undesirable. A platoon or troop
possibly, but not a regiment; certainly not a doorman.

Jeremy

Yet another friend has died and I feel as much angry as sad
at what seems like a monstrous injustice. Jeremy Madden-
Simpson – christened by Eva whose obituary I had to write
here eighteen months ago as Jeremy Madman-Simpleton
– was a dear friend and Irish nutter who hadn't long turned
forty. To see him in the Coach and Horses flailing his arms
around like a windmill while still managing to cling on to a
pint of cider, it probably wouldn't have occurred to you that
he'd been taught history by Cardinal Home at Ampleforth.
When I was on the brink last year in St Stephen's Hospital
he used to visit me every evening and bring me a croissant for
my breakfast the next day and when a piss artist takes time off
during licensed hours to visit you then you know you've got

a real friend. I teased him a few times in this column about his being barred from the Queen's Elm for an age but he was happily reinstated a few weeks ago. You wouldn't want to see a man die while he was barred from a pub.

But it wasn't all pubs and wine bars with us. In the summer – and we were planning to start again next week – we used to go to the ice-cream parlour at Harrods in the morning before opening time and giggle over strawberry milkshakes. Then, sometimes, we'd have breakfast in Fortnum and Mason. We first got really friendly after I broke a bone in my right hand on him one night in the French pub and he'd often laugh at the fact that neither of us could remember why, and he'd say, 'What on earth was *that* about?', and then add 'Well, if you can't hit a friend, who can you hit?' What's rotten is that he'd recently found a good woman and was very happy, and God's timing stinks. And why aren't the real shits dead and why do the people who've been given warnings survive? Of course, a lot of grieving isn't only grief for oneself but sheer selfishness. Frank Norman, Eva, Bryce and now Jeremy won't be walking into the Coach today, actually *pleased* to see you and showing it, and it's so bloody inconsiderate of them.

Needless to say, one thinks of one's own death constantly, and sharp, painful reminders such as friends' deaths make me wonder whether this interval on earth might be nonsense in spite of the past good days and times. The lunchtime sessions in the Coach with Jeremy and Tom Baker and Conan Nicholas were worth all the trappings of all the success stories you've ever heard and I'd rather keep down with the likes of Jeremy than keep up with the awful Joneses. Anyway, I had something of a whip-round to get some flowers for his funeral last night and contributions came from a club owner, three pornographers, an editor, a barrow boy, a shipping clerk and a publican, and in the space of fifteen minutes. He would have liked the assortment. And shuffling off this mortal coil I look around at or think of friends and it seems as though we're in a queue that's shuffling along towards a sort of bus stop. 'Who's next?' 'No, sorry. You were before me.'

There's a dreadful fellow in the French pub who once tried to make a 'book' on who in Soho was next for the long jump. I'm told he made me 5/4 favourite for the event but the long shots keep going in and, although I'm pleased to survive, it's a lousy race to have been entered for. So now, of course, as self-obsessed as the next man, Jeremy's death makes me dwell on my own wretched mortality and another birthday tomorrow compounds the morbidity. My ex-wife observed that all I thought about was myself, and she may have been very nearly right, but right now I wish to God that I believed in God. The party could go on. Different premises but no closing time. Possibly like a sterilised Colony Room Club. I wish now that I'd never snapped at Jeremy and told him to pull himself together. Thankfully he ignored the order. The trouble is that there aren't that many people about who are instant laughter, and I fear we're running out of heads to break knuckles on. He deserved better than that. I should have hit him over the head with a bottle of champagne and launched him into something much better. Fucking hell, that reminds me, he owes me a fiver.

Party spirit

The past few days have been a bit of a thrash and it's got to stop. Starting tomorrow it's all going to be different. But my birthday party and my friends threat quite overwhelmed me last weekend and I'm finding it hard to settle down again to the smooth, quiet old routine of screaming at Norman and writing my pieces in the betting shop. The weekend began badly though. My broken hand started to swell up, alarmingly for a man with sugar in his bloodstream, so I took it up to the Middlesex Hospital at closing time, where I was quite unnecessarily and childishly rude to a charming nurse in casualty called Sheila. Half an hour later I went back and apologised to her and then said: 'You must get some horrible people in here on Saturday nights; much worse than me.' She said, 'No. Not worse. In fact you're the worst I've seen for weeks.' I find that pretty hard to believe, but it could confirm my guess that being drunk is being temporarily insane. (So is falling in love, but that's another story and not a very nice one.)

But all was well the next day, I assaulted Del Monico with a cheque and dear Norman added to the booty by giving me a present of a bottle of Smirnoff – why don't these people get their own bloody PR? – and the party began before moving off to a friend's flat for the party proper. Being a geriatric suddenly didn't seem too bad at all. Friends brought presents into the Coach – books mostly – and it was all very moving. Irma Kurtz gave me something rather unusual, a gold-and-enamel money clip consisting of the seal of the President of the United States and engraved with the signature of the contemptible Richard Nixon.

And, speaking of Nixon, a lady friend taped the talks during the session in the Coach. I played it back again today, and it really is quite extraordinary to hear the nonsense most of us utter when we're holding a glass. The subject of sex cropped up immediately, of course, and one group of us were going on about just what turned us on. One woman actually said she was once excited by a man carrying some fenugreek seeds about his person. Very odd, and it reminded me of the night years ago in the Pickwick Club when someone poured an entire jugful of sauce tartare into my jacket pocket because they thought it was a good idea at the time. But I must try fenugreek, although I should have thought that money would be more sexually exciting to most women. And speaking of sauces I woke up the other morning and found my left shoe half full of the bolognese variety. It makes you wonder what on earth happens in the middle of the night.

Anyway, the party went very well. No one hit anyone and, if they had done, it wouldn't have mattered much anyway since both Doctors Finlay and Who were in attendance. Old fans of *Dr Finlay's Casebook* would have been stunned and delighted to see him dance a few Highland reels. My chicken cooked in tarragon and anointed with lemon and cream sauce went down pretty well and the drink actually held out. The next morning I was served beautifully cold bubbly in a bubble bath. I strongly recommend champagne in the bath as a way to start the day, but you can find your own waitress. The contrast between the temperatures of the bird, bath and champagne can be very invigorating and, as Norman said, I've had the punishment, now I want the nourishment. Bubbles apart, I can also recommend drinking very cold dry Martinis in a very hot bath as a way of proceeding through the afternoon towards dinner.

Well, anyway, the party's over and we now have to tread rather gingerly through another year. Epsom beckons on Wednesday and it just might be a very good Derby indeed. I can't back odds-on favourites, so El Gran Senor won't have the added burden of my money. Norman, as usual, will get that.

Snapdragon

I was delighted last Sunday to read about the New York woman who pumped five bullets into her husband. He got a divorce on the grounds that she was 'unsafe to live with'. Bliss.

How much better than the usual slow poison of marriage. I read about it on a buffetless train to Basingstoke and reflected that I should, by rights and on the law of averages, contain no less than twenty bullets. Anyway, you don't go to Basingstoke for fun, and I went there to get to Kingsclere where two good friends of mine barbecued two-and-a-half lambs. Gaston Berlemont, *le patron* of the French pub, carved the beasts, and at 3.30 p.m. I watched my £25 on Darshaan romp home in the Prix du Jockey Club – French Derby to you – at 3/1 and had a splendid day. Or did I? You see, the thing is or was, I met no less than six ex-ladies, and it breaks my bloody heart to think about what was, could have been and might have been. I felt particularly sad to meet again the lovely woman whose parting words to me years ago were 'You've snapped at me for the last time'. It was an extremely unpleasant way to get fired, and I wish she'd pumped five bullets into me instead.

Anyway, the faces from the past filled me with an awful feeling of regret, and sadness has descended on Great Portland Street this morning like some great awful wet blanket, although I shall cross the street shortly to collect £75 from my beloved bookmaker Victor Chandler. It isn't my ambition to get in Pseud's Corner again, but it has to be thought, if not written, that we're pretty awful to each other on occasion, and it's a shame. And shame is the word. What's worse is that none of us have snapped at each other for the last time and we shall go on snapping like dragons until we drop.

Apart from ex-girlfriends, there were some old men-friends I hadn't seen for years, and one of them made me squirm with that sort of patronising attitude they have when they think they've left you for dead in the rat race.

As I say, the afternoon was akin to stirring up the mud from the bottom of a clear pond. Perhaps worse than 'You've

snapped at me for the last time' are the faces you've simply
drifted away from. 'You don't bring me flowers any more'
is one of my favourite songs, but it reminds me of 'You
don't fucking telephone me any more', which is my most
unfavourite unwritten song. The recriminations in the eyes
are horrible reminders of things past. Faces shuffle with
embarrassment. Past intimacies gather in the mind and you
suddenly remember that we go on and on *hurting* each other. I
do anyway. Francis Bacon keeps telling me that the only way to
get through the business of life is to regard almost everything
as being utterly unimportant, but looking at those old faces
makes it hard to do. This is a squalid little mini-tragedy, and I
think that's about enough self-pity for one week.

The day ended cheerfully enough in the bar on Waterloo
Station of all places. If Victor Chandler had offered 25/1
against me drinking in Waterloo Station with four women and
two men while discussing sex on a Sunday evening at eight
o'clock I wouldn't have taken it. But there it is. What an amazing
jemmy to the door of the mind is a few large vodkas. Smirnoff 6
Mesmer 0. Then from Waterloo to the Coach, and yet another
old flame was rekindled. Thomas Hardy put it best. 'These
market dames, mid-aged, with lips thin drawn and tissues sere
– are they the ones we loved years agone and courted here?'
Enough of that. I write to you on Derby day and not much
else matters at the moment. Win or lose I'm off to Chantilly on
Saturday for the Prix de Diane, the French Oaks, run on Sunday.
It's a pretty little town with no old flames to bring me down.

Big noise

I keep meeting women, employed either by Lord Matthews
or Rupert Murdoch, who think that because they can type

they can therefore write. Normally, I don't bump into these
creatures, but recently I've been having to pop in and out
of Fleet Street since bread needs butter. And what a ghastly
place it is. The pubs are the pits, and the restaurants are rather
shabby. Worse, and worst, is the conversation in the pubs, if
you can call talking incessant shop conversation. Journalism is
a function, like going to the lavatory, best done at home and
not talked about. Last week I took my little niece to see an
editor in an attempt to get her lift-off in Fleet Street. The next
thing I'll know is that she'll be drinking large gins and tonic
and wearing her sunglasses on top of her head – a disgusting
female habit, being, I suppose, the female equivalent of
macho. Could there be a word for it? Facho? Whatever it is,
Germaine Greer has bundles of it. As is a red rag to a bull, a
chocolate éclair to Bernard Levin or a sheet of typing paper to
an office girl in Fleet Street, so a television camera has become
to Ms Greer. Oh, how I envy people who like themselves. One
could just sail through life.

It has always fascinated me to see and watch just what
success, 'making it' and fame do to people. The effects can
be extraordinary. With women, like Ms Greer, they just can't
stop talking and they, of course, *always* know best. Men usually,
and quite simply, become dreadfully self-important. Some of
them, idiots, crack. A few years ago, I went on the piss with
Mick Jagger and in a club called the Kismet, but known as the
Iron Lung, he suddenly burst into tears. Solicitous as a spider
to a fly, I enquired as to the cause of the dreadful stream of
tears and mucus ruining my lapels. 'I can't take it,' he howled.
'What can't you take, you fat-lipped twit?' I asked him gently.
'The success. The money and all those birds.' At the time,
I happened to be short of both requisites and suggested a
transfer of both cash and crumpet into my safekeeping. He

soon stopped crying and left without paying. My turn to cry. George Best went to pieces. I took him to lunch one day and he turned up with three girls. Three. I've done some strange things in my time but I've always found two to be quite ample. You can't get near Michael Parkinson any more, and Colin Welland, known to all and sundry in Gerry's Club as Smelly Welland, is damn-nigh certifiable.

But all this strange behaviour is the result of deep-seated fear, the cause of halitosis (or, to be more accurate, it's their friends who do the suffering). And I believe it to be fear that makes Ms Greer talk too much, and fear that has motivated her into acquiring more knowledge than you or I have on any subject in the conversational repertoire. ('Speak for yourself,' I hear someone say.) She also needs to be told that an unhappy childhood is not a suitable topic for conversation. It is not unique. I too had no sticks to my lollipops and had to wet the bed standing on my head. An introductory chapter on an unhappy childhood is permissible in an autobiography, but you should never go on television and whine to the viewers that your mother in Wagga Wagga didn't have a reading-ticket to the London Library when you were five.

It may surprise you to know that I've had a little of all this nonsense, albeit on a small circuit. In 1970, when I was the *Sporting Life* columnist, I was quite the little Jack the Lad on the racecourse. Strangers kept buying me drinks and I was pissed from Christmas to Marble Arch. But it didn't make my breath smell and I refrained from telling my hosts that my mother once clipped me over the ear for having a dip into her handbag while I thought her back was turned during an air raid. Anyway, at least my daughter thinks I'm famous still. I must be careful not to breathe all over her – just in case it's catching.

Dynamite

Last Saturday at Sandown Park I exceeded my humble expectations. The Eclipse Stakes, now the horribly named Coral Eclipse Stakes, is one of the best events in the calendar and I try not to miss it. The first man I met walking through the entrance was Robert Sangster, who is a delightful fellow in spite of having £100 million in his current account. (It's extraordinary to think that he wins the pools *every* week.) He told me that he and Vincent O'Brien strongly fancied Sadler's Wells, so I steamed in immediately and had £25 at 4/1. Not a lot, but quite a lot if that's all you're holding. Then I had a tenner on Grooming, which obliged at 3/1, and finally £50 on Special Vintage, which won at 5/2. For a moment I began to wonder whether maybe I'm not quite as daft as I know I am. I then had a quiet celebration in the bar, was driven back to London, had another private party, passed out in someone's flat and woke up at midnight surrounded by a bevy of beauties. One particular beauty seemed strangely more interested in sitting on somebody else's knee and climbing all over him than she did in your *Low Life* correspondent. Perhaps the girl who told me last week, 'You're a mean, little, alcoholic, diabetic prick,' could have been near the mark.

Then Sunday was pretty awful. I read an obituary of Flora Robson in which she was quoted as having once said, 'I have had little personal love in my life.' What an awful thing to be able to say. I brooded about that over a cocktail or two, forgot that I'd been invited to lunch by my favourite author, Alice Thomas Ellis, and spent the evening kicking myself for my bad manners and embarrassing amnesia. (I've got a lunch today, but where and who with?)

Apart from Sandown Park, the other good thing was verification of another trip to Barbados in September without anyone from the *Sun*, *Honey*, the *Guardian* woman's page or *Spare Rib*. It has taken me two weeks to recover from the thirst in Norway inflicted on me by the impenetrable handbag of a Fleet Street colleague I mentioned last week. Should my man who has fixed this West Indian jaunt inform me at the last minute that we are, after all, to be accompanied by a similarly overpaid hackette carrying a replica of Fort Knox over her shoulder, I shall take a stick of dynamite with me.

When I think of these people it comes as no surprise to read that 30 per cent of 2,000 American women recently interviewed claimed that they would do 'better than average in a fist fight'. What happened to women? Where did it all go wrong? Again, like the decline in the quality of life, I think it must have started with rock and roll. By the time the Beatles were established and the Wolfenden Report had wrecked Soho and established the porn industry, all life was low unless you happened to be holding bread. In 1962 a woman ironed a shirt for me. She didn't engage me in a fist fight. She even went to bed with me, which is the next best thing.

Looking back on that sort of behaviour, I feel as though I'm peering at a distant Restoration comedy. I think they might well have been the good old days, although most of them were spent scratching around for the price of half a pint of bitter. I didn't get trips to Barbados, and the horses I backed ran rather slowly. I was once three months late with the rent of my Suffolk cottage, which was five shillings a week. But then I remember lying on the lawn in the garden of my pub in weather like this pretending to sleep but looking up the skirts of lady tourists and just listening to the bees buzz and the ice chink in the Pimms. Their Pimms. What days they could have been in Soho and Suffolk if I'd had my enormous wealth then.

Meanwhile it's Newmarket. The sales in the morning, lunch with Charles St George and then the races in the afternoon. Days like this can be dreadfully exhausting. It's all the standing. Just you try drinking champagne for eight hours on your feet with a snatched five minutes at the table for some fresh salmon. Well, it knocks me out anyway.

Fitted up

Last week in Salonika a soldier and a labourer were each sentenced to fourteen years in jail for raping a 105-year-old woman. It reminded me of the Moroccan student I wrote about some time ago who raped a pelican and two German tourists on an Aegean island. Thank God we're saner in Britain. A friend tells me that a seventy-six-year-old man in Aberdeen appeared in court charged with indecent behaviour with two schoolgirls. He was given a suspended sentence and the judge told him he wouldn't send him to prison seeing as how the girls assaulted *him* and that anyway it was his first offence. I personally wouldn't mind all that much if two schoolgirls sexually assaulted me, but I wouldn't like to have to wait until I was seventy-six for it to happen. The fact that it happened in Aberdeen makes me suspect that they were probably just trying to get some money out of his pocket.

The other news item I read was of the death of Jim Fixx, the man who started the jogging craze. I also note that Geoffrey Cannon, the eccentric who writes about health in the *Sunday Times* and who is jogging-mad, looks seventy-six although he is nearer twenty-six. These people are courting disaster. They are also extremely narcissistic and if they choke on their bran and high fibre I don't give a fig. The only point in exercise and being fit is that it enables you to abuse yourself even more. Those people who live to tremendous ages in the Caucasus region thrive on sexual intercourse and vodka. Sex is better for the circulation than any exercise yet devised by man, and thanks to Smirnoff I have a very low cholesterol level. I can only conclude that if rabbits drank vodka they'd live to be 105 too. I suppose it's an inordinate fear of death that propels people into jogging on yoghurt-filled stomachs. We must all make way for the next generation, though. The alternative is unthinkable, unless you want to linger on and get raped by Greek soldiers or assaulted by Scottish schoolgirls.

What joggers and fibre-munchers should realise, though, is that gossip, and particularly malicious gossip, is one of the greatest progenitors of longevity. Name me a gossip who has been snatched away too soon. You can't. Benign people fade away, and joggers are benign. Put me on a desert island with a malignant. You can spot a malign unhealthy person from miles away. Like drunks, they have dodgy eyes. The whites are yellow going umber with red streaks. There's a nasty grin that plays around their wet lips when nothing whatsoever funny or amusing is being said. Their hands tremble and shake until they have plunged the metaphorical dagger between your shoulder blades. Then all is peace. They swill stories, expense lunches and unhappy memories. Above all, they understand the human condition, which is something the village idiot can't comprehend –and which is what makes him the village idiot. The village idiot is the man who mentally jogs through life. His is the mind made of the solid fibre and bran of the weather and the cost of bread and cheese. A *Sunday Times* health writer could never survive in such primitive and healthy conditions. There'd be nothing to investigate, no knocks.

Just for curiosity, I tried to do a few press-ups a few minutes ago. I couldn't manage one. Not one. I am also a failed arm wrestler. Neither of these shortcomings prevents me from not dropping dead during a jog or a dig into the cornflakes bowl. I have had alarming moments of short breath in the peace of my bed and I can no longer sprint after buses. But I still prefer to keep my hair – how did you lose yours, Geoffrey Cannon? Bad diet? Lack of shampoo? – and, as long as I can raise my arm to hail a taxi, my right arm to sign a cheque and to raise a glass, and my right foot to trip up a jogger, I shall remain moderately contented with the body I live in. The trouble is that health freaks have made the holocaust an unlikely event. It will end up with a whimper. The human race will just jog and diet off the edge of this flat earth.

Nothing doing

My typewriter keeps giving me reproachful looks and obviously thinks I'm having an affair with a pub. What dear Monica Electric de Luxe can't comprehend is that it's she who's driving me to drink. She sits there on my desk buzzing with energy and simply aching to be touched, and all I can think about is how much I need a holiday. Now, you probably think, how the hell does he need a holiday since he does damn all anyway, but you do need to get away from nothing sometimes. Doing nothing is a drudge. Anyone can cover innocent pieces of paper with words, but doing nothing requires a mite of imagination. You don't really think I'm actually listening to those bores in the Coach and Horses, do you? Good God, no. I'm sitting there trying to conjure up dreams out of thick air.

Take this morning so far. It's been hell. I lay there in the bath awhile back, listening to a concerto for two pianos by

Max Bruch. The announcer said the score had been lost, but some twit obviously found it and handed it into whatever you hand in lost scores to, which was a big mistake. After that, I lay on my bed and went through an instant replay of 1978. That wasn't very pretty and the script was awful, especially *her* lines. Then I burned my hand on the steam iron and made a cup of tea, but the milk was sour. You're with me now. Beginning to get it? You see how much better it would have been this morning if I'd simply got up at six a.m. and raped Monica Olympia immediately. It's going to get worse, though. They don't open for another hour and a half. Then, when they do, I've got to do nothing until they close. I suppose someone will tell me how they spent the bank holiday. There will be the usual ribald remarks about the England cricket team being a load of wankers. Norman will tell someone to piss off, and his mother will give me the meteorological details of the situation in Harrow-on-the-Hill early this morning. Now, wouldn't you rather have a job than have to go through all this and that? Of course you would. I don't want to overexcite you, but after the Coach closes I have to go to the *Sporting Life* to write a column, the deadline for which is five p.m. when the White Hart opens, and in there I will have to listen to a lot of hacks telling me about the scoops they got years ago. After that I will probably have to go to a Greek kebab house in Charlotte Street where I will lose my reading glasses and then be asked to leave. And you think *you* need a holiday.

Even the forthcoming trip to Barbados in four weeks isn't going to be a holiday. First, I've got to keep a diary of it for a travel magazine, and secondly that means I've got to remember what I did the day before when I sit down to write the daily entry. And the party I'm going with is a very rich mixture. Apart from trying to make sure that Richard West doesn't drown (not an easy task for a non-swimmer), you should see the ladies we're with. Have you ever taken four Dobermanns for a walk? Don't. Yes, I've got to get away from it all. But what's on the other side of nothing? I'm seriously thinking of getting a job as a computer salesman or something of that kind. Ugh. The only thing that's keeping me going at the moment is the thought of filming *Opinions* for Channel 4 in a couple of weeks' time. The director already says – smirking at my script – that there will be a lot of complaints, so we will go out at ten p.m. after the children have gone to bed. It is actually quite interesting and rather extraordinary how upset people can get over other people's lifestyles, and I wonder why. I think maybe they think your grass is greener than theirs, but heaven knows I'm living in a rubbish dump. I don't mean to offend Norman by saying that but let's face it, this isn't a formal garden at Blenheim – more a Dig for Victory allotment – we're in.

Which train of thought leads me to the war. I read a remarkable thing the other day in a book which is the history of the Prix de l'Arc de Triomphe. Apparently, when the war was declared, a steward of the Jockey Club said, 'It is unthinkable that in a sporting country like England we should declare war before the St Leger.' Of course, the St Leger was called off – it's run at the end of September – but only an Englishman could say something like that. It's also rather overrating the Leger, even though it is a classic. And he had planned his holiday to coincide with the race, too. Well, my little holiday will coincide with the Arc in October and I shall be well pleased if Reagan can keep his finger off the button until they pass the post. With All Along passing it first, of course.

Jaundiced

My body seems to have become more and more addicted to the Middlesex Hospital. Last Sunday I had to be admitted again to have a biopsy on a large lump which suddenly appeared in the mastoid region behind my left ear. From the post-operative pain I can only surmise that they have removed half my head, as opposed to taking a mere sample of it. It was the first time since my schooldays, which I can't anyway remember, that I'd had a general anaesthetic, and I don't like it. Added to which they gave me yet another local anaesthetic while I was out to the world. During the whole so-called trivial business I was also on an insulin drip, dextrose drip and a Hemanevrin drip. I had more tubes coming in and out of me than Piccadilly Circus. They seemed mildly surprised when, later, after a large injection of Valium as a bonus, I collapsed twice on their marble floor despoiling it with one of their school dinners. I feel sure that these things do not happen in the London Clinic.

But the day started badly enough and I was full of foreboding when, walking to the Middlesex, I found a dead cat in a plastic carrier bag on the doorstep of my local butcher's shop. It was a little sinister. Could it have been an inside job, or had some nasty person put it there as some sort of hint? Anyway, I arrived at the hospital and waited an interminable age to be seen by someone, and so was obliged to read the posh Sundays from cover to cover. You may imagine my horror when reading 'A Life in the Day of Rosie Swale' I came across the awful sentence: 'It's a brilliant feeling when my writing goes right – the greatest adrenalin booster in the world and better than any orgasm.'

Now I've never read any of Ms Swale's writing, so I can't really tell or know what it's like when it goes right, but I've always been suspicious and envious of people who actually enjoy the loathsome task. But more to the point I'm extremely worried as to the quality of her orgasms. It all sounds rather like a situation in which Jane Austen might have been writing in a ménage with Adolf Hitler. She also says: 'In the past I've relished my notoriety and sexy image, but now I've reclaimed my body and only do what I want with it. Nobody's using me again.' Oh, lucky Ms Swale. The last thing I wanted to do was reclaim my body from the last person who laid hands on it and I do so hope someone uses me again. What I wonder about is Ms Swale's unnatural happiness which suffuses her 'Life in the Day'. Just as village idiots wear permanent grins, I feel sure that constantly happy people are not concerned, never reflect and care very little. But good luck to her. I shall continue to be propelled by angst. Nor, unlike Ms Swale, is my idea of heaven to eat, curl up in front of the fire in the arms of the man I love, listen to music and play with the dogs. I might perhaps curl up in the arms of a dog, if I had one, and play with the man I love, if Lester Piggott would permit it, but I'd never be able to concentrate on the music.

What's always puzzled me is how the *Sunday Times* finds such innocuous people to feature. Is there a section headed 'Benign' in the *Yellow Pages*? All these people wake up in the morning and have a cup of tea or coffee, apparently, and then think about the next chapter of their book. No one, it seems, wakes up to the spine-chilling and persistently commanding ring of the doorbell to find they've run out of both tea and coffee and are therefore unable to entertain the Inland Revenue. They always take their children to school, since they're never divorced, and then they work on their books until lunchtime instead of staring at blank paper until opening time.

One of the questions they asked me at the Middlesex before they trepanned me was, had I ever been jaundiced. I said yes, fifteen years ago. I forgot to tell them it was a chronic condition. But I've opted for this mess instead of sailing round the world, single-handed, collecting owls and doing all the other things people do in the lives-in-the-day-of; and the programme *Opinions*, which goes out on 23 November on Channel 4 in which I've said just why should suitably disgust you if you're up at 11.15 p.m. watching telly and not curled up with your fire, stroking your man and planning your next chapter.

But enough of this nonsense. The Middlesex's generosity with drugs is forcing me yet again to my bed.

The fastest man on four legs

Don't ever be misled by the haggard and depressed face of Lester Piggott. He may be a little shattered at trying to keep his weight down to a unbearably uncomfortable and dehydrated 8st. 61b., but beneath the saturnine visage there lurks a wit, a brilliant putter-downer of pomposity and, last but not least, the most gifted jockey the world has ever seen.

As a long term aficionado of racing, involved with it professionally and for fun, I view the man with mixed feelings. To me, he's the guvnor sportsman in the world, a man who's dominated his game for even longer than Muhammad Ali, but every time I've met him, I've found little to say.

Suppose you met Messrs Crick and Watson at a cocktail party, it's unlikely that you'd chat to them about DNA. Every time I've ever met Lester the subject of racing has hardly come up, in spite of the fact that I may know slightly more about it than those he might call the men in the street. In fact, the last time I met Lester I told him about a painful scene I witnessed in a betting shop in Soho. An Italian waiter who put a week's wages on a Piggott-ridden horse which got well and truly beaten had an immediate breakdown. He began screaming as soon as the horses passed the post, Lester's being third.

'All my life,' he screamed, 'I've been good to my children and wife. All of them have had the shoes to their feet and the plenty to eat. Now theese bastard Piggott he keel me.' Piggott smiled and said, 'Well, these punters are stupid bastards, aren't they?' Yes, I suppose they are and I suppose he's more than a little amused at the way they follow him blindly.

It's a great pity that Lester stories are mostly unprintable because of the libel laws and they'll remain so until the sad day he weighs in for the last time, but I did like his remark when I spent the day with him last at Newmarket. He rode two horses for Henry Cecil, and at the end of the session he beckoned me back into his Mercedes to take me back to town. As we drove past the end of the gallops where they join the Bury Road in Newmarket I noticed a loose horse. Naively I thought the poor brute might break out on to the road and get injured. I turned to Lester and said, 'Look, there's a loose horse. Don't you think we ought to stop and catch it?' Lester turned to me, a wicked smile on his face, and said, 'No. Never catch a loose horse. You can end up all day holding on to the f——thing.' But I suppose my favourite, and one which sums up Lester's interest in loot was the time he rode a horse in a race sponsored by Kosset Carpets. 'Listen, Lester,' they said to him, 'if you win this race we'll give you the usual fee and percentage, but we'll also give you one of those cuddly white cats if you'd like one. Would you like one?' 'No,' he said, 'I'd rather have a monkey.' (Monkey equals £500 in cockney slang.)

When I asked the bluff and usually abrasive Capt. Ryan Price his opinion of Piggott, he said, 'Oh my God. What the hell is there to say about the man? He's done everything, he's a bloody genius. The greatest. What else can you say?'

But if you want to hear another expert who can expound at greater length on Piggott, then listen to Farnham 'Maxie' Maxwell, the retired trainer. This tremendously likeable Irishman had a really long association with Piggott. To cut the million words he uttered to me in half an hour down to the gist, it's the activity of the Piggott head that Maxie admires. 'I've known him since he was a tiny boy. The speech impediment and the partial deafness you know. And I'll tell you why I think he's great. He's got a very active brain. When he rode for me he always knew what he had to beat. For example, he'd look at one horse and he'd say to himself that that one will go on and make the running, then he'd look at another and say we'll have to keep in touch with that one. He always knew the opposition so well.'

There was an interesting sidelight to my chat with Maxie. Everyone must know that Piggott's meanness is something of a legend, but not so according to Maxie and his wife Norah. She said, 'He rode a winner for me once and sent back the 10 per cent. and told me to buy a dress with it.' Furthermore, Maxie claims, Lester digs deep into his pockets when there's a subscription for some unlucky person. He also stresses the fact that the grim-faced Lester is a bit of a wit on the quiet.

Mind you, typically and perversely, Piggott wouldn't thank you or me for advertising a soft or sunny streak. I'm positive he enjoys the tales of his penny-pinching and stone-faced outlook. But I'm proud to say I once raised a smile from him. I'd been to Doncaster for the *Sporting Life* and he kindly gave me a lift back to Newmarket. He sat next to his chauffeur studying form and smoking Havanas and, for reasons I have already explained above, I made no attempt to exploit what must have seemed like a heaven-sent opportunity to talk racing. But not a word was uttered during the entire journey. When I got out and thanked him, he eyed me quizzically. 'You're a bit of an idiot, aren't you?' he said (the language was a mite stronger). And, of course, I had to agree. Then, rare and wonderful event, he smiled hugely.

Lester Keith Piggott OBE was born on November 5, 1935, at Wantage. His father Keith then moved to Lambourn and bought him a pony when he was four. 'You couldn't frighten him away from it and he always wanted to raceride. I meant to make him a jockey and it came off,' says Keith. 'It doesn't often, but it certainly came off with him.' Lester became an apprentice to his father and he rode his first winner on The Chase in the Wigan Selling Plate at Haydock Park on August 18, 1948, when he was twelve. The next season he won six races and by 1950, although still only fourteen, he was established, having ridden fifty-two winners from a total of 404 mounts. At the end of the season he finished 11th in the jockey's table, won that year by Gordon Richards. It soon became apparent that Piggott was determined to win every race he could and he quickly developed a reputation for daredevil and reckless riding. The Stewards took note and he was first reported to them in 1950 after having ridden Barnacle to victory over Royal Oak IV ridden by Scobie Breasley at Newbury. Breasley successfully lodged an objection to Piggott, and Piggott was suspended for the rest of the season although he was allowed to ride in the Cambridgeshire. The next year he rode his first big race winner on the same Barnacle when he won the Great Metropolitan at Epsom.

The steady progression to fame, fortune and glory was now well under way. In 1952 Lester was retained by Mrs J.V. Rank and this was the year that he was to make his first and lasting impression on the Derby, a race which is now 'his' race. He was beaten three-quarters of a length by the Aga Khan's Tulyar. Riding Gay Time, Lester was thrown just past the post and then showed a side of his character which demonstrated the will to win. Completely unembarrassed by the indignity of the situation, Lester wasted no time in lodging an objection against the winner – an almost unheard-of sporting slander as far as the Derby goes – but Mrs Rank wouldn't hear of such a thing.

In 1954 Lester won his first Derby on Never Say Die. But two weeks later, riding Never Say Die again, trouble hit him in a big way, this time in the King Edward VII Stakes at Royal Ascot. Lester rode one of the roughest races many people on the Turf have ever seen. Keith Piggott showed me the film of the race and, from what I could tell, Lester tried for a space on the rails which hardly existed. Gordon Richards on Raleigh, quite rightly, wouldn't give him room to slip through and Lester switched positions to the outside and interfered with the third horse running nearest the stands. Most people who saw the race weren't satisfied that it was all Lester's fault, but the stewards found it so. In their now historic report they claimed they had 'now taken notice of his dangerous and erratic riding both this season and in previous seasons, and, that in spite of continuous warnings, he had continued to show complete disregard for the Rules of Racing and the safety of other jockeys.' They withdrew his licence to ride and made it a condition that he serve six months with some trainer other than his father. He served that spell in the Turf 'nick' with J.L. Jarvis to whom his first cousin Bill Rickaby was first jockey.

The restart of his career in 1955 saw the birth of the association between Lester and trainer Noel Murless which lasted for twelve years and must count as one of the most successful flat partnerships in the history of the game. In their

first great season, Murless and Piggott won the Derby with
Crepello and then completed the Epsom Classic double with
the Queen's Carrozza. Two seasons later Piggott won the
Oaks with Aly Khan's Petite Etoile and was a colossus who
bestrode the best horses in Europe.

In 1960 he became Champion Jockey for the first time
when he rode 170 winners from 640 mounts; the feature of
the season was his victory on St Paddy in the Derby. In 1961
he rode 164 winners against Scobie Breasley's 171, and the
following year he won only ninety-six winners and was fourth
to Breasley. In 1963 he failed by a short head when he rode
175 winners, one fewer than Breasley, but the following year
he regained the Championship when he rode 140 winners.
Now the genius became palpably apparent. He retained the
Championship for the next seven seasons. He rode 160 winners
in 1965, 191 winners, his best ever, in 1966, 117 in 1967, 139
in 1968, 163 in 1969 and 162 in both 1970 and 1971. The
world could now see, without any argument, his immense
power in a finish, using either whip or hands and heels, plus
his amazing judgement of pace. He was, indisputably, the
guvnor and those who didn't agree were the few that, through
bad judgement, judged through their pockets.

In 1966 Lester decided to break his contract with Noel
Murless and go freelance. All the pundits told him, or at least
voiced opinions to the press, that this would be the costliest
and most disastrous decision of his career. Wrong again. It was
with this decision that he was able to undertake to ride Valoris
in the 1966 Oaks for Charles Clore. Rumour has it that he
rode the filly on the condition that he was given *all* the prize
money and not just the 10 per cent. (A filly that wins a Classic
today is worth an immediate two or three million pounds at
stud.) Whatever the truth of the rumour, Valoris duly obliged.

Now, irrevocably freelance, Lester gave an exhibition lesson in how to keep a horse's stamina up its own sleeve when he won the 1968 Derby on Sir Ivor, who was considered by most people to be unable to stay the one-and-a-half miles distance. Mastery again. In 1970 he won no less than the 'Triple Crown' (2000 Guineas, Derby, St Leger) on Nijinsky and, in the same year, he won yet another Classic, the 1000 Guineas, on Humble Duty, a 'spare' ride he picked up from the Lambourn trainer Peter Walwyn.

Two other Derby stories combine to fill out Lester's profile. One, from 1972, goes some way to explaining why he is, to some, the most exasperating and unpopular jockey in the world, as well as the best. Bill Williamson, the crack Australian jockey was down to ride Vincent O'Brien's horse Roberto, but on the Monday before the race it was announced that Lester would ride the horse. Williamson had, said the reports, been injured. In fact he was fully recovered by the day of the race; nevertheless, Lester kept the ride and went on to win in one of the most exciting Derby finishes in history. Lester was, and remains, ruthless about 'jocking off' another rider if he thinks a mount well worth having.

In 1977 Lester won his eighth Derby on The Minstrel. He had virtually made the race his own. Nevertheless, one might still expect the man to be a little cock-a-hoop. So Captain Ryan Price, the trainer, was somewhat taken aback when, very shortly after dismounting, Lester was seeking him out to discuss plans for the following day when he was to ride an ordinary animal for Price at a second-class meeting. It is testimony to his insatiable will to win.

Last season saw him ride magnificently and this season? Well, there's bound to be the odd miracle or two but, sadly, and I hope to God it's not true, rumour has it that this may well be his last season. He's broken with O'Brien and will be riding freelance as usual, though mainly for the champion trainer Henry Cecil and I've a hunch that he'll be out to prove he's better than ever. Anyway, why stop? Though he is unusually tall for a jockey, he doesn't suffer physically keeping his weight down *quite* as badly as the press make out – I once saw him tucking in with a vengeance at Annabel's – and, of course he needs the money!

I reckon he must be down to his last £3 million! Speaking personally, my 1981 ambition for 'The long fellow' is for him to ride a winner on a certain two-year-old trained by James Bethell and called Colonel Mad. Meanwhile, I shall rack my brains trying to think of something intelligent to say to him about racing when we next meet, but the likely failure to do so will at least provide a rare sight – old stoneface cracking into a smile.

Trivial pursuit

Six years ago when my last wife sensibly left me I thought never again. Anyway, I'd run out of love and could only splutter from time to time as a car does when it runs out of petrol. So now what really annoys me is that I've been smitten again. The lady in question is a waitress in the Groucho club. How can I describe her? Her hair is very dark brown, almost black, and it looks like silk. Her eyes are like a summer sky and the whites of them are as clear as the sparkle of her teeth behind lips that beg kissing. Between those eyes and that mouth there is the incident of a nose. How God and genes can make perfection out of gristle is nothing short of a miracle. It is the prow of a beautiful ship. And, talking of things maritime, although it is difficult to estimate her body beneath the severe black and white costume obligatory to serve drinks in the Groucho, it would seem to be ample. Not too big, not too skinny. Somewhere half way between the *Sky Lark* and the *Titanic*. To me, she is delicious. But what on earth do you say? So far our conversation has consisted of, 'Good afternoon, sir, what would you like?' and, 'A large vodka, ice and soda, please.' I have explained that my name is Jeff and not sir and I now think that 'sir' is a way of kindly saying 'piss off.'

The whole business is steeped in paranoia. The more I look at her the more I become aware of my age, weight loss, pending hair loss, pallidness, scruffiness and general physical disintegration. How can I tell her that the inside of the top of my skull is like the ceiling of the Sistine Chapel? Or that my head rings with toccatas and fugues? I can't. All she can see is a twit who spends most of his afternoons dreaming, sometimes snoozing, sometimes arguing in a club. I need a PR badly. Perhaps infatuation like drunkenness is temporary insanity. But I am too old to shoot lines. One is like what one looks like. The *Marie Celeste*.

I know what these people want. Bettina, for that is her name, will end up with a film-maker aged about thirty who drives a Ferrari coupé, one bronzed arm nonchalantly over the driving door, and who lives in a riverside penthouse with a Burmese cat, several gold medallions, a bottle of aftershave, an extremely expensive hi-fi set and no self-doubt whatsoever. All that is so very achievable if you take yourself seriously when you're young – all you have to do is to work hard which any idiot can do – but is it worth it? For Bettina, possibly. Another odd thing is that when I've looked at her in recent days I have noticed that I get slightly short of breath. Of course, I could be having mild coronaries but I don't think so. I think it is because she is so enormously huggable. She has the majesty of an infanta. Only once have I been temporarily diverted from her presence in the club and that was one evening last week when Germaine Greer called in for refreshment. How some idiot men have got that woman all wrong is beyond belief. The Doctor is quite wonderful and is the only woman I have ever met who doesn't make me resent the fact that she immediately makes me quite aware of the fact that I am an idiot.

Speaking of which I would very much like to know just what they teach at Holland Park Comprehensive School. I went to see my daughter last week and we played a game of Trivial Pursuit. She got a very simple history question which was 'Who succeeded Lenin?' She said, 'Stanley Baldwin.' It's worrying. I used to eat history when I was her age. And now she has her first boyfriend and the fact that he's French is another worry. I suppose he talks like Maurice Chevalier and plants kisses on her all the way up from her hand to her neck. By now she probably thinks we lost Waterloo or that it is merely a railway station. But, more seriously, what shall I do about Bettina? I have nothing to offer except love, a half share in my current account, some vitamin C tablets and a bottle of Veuve Cliquot for breakfast. That is how we start the day, my landlady and I. Perhaps I should apply for a job as a waiter at the Groucho. It would be a sort of marriage. On dear, how very, very much I want to save her from falling into the hands of a really *nice* man. I could give her blood, sweat and tears.

REACH FOR THE GROUND

PART 1

Wine
Song
Soho, So Long, So Sad

Wine

I was in a tremendous hurry to grow up. Not to fulfil my
mother's or schoolmaster's ambitions and dreams for me,
but for my own yearnings – the yearnings that obsessed
me which would signal the end of the hell and prison of
childhood. I didn't miss out on wanting to be an engine-
driver or even to open the batting for England, but there was
a terrible urgency to wear long trousers, take a girl prisoner
and more than anything, to be able to go into pubs. There
was a mystique about pubs in my imagination, since they
were at once forbidden, enjoyed and somehow wicked and
therefore somehow magical. Like the first cigarette, the first
few drinks made me choke, but I had embarked on a downhill
commando course of the soul and with great impetus. My
mother took sips now and then and my father, long since
dead, drank very little indeed, as far as I know. I don't think
that genetics had anything to do with it but I soon began to
feel more at home drinking with adults – the alcohol bridged
the generation gap – and I felt also more at home in a pub
than I felt at home. In the beginning I drank half-pints of
bitter, didn't like it much, and felt cut out for better things.
But even bitter was better. I was shy, aggressive and had a lack
of self-esteem, an aching cavity. With a drink I could face a
female. With two drinks I could talk to her and with just one
or two more than that I could say what I thought and not reel
back nearly mortally wounded.

It was my introduction to Soho which gave me a taste for idleness and loafing on the fringes of Bohemia – a lifeboat of sorts for the deserter from accepted convention. From the very beginning I never really enjoyed being drunk and never have. It was only the process of becoming so that appealed and particularly that half-way stage which is all too brief. Drunkenness was and is merely an inevitable accident at the end of every day. It was the company that I kept in the pubs of those days that was such heady stuff for me. For a boy who had only just left school they were magic and already legends in an age of later developers than you see today. There were the painters John Minton, the 'Roberts' Colquhoun and McBryde, Francis Bacon, Lucian Freud, Keith Vaughan, Michael Ayrton and once I even had a drink with Matthew Smith. There were George Barker, Louis McNeice, Dylan Thomas and a hundred unpublished poets. Alan Rawsthorne and Malcolm Arnold provided the background music and men like Morris Richardson and John Davenport were extras in almost every crowd scene. It was Johnny Minton who had the money to be able to introduce me to spirits and it was whisky that helped him to suicide and much later, twenty-five years on, was to land me in the addiction unit of a mental hospital in Hanwell called St Bernard, right spelling wrong pronunciation.

In those days the undercurrent of anger, sexual frustration and the resulting self-pity were what came quickly to the surface with drink. I was difficult and a bloody bore in the way that any drunk can be, and the nights ended in fights and tears and the days began with guilt and remorse. At the time it didn't seem to me to be particularly excessive. After all, I was surrounded by people who were more judgemental about art or a man's willingness to buy his round than they were about the bad behaviour of their friends and acquaintances. As time went by, and it took me forty years to grow up a bit, the drink made me bolder, a little more outrageous, but finally often desolate.

Max Glatt and Professor 'Bunky' Jellinek, two of the founders of the modern scientific approach to alcoholism, charted the stages of the course of what might be called the downhill struggle and that feeling of desolation is just about rock bottom – complete defeat admitted. Of course there are a couple of stages on the downhill journey that I find very amusing and quite true. One of them is 'Starts drinking with social inferiors'. They could have well added 'Starts drinking with bloody bores'. At one point it is true that I would have had a drink and passed the time of day with almost anybody although I loathe unsolicited conversations in pubs with strangers. Alcoholics seek each other out and recognise each other at first sight. There is a flash of recognition that lights up on their faces as they see each other in their thousands and all over England as the bolts slide back on all those doors at opening time. As it felt better at school to be in trouble with another boy and not to be the only one caned so it is to be with almost any company groping one's way through the fog and loneliness of the boozer's day.

A nasty and tedious stage of the descent is the business of attempting suicide. It makes me cringe and curl up with embarrassment to think of it now, but I tried it a handful of times thirty years ago and I meant every attempt at the time, and was not just 'crying for help'. The cry for help has become a joke that I share with Richard Ingrams and was an oft-used phrase in *Private Eye*. If I did cry for help it was done once and finally for real and it led straight to St Bernard's Hospital in Hanwell. Wandering through Kensington one morning at an extremely low ebb, I called into a tobacconist to buy some cigarettes. The man behind the counter asked, 'Can I help you, sir?', and in reply I just burst into tears and because to both our horror I couldn't stop crying he went over the road to fetch a conveniently placed doctor who turned out to be also very conveniently an Irishman, a racing fanatic and a man not averse to a gargle himself. He arranged for the addiction unit at the hospital to accept me as an inpatient immediately. I was met there, still in tears, by a male nurse who looked like Joe Frazier who turned out to be a King Kong with a heart of gold. They gave me heavy doses of Parentrovite and Largactil and more or less knocked me out for a week, only waking me to feed me.

What a strange place it turned out to be. Physically on the mend I woke up to find myself in the next bed to Jumbo who had, it seems, contrived to land a Boeing jet on the same runway as another jet trying to take off in the opposite direction. The airline in their wisdom, suspecting our new friend Jumbo might be an alcoholic, put him in charge of traffic control at Nairobi airport. He had been showing some signs of anxiety since the Battle of Britain and now here he was lying next to me as happy as a sandboy with the dreaded and irreversible Korsakov's Syndrome, a jolly, laughing cabbage. He would die there.

Nearly everybody had such a bizarre story to tell that they were all fascinating and only two of them were classic bores whereas drug addicts were and are all of them boring. At least most alcoholics, although consumed with self-pity, do have a sense of the absurd and are well aware of their sometimes ridiculous situation. I was to learn that the types in these addiction units varied very little. There is always, for example, the obligatory BBC producer, a sprinkling of Celtic ne'er-do-wells, sometimes a journalist like myself, and there was a panic-struck Indian civil servant who thought he had gone over the top when he had just three lagers for lunch one day. The women I met in group therapy sessions from the female ward were usually rather respectable, mostly middle-class women whose guilt revolved around having given their bodies to almost anybody in return for a drink. A notable exception was a young woman I took a fancy to who had been a sister in the emergency department of a hospital, fond of secretly sipping vodka all through the horror of her shifts and who had been tumbled one day when she inadvertently sprayed the face of a patient with very bad eczema with vaginal deodorant.

It was one day during a psychotherapy session I had the thrill of nearly killing a man. He was one of those boring suburban men with a pebble-dashed mind to go with it. He listened to me spouting some autobiographical nonsense – that's all we talked – and then made a sneering remark to the effect that, in his opinion, I had always made the mistake of aiming too high, i.e. the moon. I jumped across the room, leapt on him, got my hands round his throat and began to throttle him. After other patients and the nurses pulled me off him and my temper subsided, I felt as refreshed as anyone could look bathing in a mountain stream in a television commercial. I wore a beatific smile for a week.

Most of the time, though, was spent talking in what they called the day room to the two friends I made there, one of them whom I still see and who is a dry alcoholic and the other, a Scotsman, who worked his way south from Glasgow to London over a period of fifteen years, stopping at various prisons on the way. Three-quarters of the patients there were Celts and there always are that number of them in any alcohol addiction unit. Irishmen tend to blame their matriarchal society and the Scotsmen usually point to their poor, squalid and violent upbringing. And yet very few drunks simply admit to either enjoying heavy drinking or to having what men like Professor Glatt would call personality defects. But to make only two friends in that time among so many patients is some indication that alcoholics are very nearly as boring as drug addicts.

Eventually, when I came out at the end of the three-month stint, I went straight to the French House in Soho for a drink to celebrate the fact that I no longer drank. From then on, in spite of my good and sincere intentions, I began to use phrases such as 'Just the one' more and more and I began to have to keep drink at home and to know that if I went out and wherever I went that there would be a drink there at the end of whatever journey I made, were it round the corner or miles away. I went back to whisky and drank even more than I had before my spell in St Bernard's.

One day I woke up lying on my sofa in the sitting-room of my cottage in Suffolk. The place seemed almost empty and after a few minutes of looking and searching I realised that my wife and daughter had left. The finality of it, the realisation that all attempts had failed, the emptiness, the desolation and the too-lateness of yet one more chance, one more new leaf to turn over, made my chest ache so much that I as good as gasped for breath. Love ebbs but on that occasion it was wrenched away like a rotten tooth. From that moment on I drank for oblivion.

To some extent writing some pieces for the *New Statesman* at the behest of Anthony Howard saved me from going quite insane and also I had to be sober at times to go on doing so and earn a living, writing features for things like the *Sunday Times* colour magazine and the odd crumbs that Mike Molloy would feed me from the *Daily Mirror* out of what I am sure was pure kindness. I also was never in a complete haze since my sex drive was as strong as ever if not made even stronger by the desperation of loneliness and I had to be able to do the deed. Oddly enough, had I been a teenager counting heads

I would have been pleased with myself since I embarked on the most promiscuous period of my life and with a courage derived from Scotch but attributed to the Dutch I became a veritable ladies' man. Scrubbers' man too. I fell in love just once more and for the last time in 1978. For her I made another futile attempt and by that time I had not only *Private Eye* but a certain amount of success with the *Spectator* 'Low Life' column to keep me from the gutter and the madhouse, but that marriage was to fall apart as well in 1981.

Life went on and now it was sustained by a vodka drip and a feeling of enormous relief that I had seemingly almost suddenly been given an identity by the *Spectator*. It felt much better to be 'Jeffrey Bernard, the drunk' than just 'that drunk'. Of course, I didn't drink less, but I somehow managed to keep my head above vodka. But I had still not managed to pull off the trick to be able to change and settle down as my wives and other women had hoped I would for so many years.

Then, in 1989, Keith Waterhouse announced one afternoon in the Groucho Club that he intended to write a play based on my *Spectator* columns, to be called 'Jeffrey Bernard Is Unwell', so confirming my suspicion that he was stark-raving mad. What he was was clever. The play, mostly about my drinking, made drink somewhat paradoxically a thing of secondary importance to the very first taste of self-esteem I had experienced off a school cricket field or later in a lady's chamber. It was suddenly like being able to walk without crutches albeit hobbling for most of the time. The immediate success of the play was heady stuff for me and although it didn't accelerate my drinking, my intake was a steady two years of celebration. First night after first night.

The booze was now affecting me more physically than it had before, and apart from my pancreatitis having reached the chronic stage I was wasting and my legs were beginning to give way. First there was the present of a walking stick with a silver band engraved 'To Jeffrey Bernard from the *Spectator*' and then there were accidents from stumbling and falling even when stone-cold sober and eventually septicaemia which led to the below-knee amputation of my right leg. I felt more angry than depressed about it and what with my now ageing face I became acutely and horribly aware of the fact that it was highly unlikely that any woman would ever want me again.

But something else was happening that was odd and entirely new to me and it still does give me an odd feeling of surprise. I was actually becoming bored with drinking a lot. Plain bored. After years of pub-going I now knew more or less exactly who was in what pub at almost any given time of day or night, and I knew the conversations so well that would be going on in them. At last I could stay away from places like the Coach and Horses, the French House and the Groucho Club without feeling that I was missing a treat, a party, maybe Miss Right or some wonderful happening or other. I was, so to speak, pulling up lame in some sort of rat-race. Maybe this is the early retirement, although God alone knows I've been working towards it for long enough. There isn't the same sense of urgency any more and only very recently I remember one day feeling almost worried that I might live for too long. The idea of being old, broke and alone would have anyone reaching for the bottle and then to not be able to pay for it, God forbid. Now they tell me that my pancreas consists largely of scar tissue. I think maybe my brain does also for the memories are scars of a sort.

In the past and at my lowest ebbs I used to think that maybe drink had destroyed my life, but that was dramatic nonsense and temporary gloom. Without alcohol I could have been a shop-assistant, a business executive, or a lone bachelor bank clerk. But why pick on bank clerks? The side effects and the spin-offs produced by my chosen anaesthetic have at least produced a few wonderful dreams that turned out to be reality. Even the hangover from the nightmare contains some sweet nostalgia.

Song

It was not long after the Groucho Club opened that I became a member. It was too expensive for me but it was clean, comfortable and there were no lager louts and only the very occasional tourist brought in by a member. Of course there were and are, sadly, an increasing amount of suits – advertising people and pop music producers. There were also a few actors and writers that I knew and liked who used the place and I began to use it as my afternoon drinking club.

One afternoon I bumped into Keith Waterhouse in there and while we had a drink together he told me that he was thinking of writing a play based on my *Spectator* columns. As I have already mentioned, I thought he was mad. For the next few weeks I gave it very little thought indeed. If I did think about it at all I simply thought that it was another pipe dream that would come to nothing. I was feeling generally unlucky. Then, when Keith finally got it off the ground and told me that Peter O'Toole was to play me in it, I felt strangely elated but I still couldn't quite believe it and I felt so pessimistic that I thought if it does come off it will indeed come off and after only a few performances. Any paranoia I felt was fuelled by the fact that I knew that there were whispers going around Soho that almost anything to do with me must fail. And then at last it really was going to happen and we came under starter's orders. There were a couple of interviews and some photo calls involving Peter O'Toole and myself and at last I was beginning to feel some real excitement about the project. Peter turned up for the first day of rehearsals quite incredibly and amazingly word-perfect. He liked the play so much, referred to it already as 'my play' and he told me that he was driving his young son Lorcan mad by continually directing his speeches from the play at him.

The play was to open in Brighton where it was to run for two weeks and I was now beginning to hold my breath, as it were, for longer and longer periods. The play opened at the Theatre Royal and the house was packed. A lot of friends and acquaintances had come down from London for the first night and I remember having trouble in recognising Fenella Fielding, either because of my failing eyesight or because I had already celebrated that first night a little in advance.

The following morning the papers, as the audience had done the night before, declared it a hit. I went round to see Peter as soon as I woke up the next day, taking the local newspapers with me, and he read them over our coffee in a very cool way that surprised me considerably. He had obviously had no doubts whatsoever that he and the play had been headed all the way towards a great success. I was interviewed by radio and press as I was when the play moved to Bath a fortnight later, and for once I wasn't just being asked what it was like to be a well-known piss artist. I was now a little more than an animated bottle of vodka named Smirnoff. As Keith was to say later, we were a smash hit before we opened.

I was somewhat childishly pleased at the fact that so many people who had predicted disaster would now have to eat their words. Even John Hurt, a friend of sorts, had more or less dismissed it after having been originally offered the part by Keith, saying to me that he thought it might make quite a good radio play but that it wasn't for him. I personally thought that his bottle had gone as far as stage acting was concerned and where there were no retakes.

It was all one hell of a heady experience for me though. Sometimes I would walk down Shaftesbury Avenue from the Coach and Horses and stand opposite the Apollo to gaze at my name in lights. I got a tremendous kick out of that and anyone else in the same position who denied that would be a bloody liar. Apart from the thrill of seeing 'Jeffrey Bernard' in red neon I had some mixed feelings about it. I found myself wishing that my mother had been alive to see it and also some very close and dear friends who were now dead and who would have been proud of me. Also, on a more childish level, I wanted very much to have rubbed it in to those who had always been sure that I would simply fade away, from schoolmasters to those with mean-spirited envy.

Looking at my name in lights I also was extremely conscious of a sort of absurdity about the situation. After all, I was still the same person who had worked on those building sites, worked in those steamy kitchens, fought professionally for a fiver, and lived in the greatest dosshouse of them all, the Camden Town branch of Rowton House. And now here I was being congratulated by strangers in the stalls bar and being asked for autographs and being bought drinks. All of this could make a man who took himself seriously quite mad, but a day has never passed in forty years in which I have not remembered the ghastly beginnings of it all. Sometimes I would go round after curtain-down to see Peter in his dressing-room. He was always utterly charming and he was also delightful to my daughter or any other friends or relations I took with me. The star who hadn't had a drink for years himself always handed me one full to the brim.

But in spite of all the bright lights, the flattery, the publicity and the more and more familiar name there were still aspects of life that confirmed my belief that it was and is a bowl of shit and not cherries. Now there was beginning to be some sniping from the wings. At the very beginning a Brighton journalist, Mike Howard, although describing Peter's performance as having been magic added, 'The underlying morality of portraying such a man on stage is questionable.' A Hilary Bonner said that we shouldn't be laughing at a man drinking himself to death, but Peter loyally wouldn't have it that I had wasted my life. 'Waster? Jeffrey is a gutter poet,' he told the *Evening Standard*. In the *Financial Times* Michael Coveney said that the play owed little to me and remarked, 'The man in question is very probably a shit of the first order.' Even in the *Spectator* Christopher Edwards said that I was full of self-pity and self-censure, the latter being, as Doctor Johnson remarked, 'an invidious form of self-love'. The *Sunday Times* magazine captioned a photograph of me with the words, 'Jeffrey Bernard could have been a seam bowler, but ended up plain seamy.' Milton Schulman in the *Evening Standard* said that there was dead cynicism behind my eyes, and John Gross wrote in his *Sunday Telegraph* review, 'Possibly we are being given a sanitised version of the real Jeffrey Bernard, I occasionally find something menacing and a bit unpleasant in the columns.' Jack Tinker, while admiring the play and referring to me as a skeletal Falstaff and a hero for our own times, went on to say, 'To be honest, I move tables in restaurants in order not to sit next to this self-same Bernard. He cannot be guaranteed to be the amusing creature of his own stage legend; and unfortunately I have never seen him behaving as anything other than a sad, old, drunken bore.' Nastiest of all was the *Sunday Telegraph*'s piece, very probably written by the then editor, Peregrine Worsthorne, who referred to my modest talent, described me as an absurd amateur and said that I was just a drunk. 'There is *no* more to him than that.' He also drew attention to my 'unpleasant temper and darker side of his personality, offensive to those who can't answer back and ingratiating to those who can'. He also sneered at me for 'sucking up' to Graham Greene. This was not by any means, incidentally, the first or last time that my short but genuine friendship with Graham Greene had caused so much resentment – envy in my opinion – in other journalists. Had any of them stopped to think they would not have wondered that a low life column would have very much appealed to Greene. He did once say, 'When I first met Jeffrey Bernard I felt as though I had known him for years,' and he kindly wrote in a blurb for the book *Low Life*, 'In all the years I have never once been bored by Jeffrey Bernard.' Even the Salvation Army's paper *War Cry* had a go at me with a front page leader headlined 'Jeffrey Could Be Better' and a contributor to *Hospital Doctor* magazine wrote about me under the headline 'Alcoholism Is No Laughing Matter'.

In spite of all this sort of criticism, among the people who enjoyed it tremendously and who were spotted in the hospitality room off the stage and in the stalls bar were Placido Domingo, Rupert Murdoch, Cliff Richard and the King of Norway, and Princess Margaret and I myself met and drank with Jane Russell and Jack Lemmon in the stalls bar, and we were also visited by two prime ministers. In time we won the *Evening Standard* Comedy of the Year Award and I jokingly told Keith that I would like to borrow the statuette for six months of the year. I have to admit that I was only half joking. I had, after all, written most of it. After a while Peter O'Toole had to move on to continue his film career, but the show went on and

Tom Conti successfully took over, although I didn't much like his performance, believing him to be totally out of sympathy with the character he was playing. And then James Bolam took over and the audiences still laughed and we hadn't finished yet, because Peter came back for an amazing ten-week season at the Shaftesbury where he again broke all theatre records by filling 1,400 seats every night and with the crowds of people fighting their way through ticket touts. Again the play attracted rave reviews and there was more to come. Dennis Waterman took the show to Australia and I went out to see it. The two weeks that I took off from the *Sunday Mirror* to do so earned me the sack which was a financial blow, but almost worth it to see Sydney again and to watch Dennis performing in the last night there. There was a short run after that in Dublin where it didn't go down that well, and someone, I believe coincidentally called Jeffrey Bernard, fled with the takings, and then the play was put on in Scandinavia and Italy and who knows – it might even come back again here one of these days. For a short while it did fairly well in Buffalo, New York, where it was directed by Keith's son. Now there is occasional talk of it being adapted for television even six years after that first night in Brighton, but who knows what will happen. I don't know. All I know is that it has, as I have already said, changed my life, and even the spin-offs, like being asked to do *Desert Island Discs*, have been enjoyable, and a portrait that was painted of me by Michael Corkrey hung for a while in the National Portrait Gallery.

I came back down to earth on the afternoon of 8 February 1994, when my right leg was amputated at the Middlesex Hospital. Just one of God's custard pies. Jeffrey Bernard really was unwell. Sometimes these days somebody like Londoner's Diary in the *Evening Standard* will telephone me to ask my opinion on the most irrelevant and trivial subjects, but I think that they really telephone to see whether I am still alive. Twenty-odd years ago a bookmaker in the French House in Dean Street made me a 5/4 on favourite to be the next person in Soho to die. He lost his money several times over. I am not quite ready yet, and Keith Waterhouse, God willing, will have to wait to write a posthumous play about me if he wants to.

Soho, so long, so sad

Soho is dying. She lingers on doggedly but she has been a terminal case ever since the day Lord Wolfenden published his report which drove prostitutes from the streets. In their place there sprung up the industry of pornography. Dirty bookshops, blue cinemas and strip clubs, and in very nearly every instance where they now stand there was once a café, bistro, restaurant or delicatessen. Now it is only the pornographers who can afford to pay the rents and rates of these once delightful premises.

The decline of the quality of life has really taken a fancy to dear old Soho. I first came to Soho in 1948 when I was sixteen years old. It was love at first sight. I became immediately addicted. My brother was a student at St Martin's School of Art at the time and one day he asked me up there to meet him in the café where the students had their coffee breaks. I thought I was in Disneyland after two fairly disastrous years in a strict public school. The Swiss Café, as it was known, was in Manette Street by the side of Foyles. I found myself in the midst of would-be poets and painters, writers, layabouts, café philosophers, bums, a few genuine Bohemians, a vanished breed, actors and some very pretty girls.

It represented everything I was brought up to think was wicked so, of course, it was magic. I was introduced to sex, drinking and horse-racing in no time at all. Yes, 1948 was a very heady year. As time went by and I became less socially gauche I spread my wings and got to know the Soho beyond Manette Street. Soho proper was and is enclosed by Oxford Street, Charing Cross Road, Shaftesbury Avenue and Berwick Street market. In Dean Street the York Minster (sometimes known as the French) had a genuine feel of Parisian café society. In the morning the local tradesmen and shopkeepers plus the mostly French prostitutes who Wolfenden thought so outrageous would come in, sip the Amer Picon or Ricard and chat and gossip and discuss the village of Soho.

It was charming. The French girls were elegant, polite, bought their round and never solicited for custom. Madame Valerie who owned the patisserie around the corner – still there – held court and poured great quantities of Guinness into her gigantic body. Later on, and for quite a while, I would have a routine drink every morning with Dylan Thomas who was usually a bit hungover. Nice man sober, impossible drunk. But most of the poets and writers used the Highlander further up the street. And what a different bunch they were to the mostly awful advertising yuppies who use it now. Apart from Dylan there was Louis McNeice, George Barker, John Heath Stubbs, David Wright – I can't remember them all, but it was a who's who of modern poets. Then, as we've seen, there were the painters Roberts Colquhoun and McBryde, John Minton, Lucian Freud, Keith Vaughan, Francis Bacon – not a millionaire then – all of them now represented in the Tate.

Such people intermingled with a very different bunch who could have come straight out of William Saroyan. Ironfoot Jack, Handbag Johnny, Sid the Swimmer and The Fox. The one place they couldn't get into, though, was the slightly exclusive Gargoyle Club on the corner of Meard Street. It was a beautiful place and the interior had been designed by Matisse. It was a bit up-market but they put up with what were then Bohemians. On a good night it was fascinating to see people like Robert Newton ranting and roaring into the early hours. After that it was across the road to recover at an all-night coffee stall on what was then a bombed site. Gaston Berlemont, the guvnor of the French pub, said that the fire which destroyed the wine merchant there had improved some wine found still intact in the cellar by years.

I worked as a navvy building the block which replaced it and customers from the French would sometimes pass a glass of Pernod to me over the wall to the intense annoyance of the site foreman. But I could still keep in touch with all these people even when doing nasty jobs. I worked for a while as a dishwasher in the famous Mandrake Club in Meard Street.

The Mandrake started out as a chess club with coffee only in a one-roomed cellar. Boris Watson, the enormous Russian with an uncertain temper who owned it, reputedly killed one of his customers in his previous club, the notorious Coffee Ann. Eventually he was granted a licence and expanded the club to a further six cellars so that it extended right under Dean Street. I would collect my wages there and move immediately into the bar to spend them in company with some legendary Fleet Street men like Cyril Connolly, Maurice Richardson and John Davenport.

A few yards away there was the famous Colony Room Club known to all as Muriel's. It is still there but Muriel who held court is dead and the place has gone to seed. It was oddly enough a rather smart club then and expensive for its time. Muriel only really liked famous and rich people in there and I think she allowed me in there because I could make her laugh. And what an odd assorted bunch that used it. It was largely a homosexuals' watering hole and I have drunk with Noël Coward, E.M. Forster and Tom Driberg in there. More recently the Kray twins used it. Strangely enough they were social climbers and they tried to climb by giving money to charities. I didn't realise who they were when I first met them and was rather rude to Ronnie. I sometimes wonder how I am still alive.

But Soho was never as full of villains as the Sunday papers made out. The famous knife fight between Jack Spot and Italian Albert Dimes was strictly personal, as was the shooting dead of Tony Muller by a friend. What I mean is that they represented no threat to the likes of you and me or a passing tourist.

Being flat broke in those days, the one thing I didn't get many helpings of was the great food that abounded in Soho. The generosity of friends gave me glimpses of it though. The best restaurant I could eat frequently in was the upstairs restaurant at the French pub. Never mind the atmosphere downstairs, upstairs you could believe you were in Paris. It was all of £1 5s for an excellent three-course meal and a bottle of good wine. They had a nutty waiter there too who thought he was a good spoof player and would like to play you double or quits for the bill. I am glad I was streetwise by then.

What is awful is that more than half the people I have mentioned here are now dead. I fear Soho will follow shortly. Now I sit and tipple in the Coach and Horses, or the Groucho Club, and think that most clichés have an element of truth about them. They were indeed the 'good old days'.

PART 2

Low Life
6 January 1990 –
31 December 1994

Culture shock

A friend of mine who is well acquainted with Scotland tells me that the reaction of the inhabitants to having Glasgow made the Cultural Capital of Europe this year is a very healthy one. They are quite simply terrified that it will put 20p on the price of a pint of bitter. The attic that I write from is steeped in culture. The walls are alive with the sound of music. Mostly Mozart. I have a few very heavy books and my telephone only answers to intellectual friends and so I know how these people feel. I sit here sweating or lie here trembling at the thought of International Distillers & Vintners Ltd putting 20p on the price of a bottle of Smirnoff because they may hear *Cosi fan tutte* leaking out of the window. I may even become a tourist attraction. What a way to end.

The marmalade on my typewriter tells me that this isn't exactly a stately home but it does have its little pretensions and I don't much like them when I see them in the sober light of about three a.m. We know that Hermann Göring was a vile pig but I know what he meant when he said, 'Every time I hear the word culture I reach for my gun.' Governments, as time goes by, seem to be ramming culture down everyone's throats just as the likes of Jane Fonda would force-feed us with bran if they had their way. I cannot for the life of me see why a perfectly ordinary Glaswegian psychopath should have to subsidise a string quartet or a watercolour. Living as I do nearly next door to the Royal Opera House I see the people who queue up for subsidised opera when I go out to Bertorelli's for tepid pasta – the price of being too lazy or feeble to cook is colossal after a while – and I wouldn't give any of them a penny. Give me a Glaswegian wino who thinks that Beethoven was a sprinter once owned by Phil Bull. (He was so fast he couldn't even stay the minimum distance of five furlongs.) No, I don't like people who wear their culture on their sleeves. It should be a little more private, I think, like a lot of self-indulgences. I suppose Glasgow owes it to its excellent architecture that it was picked as being the Cultural Capital of Europe this year. But the Scots are resilient, as we saw at Waterloo and the Somme, and I am sure they will get over it.

Meanwhile, if television is a culture of a sort, I have had a dose of it. NBC filmed an interview with Peter O'Toole – excellent I am told – and then they did likewise with me in the pub last Monday. On Tuesday they came to the attic to film me typing a sentence, whence we went to Romilly Street to film me walking into the Coach and Horses. It is doubtful that it will be the most exciting footage filmed in 1990 but I think it should be shown in Glasgow and not just New York. I would like to see Peter on the video but I certainly do not wish to see the rest of it.

I have slightly gone off Americans anyway since they went anti-smoking and drinking and got on to health. That is their culture now. They won't make many inroads into Glasgow with that one. I have smoked twenty cigarettes since five a.m. this morning and I am on my second sip. I feel as fit as a fiddle. Nathan Milstein's one which wakes up my landlord in the middle of the night. Yes, there is a lot of culture here in Covent Garden and anyone wishing to sit in my armchair and listen to a bit of chamber music and have a gargle can send me £15, the price of a stalls seat at the Apollo Theatre. I am open from closing time until opening time. Why bother to go all the way to Glasgow?

Past caring

As is my occasional habit I went down to the stalls bar for a drink last week to see what was buzzing and who should be there but she who would once drown in my eyes. She hasn't changed. She still looks like a walking jumble sale. Now she is busy treading water in someone else's eyes. But it all came back to me. The time we stayed with Alice Thomas Ellis in Wales when she said to me, 'Run me through the meadows to the river's edge and sweep me into your arms,' and the time I threw her a shirt to iron and she got on her little but high horse, pulled a daft face of outrage and said, 'I am Carmen, not Mary Poppins.' What laughs we had. I did anyway. I quite miss those notes she used to leave me on the mantelshelf which always used to read, 'Why do you treat me like a shit?' Of course I didn't. I treated her like Mary Poppins and nearly went bankrupt taking her to a Greek restaurant in Cleveland Street every night.

Oh well, that's all tears under the bridge. It was also interesting to meet Jack Lemmon in the bar during the interval. He is as delightful as you may imagine. And I met my old friend Joan who was the boss barmaid at the races in the old days and what a good lady she is. (She could reveal some startling things about stuck-up owners and trainers.) But the strange spin-off of the play is the amount of rather odd people I have met when I have lurched down the stairs into the stalls bar. It is my bad luck not to look like Peter O'Toole but nevertheless people seem to recognise me and I have met many pleasant oddballs.

These are quite jolly times. How long will they last? Don't ask. The other side of the coin – and there always is one – is that I have to leave my Covent Garden attic because the lease is up and I am at my wits' end to know where to go. My wits' end is not a long way to go, but it is all very alarming. I still remember the horror of living all over the place and out of carrier bags in 1987.

I keep wondering whether or not to live abroad. Ireland or Barbados, where they speak English. But I would miss my mates and the more I think about it I would probably miss even the *bores* I know in the Coach and Horses. Perhaps bores can become soothing when you know them. A sort of balm. There is a man in the Coach who blots out all thoughts of the Inland Revenue and that is more than vodka can do. And just ten minutes ago I received a letter telling me of a studio flat in Soho which is going. I telephoned and apparently it went yesterday. Is God a joker? Never mind. I thank him for my resilience. Together with that letter I got a bill for £15,850. I feel almost past caring. Perhaps it is the hangover from dinner last night with Charles St George. (Also present was she who would once iron fourteen shirts at a standing, which is always a bonus.)

But, as I say, I am almost past caring. You can expect to be bowled a bumper per over so I suppose one must expect to be kicked in the balls once every six days. In a strange sort of way I think I may even be winning and the next bouncer God delivers me will be hooked to square leg for six. And yesterday, out of the blue, I got a letter from a man I was banged up with in 1972 in the drying-out bin. He sounded so well, which was marvellous. It makes me want to invite him out for a drink. But that would be wicked, wouldn't it? After all these years. He obviously hasn't been bowled his fair share of bouncers by his nibs up there.

Still functioning

I wanted very much to accompany Anna Haycraft to Rosamond Lehmann's funeral but I was trapped in a sick-bed. What a delightful woman Rosamond was. Some old ladies can be quite daunting if not scary but she was utterly charming, entertaining and funny. I went to see her sometimes in her house in the afternoons to have tea with her and I felt it was a privilege to be invited. It was a surprise if not something of a mystery to me that she actually read this column. At least she won't have been in the slightest bit frightened of dying. I don't think death existed for her.

It was a sad end, though, to a bizarre week. I get some strange letters from time to time and I received a couple of real weirdos. Saab motor cars wrote to me to inform me that they have a new model that has 150 bhp and can do 127 mph and would I care to test-drive it. They have to be mad. In my present condition I couldn't test-drive a lawnmower. I wondered if they would have liked me to take this car through its paces after the cocktail hour and I can only assume that they are prepared to write off one of these £15,000 cars. I wonder why.

The second crazy letter I received was from a medical clinic the name of which I have forgotten. It was an unsolicited missive and a damned impertinent one. They offered to cure me of impotence and premature ejaculation. Where on earth did they pick my name from? I have never complained of either malfunction and if I did suffer from premature ejaculation how could I possibly be impotent? I have made facetious remarks in the past about giving up the chase and the struggle but there is a world of difference between indifference and impotence. Furthermore it is 100/1 that a man of fifty-seven could suffer from premature ejaculation. They must have drawn my name out of a hat. Other than that someone is stirring it. It matters not but I would quite like to see what sort of letters they address to women.

Last Sunday morning I managed to move at last to a new flat and what a gargantuan struggle that was. Of course I couldn't move a muscle never mind help carry anything, so I sat and watched the noble removal men. What a marvellous team they were, not professionals but the gang from the Coach and Horses. Heroes. They were dripping sweat at both ends of the move and they had all of them volunteered to do the job. That's friends.

The flat is a nice self-contained place just suitable for me and it has a lift which compensates for my having hardly any legs left. It even has a small balcony which I shall sit on during the summer months. I am not quite sure about the location, though. Maida Vale isn't exactly exciting and it is some way from the West End. But it is a vast improvement on my last place and even has a washing machine. My niece who lives around the corner has put me in touch with a cleaning woman, who is going to come in twice a week owing to my being more or less disabled, but she tells me that the woman is on antidepressants. I am not quite sure how I will greet the sight of a depressive armed with a Hoover. With luck she may have her manic moments.

What I do look forward to now is being able to take up cooking again. Sharing a kitchen just didn't work and this place will work.

A slap in the belly

Richards, the fresh and wet fishmonger in Brewer Street, was forced to close down last week and it is a minor tragedy. A preservation order should be slapped on all of old Soho before it becomes a vast strip club. And something should be done to curb the greed of Soho landlords. God knows what, though. The boss told me that he had looked at alternative premises further along the street, but they were asking for a rent of £45,000 a year.

Of course, the public is mad too to support these clip joints. How anyone can prefer to stare at two tits rather than feast their eyes and then their stomachs on that display of the fruits of the ocean is beyond me. Anyway, once you have seen two or three tits you have seen them all. I walked past the shop the day after they closed it and the staff were standing outside on the pavement looking extremely gloomy as a team of builders filleted the place. And why do the people who own these buildings sell out to property spivs? The man who owns that good bar P.J. Clarke's in New York has reputedly turned down millions of dollars for that prime site.

But Soho is falling apart and so are a few of its denizens. The old faces are being replaced by some pretty awful new ones. Above Richards there used to be the first tailor I ever went to, Manny Goldshaker, who confessed to me that he was a secret ham and bacon eater. Opposite there was a very nice prostitute who would lean out of her window when she wasn't working and her blonde hair cascaded over the windowsill. She was murdered and they never caught the man. He probably frequents the awful peep show that is now beneath her old flat. It is all very depressing.

On top of that, my niece has just telephoned to tell me that her sister has just been taken to hospital where they have diagnosed diabetes. It is rotten for her particularly since she is a young dancer and not an old layabout. At least she is sensible and organised and will not forget to take her insulin, and a glance at the wreckage I live in will keep her on the straight and narrow. What a nasty, bloody little organ the pancreas is. You would think that giving yourself a couple of jabs a day would soon become a habit.

Diabetes is incurable but they have just found a way in which to electrocute sperm. It rather reminds me of my own research work in the chemistry lab when I was twelve years old. I discovered that you could kill goldfish by dropping some potassium permanganate in their bowls. It looked like pink gin with the bitters left in. But I wonder if diabetes runs in our family. Neither of my parents had it but they died young. I gather that longevity is hereditary and I wonder if the opposite is true. I shall be fifty-eight next week and my father was fifty-eight when he died. Like most gamblers I am horribly superstitious.

I ponder these things staring out of the window and looking down at Maida Vale. I should have been looking out of the window next week and seeing New Zealand, but that trip I was so looking forward to has been cancelled. The book I was to have helped launch has run into legal difficulties. And they were going to fly me on to Sydney. So that is more fish I won't see. Richards in Brewer Street has gone but if the Aussies ever close down Doyle's in Sydney it will be a calamity.

Pretty wobbly

I haven't washed my face since I went into make-up yesterday to go on Derek Jameson's chat show on Sky television. It is a tremendous improvement and I must learn how to do it for myself. I no longer look quite like a crumpled, leftover meringue. It was a pity, though, that they couldn't do anything about the legs. Negotiating the stairs to get on and off the stage was an embarrassment. With a drink in one hand, a cigarette in the other, sans bannister it was a shaky progress. How much more civilised they all were than the teetotal, anti-smoking BBC and ITV people. A vodka and soda looks like a glass of water and I doubt that my smoking a fag is going to make the kiddiewinkies rush out to buy a packet at ten pm.

I haven't liked Derek Jameson very much ever since he sacked me from the *Daily Express* when he took over about fourteen years ago. It was a serious financial wound. But yesterday he was aces and he is the only television interviewer I have come across who lets you get a few words in edgewise. The rest of them are doing you a favour. Well, it's *their* show, isn't it?

After the show I went to the Royal Academy to see an exhibition to commemorate the work of Elinor Bellingham-Smith. What a good woman she was in every sort of way. Elinor put me up in her house in Chelsea years ago when I was homeless and more recently we were neighbours in Suffolk. It was routine to call in on her when in the village of Bildeston. She would be sitting at the kitchen table, elegant in her cashmere, with a drink in one hand, and we would tipple and giggle like children sometimes at the absurdity of life. She once gave me a copy of the collected poems of W.B. Yeats and a copy of *The Unquiet Grave*. A nice mixture. Dear Elinor.

But all that was yesteryear and yesterday. Now I have been up since dawn clearing up my flat in readiness for the cleaning woman who comes at ten a.m. Why have I got a cleaning woman when the very thought of her compels me to wash up and wipe the surfaces? You might as well extract your own teeth for fear of troubling the dentist. I should go the whole hog, do the hoovering and then we could just sit down and drink cups of tea for the two hours she is here. Turn her into a paid companion. That would be better because she certainly isn't cut out to be what I remember charladies as long ago when I was a boy. This one isn't ugly or old enough and she hasn't got a smoker's cough, neither does she shuffle about and moan. Nor does she stop work for tea, although I did once inflict a vodka on her. (The sun in Maida Vale is over the yardarm before you can say Jack Robinson. It is the northerly latitude.)

I suppose I should go and wash the make-up off now before she arrives and go back to looking as transparent as an amoeba again. Come to think of it there is an amoeba who comes into the Coach and Horses and I suppose you could call his best friend a molecule. The pipsqueak doesn't come in any more and drinks in Lamb's Conduit Street now. Norman, the atom of hot air, is on holiday and the place is almost empty. I like it that way as long as they keep cashing the cheques.

Dear God, the cleaning woman has just this minute phoned to say she can't make it today. Why oh why did I wash up and hide my dirty socks? She says she is coming in two days' time and I intend to make the place filthy by then. I want my money's worth.

Gathering gloom

I am writing to you on the morning of Derby Day and a pretty damp and miserable morning it is. I switched this wretched typewriter on at six a.m. and we have been trying to outstare each other for two hours now. The jasmine finally died in the night and I see that my palm trees may be on the way out. A few leaves are turning brown and I don't quite know if I am giving them too much or too little water. I am not even sure that I can last the day. I have had to pour myself a drink to stop my smoker's cough and it is far too early for that. I have had a patch in my throat for the past five years and only a drink will stop the awful dry tickle. I asked a doctor why that should be and he said it was because a drink or two anaesthetises the spot. That's not all it anaesthetises, I can tell you.

Then I have just had a note slipped under the door from the man who lives above me. He requests me not to play Mozart's Requiem at three a.m. I never thought he could hear it, but that's that. A pity because it is a good piece in the middle of a sleepless, pitch-black night. I shall have to hum to myself under the duvet from now on.

Gloom is gathering like distant storm clouds. The cleaning woman came in yesterday after two weeks' absence suffering from depression and I think I may have caught it from her when she was last here. For those two weeks I have been staring at a piece of toast on the carpet utterly unable to pick it up. That sort of inertia and inability to make any effort whatsoever gets worse as time goes by. I am pretty sure it has its roots in chemistry because life, in fact, isn't at all bad and I have had good news of *Jeffrey Bernard is Unwell* and its future. Superstition forbids me to say what that is.

The Derby runners will have been up and out now, cantering a few furlongs since daybreak. It is a good sight and the crack of dawn is the time to be at Epsom on Derby Day. Sitting here in Maida Vale, cocooned in concrete, I see it as though I am there. It is a marvellous sight to see a horse turn on to the course and then stretch out on the bit. In the middle of the course those wretched food stalls will be all of a fizzle with horrible hot dogs and hamburgers. What I do like out there are the fortune-tellers in their tatty tents. What a shame they can't read a horse's hoof. 'You will soon win a big race and afterwards cover forty-five mares a year.'

But now I must shake off the inertia and sloth. Two chums are coming for lunch and to watch the race. I must go shopping and that's an awful effort. But it will be amusing to hear them talk complete bollocks all afternoon. One of them has had the longest losing run I have ever known and it must come to an end.

I shall have one more drink, go to Marks and Sparks and probably switch my allegiance to Robert Sangster's Blue Stag, or I might not bet at all and just listen to my mates waffling and swearing at each other in obscene banter. But to hell with Epsom. I shall pick out a winner at Beverley which will pass almost unnoticed. And I hope the rest of the week does just that too.

A woman's touch

I only found out the other day that the tax inspector who is hounding me nigh unto death is a woman. When my accountant informed me of the fact I gave what I can only describe as a cynical shrug of my drooping shoulders. There has been some sort of acid in my mouth ever since. I thought I had got rid of women once and for all. It is quite extraordinary that when things have been going well and smoothly a woman will appear and bring me to a halt with a short, sharp jolt.

I remember some years ago winning £100 on a horse at Newbury, a bundle at the time, and standing in the bar toasting my good fortune when my then wife walked in and said, 'You'll be able to buy that Hoover now.' That anybody can seriously believe that money is for Hoovers or for a rainy day is beyond my comprehension. Every day is a rainy day. No, income tax inspector is a very suitable job for a woman and it is surprising that no Chancellor of the Exchequer has ever been a woman. In that event a large vodka would cost £100.

But there are other aspects of money which are troubling me at the moment. A month ago, I had to write to an old friend to ask him for £1,000 he has owed me for a while. I have erected a wall of silence. He can keep it, but I do not like having the piss taken out of me in that sort of way. Three years ago I *gave* an old friend £500 and he hasn't spoken to me since and, in fact, he doesn't even come into the Coach and Horses any more. Just think of how many people you could get rid of with £1 million. Why can't this woman income tax inspector go away and leave me alone? What she wants is ridiculous, and *Jeffrey Bernard is Unwell* is not *The Mousetrap*. Incidentally, Norman says that *The Mousetrap* is a better play than *King Lear*. I asked him how come and he said, 'It's had a longer run.' There is no answer to that.

Last week he was sitting this side of the bar looking particularly gloomy and I overpaid him with a penny for his thoughts. He said, 'I just wish I could see England beat the West Indies 5-0 in a Test series before I die.' He then asked me what I would like to see before I die and I told him a barman in his employ who knew what he was doing and who could speak English. In recent weeks he has taken to employing Serbo-Croats who have been bitten by long-range tsetse flies. It is the only pub I know of in which prudent customers carry a hip flask. But I suppose it is somewhere for an aimless man to go. I sometimes wonder what Charles Dickens would make of the place were he alive today. It is almost certain that he drank in the Coach. He did a lot of pub-crawling between the Lamb and Flag in Covent Garden and Soho. Fagin was probably based on a publican and if he was he has been reincarnated.

So, what with Norman, the woman income tax inspector, my missing £1,000, the weather, the play coming off before *The Mousetrap* does and my landlady kicking me out to sell the flat, I reach for a drink and strangely find myself not giving a damn about any of it. In fact I am very nearly singing in the

rain. Humming anyway. And there will be no insomnia thanks
to the World Cup on television.

My only interest left in that event, and I am not vindictive
by nature, just malignant, is to see whether Maradona breaks a
leg on Sunday. The McEnroe of football and by now probably
as mad as Mike Tyson. Dear God, what fame does to some
people. Like money it is dished out to the wrong people a lot
of the time. I read somewhere that Maradona paid £25,000
for his earring. At that I reached for yet another drink. One is
truly driven to the stuff.

A bleeding shame

I was irritated last week to read here that 'Jeffrey Bernard
is unwell'. I had, in fact, had an accident which is quite a
different thing. Unwell implies drunk and would to God I had
been drunk. In that event I would not have been in agony. I
got hit by a Royal Mail van in Brewer Street which then went
on its merry way without stopping. My head hit the pavement
with an almighty crack and was cut in four places and, worse
than that, my right-hand rib cage was smashed and I had six
broken ribs. That caused an internal haemorrhage.

Luckily, I am not short of blood but the pain is still making
me feel sick. The Westminster Hospital kept me in for a week
to make sure I didn't get pneumonia and at least they were
not as mean as some hospitals when it came to dishing out
painkillers. Six injections into the back with an extremely long
needle are not nice if you are squeamish. I am not, thank
heavens. I stood next to the charming consultant as he put
the X-ray of my chest on to the light box and he said, 'God
almighty. Thank God it's your chest and not mine.' I liked
that. No bullshit.

So here I am at liberty again and writing to you from the Groucho Club where they are temporarily very kindly taking care of me. And yesterday, three hours after leaving the hospital, a motorbike missed me by about six inches as I was crossing Old Compton Street. Somebody up there must hate me.

But what a strange time I had of it in the Westminster. We were not allowed to smoke, of course, and those of us who wished to had to do so sitting about on the landing by the lifts and outside the wards. I was one of the very few men on that floor who did so and I spent the week surrounded by the zaniest bunch of chain-smoking women I have come across, all patients from the gynaecological ward. They talked about nothing but their operations and complaints and they seemed to really enjoy doing so. I was a little surprised that they talked to me so openly, but it would have been one hell of a job to stop them. I could now draw you a detailed and accurate map of Mrs Griffin's fallopian tubes. I also know Mrs Carter's womb inside out and I wish I knew it better inside than out. One morning, a lady called Betty nudged me in the ribs – the left-hand side thank God – and confided, 'D'you know, Jeffrey, I've been bleeding since 10th March.' There was nothing to say to that. I finished my cigarette feeling suddenly saddened by the thought of how many wombs have been incinerated and washed out to sea in my own lifetime. We blokes have very few problems in that area, although I was alarmed a little to see, while watching the Test Match on the television the other day, a sentence flash up on the screen when Sharma was out stating quite simply, 'Sharma, two balls, one minute.' Quite.

Well, I suppose there aren't many hospitals left in London that I haven't been to now. The Westminster I rate quite highly and give it three crossed scalpels. I was lucky to be pestered a little by the press on my first day there because it prompted them to give me a private room. So at least, awake for most of the night, I didn't have to listen to the coughing, farting and moaning of the dying. A kind woman from the *Daily Express* brought me in a cassette player with a Mozart tape and that mixed with my vodka sips saved me. But the real angel of mercy was our own Jennifer Paterson who brought me a box of ice every morning. In a nasty hot week it nearly made me feel quite well.

Shock treatment

There were two nasty shocks waiting for me when I came home from hospital. No, not buff envelopes. I discovered that the woman who lives above me on the first floor is addicted to pop music which she plays fairly loudly on her radio, and that the woman who lives beneath me in the basement has a Rottweiler. Added to that there is another woman who lives opposite who also plays pop music very loudly all weekend with her windows wide open and I can't tell her off because she is black. I resent that. Not being able to tell her off, I mean.

On Sunday I played Beethoven's Choral Symphony twice, not to counter-attack the woman upstairs, but to block her out. There are some loud passages in that work but I also resented playing it since I didn't particularly want to hear it. Not twice anyway. The Rottweiler bothers me less, although I would dearly like to feed him a hand grenade. At least he has his separate entrance but if I sit by my bedroom window and gaze into his garden he looks at me as though he has just heard the word 'bone'.

It has been an appalling week one way and another. The broken ribs are so painful that I have been eating painkillers as if they were jelly babies and I am incapacitated. It even hurts to peel a potato and mashing the wretched things is nigh impossible. It would have been worse a few years ago. As it is my accountant has just held back enough of my money from the Inland Revenue to allow me to take a holiday. What a thing it is when you have to more or less beg for your own money.

So I am going off for a week or two. Where to? I am not sure. Kuwait springs to mind. It is warmer than Belfast. An American couple who read the *Spectator* have kindly offered me the loan of their house on the Florida Keys, but I have lost their address. This is either premature Alzheimer's syndrome or the skull has hit the pavement once too often. But wedged here in West Hampstead 'twixt pop and dog even a week in the ghastly Canary Islands might seem pleasant.

On my short list at the moment are Corsica, Crete and Istanbul. My brother Oliver, who lived and worked in Corsica once for quite a time, and Graham Lord who has recently holidayed in Corsica have told me that my spindly legs would not stand up to the hills and steeps of the island. That worries me less than the constant reminders one would see of that monumental shit Napoleon. What Dan Farson has written and told me about the low life of Istanbul appeals tremendously. I am told that Crete, away from tourist haunts, is beautiful, but how do you get around? It irritates me tremendously that newspaper and magazine travel editors and writers always assume that you have a car and drive it. The *Sunday Times* travel section is the most guilty of those parties. I realise that under Mrs Thatcher it is a crime to be broke, but do we all have to have cars as well?

Happy days

When and where were you happiest? That is being asked of me in a questionnaire I am to fill in and I am damned if I know the answer to it. In fact I have been wondering about it for five days now. Last Sunday I mentioned my quandary to our own Christopher Howse and he said, 'Well, have you *ever* been happy?' That set my brain seething even more.

There have been brief moments of joy and respites from anxiety but, as I say, I am damned if I can think of any that stand out beyond the trivial. Certainly not before the ancient age of sixteen. It was then, coming home from school for the summer holidays, that my mother asked me, 'Did you have a good term?' It triggered something off because I burst into tears. She then said, 'It's all right, I'll never send you back to school again.' I can hear her say it now and to come up from the depths to hear those words gave me the emotional bends. But for pure joy, and that is how my dictionary defines happiness, it doesn't, in retrospect, beat a catch I held running in twenty yards from deep mid-off to extra cover. And that was only fifteen years ago.

When I first looked at the question I thought that the answer must lie somewhere amidst the girls and women I have been involved with, but it doesn't. That is probably, more like certainly, because it always ended in tears. Mine. Getting out of the army with a pay-book stamped 'Mental stability nil' was a day of great happiness. What a relief, equalled only by discovering a bar with a lavatory in the Valley of the Kings one furnace-like day four years ago. A cheque in the post can nudge one towards happiness, but it is really only temporary relief like backing a winner.

I remember sitting in a hotel in Brighton, drinking coffee with Peter O'Toole on the morning after the first night of *Jeffrey Bernard is Unwell* and him reading out the notices. That was excellent, as was the first night at the Apollo Theatre. And, speaking of the theatre, there was a night Marlene Dietrich came to see it. I met her later that night in the

Pickwick Club where she came over to my perch at the bar, bought me a drink and said, 'I just want to say that I think you are wonderful.' She even bought me another drink and the tycoons at her table looked very annoyed. I couldn't sleep that night and lay wide awake in bed thinking, 'Christ almighty, Marlene Dietrich thinks I'm wonderful.' I realise people say such things to each other all the time but at *that* time it gave me one hell of a buzz. Heady stuff.

It is odd that my daughter does not feature much in my list of happy memories, but that is because of the guilt I still feel about trying to drown myself in whisky when she was a baby. No number of the endearing reassurances she gives me nowadays can obliterate all that.

Now here's a thought. Why didn't they ask when and where were your unhappiest moments? Well, they stick out like so many sore thumbs. They could take their pick from deaths and divorces to Gower being out for a duck or hearing Norman shouting, 'Last orders, please.' Actually, he doesn't say it quite as politely as that.

Greene and pleasant land

This year's break was definitely beta minus and I have just come home after only five days on the Côte d'Azur. I was shoved from hotel to hotel. Every one that I booked into told me that I could only have a room for one night because they were booked up, usually by groups of Germans. And what awful-looking groups. I should have thought that they would want to get away from each other, but it must be ingrained in them to want to stamp *en masse* all over Europe.

To choose Nice as a base was not very clever of me either. The streets were jammed with window-shoppers wearing silly tee-shirts and a vodka was £4. I should have saved my money for the forthcoming sunset in a nursing home.

The best thing that happened was meeting Graham Greene again. I had lost his telephone number but I went to Antibes one morning on the off-chance of seeing him and, lo and behold, there he was sitting in his favourite restaurant and he made me welcome. It is not only a pleasure to know the man but also a privilege. He said some very amusing things about some well-known people and it is bad luck on you that I won't repeat them. I do not think it would be right but there must have been some burning ears in Grub Street. He may be moving to Switzerland in which case I shall have to overcome my prejudice about that country to go on the piste with him.

The next day I travelled along the coast in the opposite direction and visited Roquebrune at Cap St Martin before going to Menton for lunch. Dear God, there is something awful about resorts. But the lunch was memorable and the helpings very generous: six grilled sardines followed by six lamb cutlets. A sniff of the claret told me that it was so good that I didn't give it the chance to breathe. Incidentally, I don't see why the wine is as expensive as it is in the country that makes the stuff. Perhaps they can see you coming.

That evening an odd thing happened. I went to a bar that had quickly become my favourite in Nice and to my utter amazement a middle-aged homosexual actually made a pass at me. You don't need to be fluent in French to know when somebody is making a pass. Being as vain as the next man I felt rather flattered and then it slowly dawned on me that the man must have been a necrophiliac. I took a close look at myself in the mirror and to be sure all that is left of me is my hair. But he bought me a drink and he may be the first and only Frenchman to have done that.

When he realised that I was not gay – I was paying a lot of attention to two stunning-looking women at the next table – he tried to fix me up with one of them. They were prostitutes. I hadn't realised, since you don't see them any more in London, and I am not used to them ever since Lord Wolfenden banished them from the public view. But what is very odd is that in spite of all the nuts, rogues and villains I have met over the years never have I come across a homosexual pimp before. When I turned him down and then the two lovely whores he shrugged as if to say I was the last straw, mad and English as well. I am a bad ambassador perhaps and no wonder the French think we are lousy lovers, staid and unromantic. Perhaps all three of them took some consolation from the fact that I look as though I am HIV positive.

On reflection I rather wish I had gone with one of the two women. I haven't done that since 1949 in Paris when I was seventeen and John Minton paid for my visits to see Mimi in her room two floors above a café called Ambience. I must have been very fit then because I remember being up and down her stairs like a rat up a drain. But I am no longer a rat and in any race I now compete in I usually end up as an 'also ran'.

Thin walls

Every morning I lie in bed and wait for it. At 6.55 a.m. precisely, the person who lives above me gets out of bed, walks to the bathroom and then urinates. That is how thin the walls and floors of this house are. Now, I am not in the slightest bit squeamish, particularly about bodily functions and I could nurse the sick, but what I don't like is the feeling that I am unwittingly invading another person's privacy. Also I am irritated that listening to somebody urinating above me every day for the past three months has put me in mind of that old song, 'Pennies from Heaven' and I hate to have a tune, any tune, on my brain.

This person then goes to the kitchen and puts the kettle on for tea. It would be an exaggeration to say that I could hear how many teaspoons of tea are put in the pot but, having read Sherlock Holmes for my PhD thesis, I can assure you that there is not much that goes on upstairs which can be kept secret from me. I have tried blotting out the piddling noise by turning up the shipping forecast to full blast on Radio 4 but I do not think the onus should be on me. What did occur to me this morning was that I should push a note under the door suggesting that this person buy a cat litter tray or a quantity of blotting paper. But then, in the event of a cat litter tray, I suppose I would be subjected to the noise of scratching. But sounds and noises penetrate in a downward direction and less of an upward one, so I wonder what the woman who lives in the basement can deduce from the noises I make. Not a lot.

The all too occasional noise of this typewriter at work? But pouring a drink is as silent as pouring oil, I suppose the noise of the electric juice squeezer indicates how many drinks I have had, since it is one orange per vodka, but it is doubtful that she can hear my brain seething. For me, it is a deafening noise. Anyway, considering I am so aware of these trivial things – the upstairs peeing person was half an hour late for work this morning – you can see that my life is rather thin, not to say almost empty. All the more reason to wonder that the nice Austrian woman, Renate, should have picked on me as the subject of her PhD thesis. At least she has got something out of it already in the way of a jolly little trip I believe she enjoyed.

The *Mail on Sunday* flew her over from Vienna the other day so that they could interview and photograph the two of us together in the Coach and Horses. (What an awful picture of me: Dorian Gray in reverse.) But, if she can get a PhD writing about a man who listens either to 'Pennies from Heaven' or 'Raindrops are Falling' every morning and then pours oil on his troubled waters before phoning for a minicab to the West End for a few drinks and to shamble aimlessly about until the evening, then good luck to her.

If she gets this PhD I shall fly to Vienna and we shall have a splendid lunch party. I have never been to Austria and the only thing I dread is a surfeit of Strauss waltzes. I am sure they seep from every wall. Better, maybe, to listen to the urinating at the crack of dawn in horrible Hampstead. Incidentally, I have been wondering why Anthony Burgess will insist on using the word 'micturate'. I conclude that he is an English language swank. Whether it is correct or not is neither here nor there. What's wrong with piss?

Meanwhile, I await with no little anticipation the noise of the first fart of winter from upstairs. When I do hear it, I shall write a letter to *The Times* on the lines of 'on hearing the first cuckoo of spring'.

Eggs over easy

Last Monday I went to the *Sunday Express* Book of the Year Award at the Café Royal and sat at Frank Muir's table. What a charming man he is. But I couldn't help wondering, every time I looked at him, what on earth must it be like to be Geoffrey Wheatcroft's father-in-law. It makes me wonder which unlikely journalist will lay siege to my daughter one day. My brother, Bruce, has suggested the wine correspondent of the *Cork Examiner* but it doesn't really matter as long as my son-in-law-to-be does not work for the *Sun*.

These lunches, like the *Evening Standard* Drama Awards one,
are strange dos. You see the same faces at most of them. I think
that maybe Ned Sherrin is sustained by 365 of them every year.
Laurie Lee was at the Café Royal again but he sat too far away
from me to keep an eye on him. Last year I sat next to him and
he shovelled four lamb cutlets into his jacket pocket without
even bothering to wrap them up in a napkin. I said to him, 'I
didn't know you had a dog.' He said, 'I haven't. They're for me.
I shall heat them up again tonight for my supper.' I should have
thought that the royalties from such works as *Cider With Rosie*
would bring in enough to pay for food instead of having to wash
old chops covered with fluff and bits of tobacco from a jacket
pocket. This year we had roast lamb served with a thick brown
gravy, so God alone knows the state of his pockets the next day.

The day after the *Sunday Express* lunch, a BBC television
crew came into the Coach and Horses. *Arena* are making a film
about that hero, Keith Waterhouse. They gave me a walk-on
part and I even managed to bungle that. Keith performed the
now famous egg trick from the play to perfection. When it
came to my turn I followed through too hard in the manner of
an off drive and knocked the pint of water over, although the
egg remained intact. That let the side down for, as Keith said,
'You should be able to do it if you are over fifty and pissed.'

Also this week a man came in from BBC Radio 4 to
interview me about my feelings about Boxing Day. I don't
have any. Boxing Day is quite simply 26 December to me. He
also asked me for hangover cures. I haven't had a hangover
since I gave up drinking whisky some twelve years ago. I had
to cast my mind back some way. The best barmen in London
always included crème de menthe to settle the stomach, I
know, but a simple hair of the dog will do. Hangovers are
caused by an absence of alcohol.

Unlike the *Arena* film team who were very hospitable, this bloke didn't offer to buy me a drink in forty-five minutes. Don't they teach young men anything when they join the BBC? I wonder what on earth the qualifications are to get a job at Broadcasting House. With arms as short as his and pockets as deep one thing is certain. He will definitely not have a hangover on Boxing Day.

Party pris

God preserve us from the Christmas office party. Almost any party. I liked them when I was younger and used to go along in the hope of leaving them at the end of the day with a one-night stand. Now, I am delighted if I can procure a taxi to take me home at the end of the thrash. Anyway, I only know of three men capable of giving a good party and they are Charles St George, Peter Walwyn and Robert Sangster. Why they should all be racing men I don't quite know, although a day at the races frequently develops into an alfresco party.

Oh for those bygone summer days. Now I am faced with newspaper and magazine parties which I detest. So why am I going to one tonight? It is probably an unconscious desire to keep 'in touch' with all those awful people who say, 'We must have lunch one day,' or, 'You must write something for us soon,' and who you never hear from again.

Nevertheless I have at last stopped knocking the business of Christmas. In fact, even living alone as I do, I am considering buying a small Christmas tree and putting it in front of my television set to block out the millionth screenings of *The Magnificent Seven* and *The Sound of Music* plus the awful Terry Wogan et al. My daughter is coming over for lunch and so is

an old friend who I kibitz with in the Coach and Horses. I sit
here wondering what my ex-wives will be doing. Never mind.
They have now fallen on better feet than mine.

One good thing about this year is that no one has asked me to
write a Christmas piece. It used to be obligatory in Fleet Street
for hacks to do so. On one newspaper I worked for some years
ago the editor would walk around the open-plan office like a
schoolmaster supervising prep asking all the writers, 'Have you
done your Christmas piece yet?' My annual contribution was
always the one about waking up on Christmas Day morning
flat broke in a Camden Town dosshouse with nowhere to go.
It makes me yawn now to think about it.

Another awful thing about these Christmas office parties
can be coming face to face with a hackette or secretary that
you featured with twenty years ago. Embarrassing for both
parties but less so for the one with the worse memory. There
are women who have etched in their eyes the unspoken
question, 'Why didn't you telephone?'

I suppose one thing that can be faintly amusing to observe
at these dos are the hacks who, because of the season and the
unfamiliar booze that goes with it, are compelled to tell their
bosses home truths. Mike Molloy got so fed up with getting
that when he became editor of the *Daily Mirror* that he had to
stop going into the pub and I am afraid I have to plead guilty
in his case. Thank God I don't do that any more. I don't have
to. Editors can tell perfectly well just what I think of them
when I give them a wintry smile.

And now, of graver consideration than an office party is the
second Test Match starting on Boxing Day in Australia. Alan
Lee has made a good point in *The Times*. England don't need to
work harder or make more effort, that would be like asking a sick
man to run round the block. All we need is to find some *quality*. I

shall be glued to Radio 3 listening to the commentary, cracking walnuts, eating satsumas and leftover goose. But I draw the line at paper hats. And a happy Christmas to both my readers.

My night at the opera

It was with a mixture of amusement and irritation that I received the news that Taki had written in the *Sunday Express* that I was decadent and that Geoffrey Wheatcroft had written in the *Daily Telegraph* that he found it odd that I should have included 'listening to Mozart' among my hobbies listed in *Who's Who*. Odd, he said, because he had never seen me in the Royal Opera House.

I know full well that it is sometimes extremely hard for a journalist to find anything to write about, but for a man who has served a prison sentence for smuggling cocaine to call me decadent – morally corrupt – indicates a hack of little information, mean understanding and uncertain temper. As for Geoffrey Wheatcroft never having seen me in the Royal Opera House, I am not in the least surprised. You have to keep your eyes open to see somebody, especially if they are as diminutive as I am, and that can be difficult after a hard afternoon in the Garrick Club.

But just for the record I must tell you that I have always had connections, however tenuous, with the Royal Opera House. My father was resident scenic designer there in the days of Caruso. They often lunched together and, although I was not alive to have witnessed those meals, I had the word of my mother – an opera singer – on it. Later, when I was a decadent baby, Sir Thomas Beecham used to spend the odd weekend with us. I never spoke to him myself because I always had either a thumb or a bottle in my mouth. Years later, when

Wheatcroft was still at school and planning his meteoric rise
to fame, I worked for a while as a stage hand at the Opera
House, so I know the place well. It is next to the Nag's Head
and opposite Bow Street Magistrates' Court. Mozart himself
couldn't have arranged it better.

But you don't, of course, have to go the Royal Opera
House to listen to Mozart. As every opera critic should know,
they have things called compact discs these days. If Geoffrey
Wheatcroft had been in West Hampstead last Sunday with
his eyes open he could have seen me listening to a private
performance of *Cosi fan tutte* in my own sitting room. I have
a splendid auditorium here. A man may smoke without
making the singers cough and the bar never closes. It must
also be remembered by musicologists that Mozart wrote music
other than opera. You know, symphonies, concertos, chamber
music, all sorts of stuff like that.

Anyway, apart from Taki and Wheatcroft another sniper
emerged last week in the pages of the *Observer*. This particular
marksman or markswoman described me in a subtitle as
being a 'seasoned barfly'. I didn't care for that. If anything I
am a lounge lizard. We eat barflies for breakfast. In any case
the word barfly implies that a man is hanging about with the
intention of cadging and sponging drinks from other people.
There was a time – but I can buy my own now. Especially if
the accusing *Observer* paid me my bloody fee.

So who else wants to have a go? I also put in my list of
hobbies cricket and cooking. I haven't been to Lords for
seven years now, and then when I did, I left in disgust after I
dropped my thermos of vodka. And as for cooking, well, what
can I say? Last night I had a Marks and Spencer Cumberland
pie with some of their ratatouille. Call that cooking? Yes. The
timing is of the essence just as it is in cricket and Mozart.

Cocktails in Greeneland

Perhaps enough has already been written about Graham Greene, but he has been on my mind ever since the day that I heard he had died. I still can't quite believe that I knew him and had all those lunches with him in his favourite restaurant, the Félix au Port in Antibes, and sipped all those massive cocktails he poured in his flat there and in the Ritz when he stayed there.

I first met him at a *Spectator* lunch and I was not very impressed, although I was in awe of him. Led on by the other guests he spoke largely about spying, which is a subject not dear to my heart. Two years later I planned a trip to the South of France and somehow plucked up the courage to phone him and ask if I could pay him a visit. He was charming and he invited me to the Félix for lunch. When I arrived he was sitting at a table outside with his companion, Yvonne. She spoke English very well but her pronunciation resulted in her calling him Gram, and when she referred to him with strangers she called him Gram Grin. She drove him the odd half mile to the Félix every day for his lunch. That day I remember we both had steak with purée de pommes and vin rosé. I only mention that because as it turned out we discovered we were both mashed potato freaks. That broke the ice. He didn't want to talk about the likes of Henry James all day. At the end of that lunch I felt a little sad thinking that I might never see the great man again. In the afternoon I was amazed when he telephoned me at my hotel and invited me to his flat for drinks that evening. It was a pretty ordinary flat. What you might call superior council. He poured enormous measures of vodka for us both.

Then the subject of spying cropped up again, albeit briefly. Reminiscing about the people he had known over the years he chanced to say that Malcolm Muggeridge was the worst spy he had ever recruited. He said, 'Malcolm once claimed that through his own very efficient intelligence network he had effected the sinking of a German U-boat in the Mediterranean. Impossible. It must have been a very large fish. Probably a tuna.' For four days I metaphorically sat spellbound at his feet, sipping his bumper drinks while he dished out gossip about the literati of the past.

A year later he telephoned me out of the blue and told me he was staying in the Ritz and would I join him for a cocktail. More tumblers filled to the brim. He told me that I should have a go at writing short stories. Then he offered to write a blurb for the paperback edition of *Low Life*. I was a little taken aback. Flattered too. He was a regular *Spectator* reader though and he said that there was more than a streak of the low life in him.

I last saw him six months ago when I was in France again. I went to the Félix again on the off-chance of seeing him and there he was lunching as ever with Yvonne. He looked well enough, although frail and a little shaky. He said that his doctor had just restricted him to one drink at lunchtime. 'And here it is,' he said, raising the largest vodka I have ever seen. His eyes twinkled. Usually they were rather sad. I don't want to go to Antibes again and I shall miss a man I knew briefly but whom I regarded with admiration and great affection.

Across a crowded room

A man came into the pub the other day carrying one of those awful mobile telephones. I asked him if I could use it and he kindly obliged and asked me what number I wanted. I gave him the number of the pub. Norman was standing no more than six feet away from me and when he answered the call he barked, 'Coach and Horses. Hallo.' I said, 'Is there any chance of being served a bloody drink in this ghastly pub?' My language was a little stronger than that. He twigged immediately, spun round and said, 'You bastard.' Then he laughed and served me. He rarely does that but he was unnerved for a second or two there. So these telephones do have their uses. It could be interesting to phone a woman in a pub and watch her as you chatted to her.

I remember once being served by an Irishman at a Derby lunch in the Dorchester when I spotted Sally, the Begum Aga Khan, a couple of tables away. I asked the man to deliver her a note without a word in her ear. I had written on it, 'Although I am only a humble Irish waiter, I think I am in love with you.' She looked astounded when she read it. Her face was a picture and always was. But I gave it away by smiling when she looked up. Even so when the waiter served the pudding he handed me a note in the royal writing which said, 'I love you too.' Would that it had been true. Anyway, it was nice to catch Norman off his guard and that is about all I can remember in what has been a week of boredom transcending even the week I spent locked up in the guardhouse years ago in Catterick Camp.

They not only taught me how to drive up there, they taught me how to wash and polish coal and to paint the fireplace in the sergeant's mess white before lighting the fire with the gleaming coal. Surprisingly they let me out of my cell one night to listen to the commentary of the first Randolph Turpin *v.* Sugar Ray Robinson fight on their radio. What strange people they were. I seem to remember that the regiment, the 14/20 King's Hussars who have just performed in the Gulf, only had one trophy to speak of and that was a silver chamberpot that once belonged to Napoleon. I believe the officers drank champagne out of it on special occasions. It would have to be a very special occasion indeed for me to drink even a single vodka from the pot which once supported those historic piles.

But what a dreadful place Catterick was and probably still is. Freezing in the winter and shaving in almost total darkness with cold water. Cold fried eggs resembling jellyfish for breakfast. We had the dubious honour once of being inspected one day by the Duke of Gloucester, George VI's brother and a right old pisspot by all accounts. He had the trooper standing next to me put on a charge for not having polished the *back* of his cap badge. The said trooper might have got a little bit more sympathy if he had said that he couldn't have polished it because he had run out of Brasso due to having drunk it all. Never tried it myself.

What any of this sort of nonsense has to do with soldiering I shall never know. When a medical board asked me what I intended doing after my discharge and I said, 'Write,' they promptly stamped my pay-book with the legend, 'Mental Stability Nil'. Quite right.

Down the drain

Murphys have been digging up Dean Street in an attempt to recover a shovel an Irish navvy left there some weeks ago when they were working on the drains. That is what I have been told anyway. And another odd thing. A man who comes into the Coach and Horses told me yesterday that he was walking home last week at two a.m. when he saw an old woman feeding scraps and titbits to an enormous rat. He said, 'What on earth are you doing?' and she said, 'Feeding the cat. He always comes here at two in the morning.' He tried to shoo the horrid thing away but it had eaten so much it couldn't run. So he kicked it to death.

I could put you in touch with several people in Soho with equally bizarre tales to tell. But I did see an odd thing with my own eyes this week. Norman's dear old mum came into the pub one morning complaining that it was too hot. She was wearing a mink coat. A mink coat in June, I ask you. I admit it has been an awful June so far and my wretched landlord has still not had the gas boiler mended. I have to go to the Groucho Club to get a bath and I have been shaving in various club and pub gent's lavatories. Yesterday I was so cold and ill I had to come home and go back to bed in the late morning. I telephoned my daughter and she came over with some tinned soup which I felt too weak to open and heat up myself. She even very thoughtfully brought me some oranges to squeeze into any vodka I might have had, which I did. I am delighted that she has become so affectionate now that we see a lot of each other and she is a great comfort.

What hasn't given me much comfort was the phone call I received from a newspaper asking me to write a joke piece: my own obituary. I shall, of course, do it because I need the work, but I am very superstitious about it and prefer to tempt the fates on a racecourse. I wish I could use some of those obituary clichés such as, 'He never married', but I suppose I can say, 'He was a good companion', meaning he was pissed from breakfast to Christmas. But that wouldn't be true. That is just a rumour put about by Keith Waterhouse.

The good news is that the brewers have renewed Norman's lease and given him another five years. He touchingly said that my ramblings, as one critic put it, had helped. But in five years it will be against the law to smoke or drink and food shops will stock nothing but muesli. It will also be against the

law to die. I am not quite sure how they will punish people
for that but they will, they will. What this country needs is an
alcoholic Minister for Health. At least Norman gives the staff
of the Middlesex Hospital something to practise on. He is very
nearly a body-snatcher.

Which reminds me. He came out with a good one the
other day. Watching his staff from the customer's side of the
jump he turned to me and said, 'The service here is so slow
you'd think they were pouring glue.' Anyway, I am writing this
column on the morning of Derby Day and, although I don't
much mind not being able to go, I shall be extremely put out
if the television room in the Groucho has been taken over by
a load of advertising yuppies having a conference. The pub is
not much good for watching television, being a little noisy, but
worse is having to put up with listening to the asinine comments
of customers who haven't a clue as to how to read a race.

But I have to go out. It is so cold here I think it may snow
in the kitchen this afternoon.

Thin gravy

I am so weak now that I could barely get out of the bath this
morning. I ended up flapping on the floor like a fish out of
water. The only thing for it is to find a good sauna and sit in
it on a rubber cushion and tipple iced drinks in the steam.
The last time I had a sauna was long ago and in a private
house in Ireland. Sean Kenny was there with a beautiful girl
and one day they shared a bottle of whisky in nearly 100
degrees plus each other. No wonder the poor sod died of a
heart attack. He was a good man and very amusing. He once
offered me some advice as to the best way to meet a deadline.
He suggested I move into a really good and expensive hotel

like the Connaught without a penny, indulge myself via room service and then the fear of being arrested for failure to pay the bill would spur me on. Well, it wouldn't. The sword of Damocles has been hanging over my nut for some years now and I take no more notice of it than I do of my shadow. I think Sean may have had his tongue in his cheek when he came up with that one.

But the bath is no longer a pleasure. Thanks to being so bony it is more than uncomfortable, it is painful. I suppose I could get my own mini-sauna as some jockeys have. The danger there would be passing out in it and being reduced to stock or thin gravy. Yes, nearly everything except for lying down becomes a mammoth task when you are an invalid.

Yesterday I got trapped inside a rollneck jersey when I tried to take it off. It is too small and it stuck over my face. It was very claustrophobic and I thought I would suffocate. Even that had me sitting down and panting for ten minutes. And to think that I once had a girlfriend who used to call me 'tiger'. All this is doubly depressing because I would very much like to get not only my body in shape but also my face. I am smitten by a young woman so much so that I would like to make a comeback. I am fed up with walking into the sunset by myself. Just me and my hip flask.

But at least my dear niece Emma has just turned up to clear away two weeks of debris and rubbish in my kitchen. In the horrible pile of the stuff I see that there are vast quantities of orange skins left over from the juice I squeeze for the vodka. Almost mountains of them. It is a fallacy dished up by health freaks that you can't have enough of it. Some time ago a post-mortem revealed that a man had died because he overdosed himself with carrot juice. That being the case Jane Fonda must have one and a half feet in the grave. You don't need vitamin supplements if you eat properly and the acid from the oranges is playing havoc with my stomach lining. It isn't the vodka. Four years ago the hospital told me to stop putting lime in my drinks.

All of this will be irrelevant to healthy *Spectator* readers who sit down to breakfast every morning in their grey suits and take their oranges in the form of marmalade. I never understood why those poking fun at young fogeys on the *Spectator* should pick on the fact that they all supposedly like marmalade. Is it symbolic of the middle classes? I shall put a spoonful of the stuff in a blender with a large measure of vodka and to hell with what the diabetic clinic says.

Bowled over

Last Sunday there was a cricket match to celebrate the centenary of the Chelsea Arts Club. It was a glorious day and the game was played on a lovely and well maintained ground at St Leonard's Terrace between the King's Road and the Royal Hospital. A couple of old pros turned up, Butcher of Surrey and Clive Radley of Middlesex and England, but there was some sparkling batting from nearly everyone. They asked me to do a spell of umpiring with Peter O'Toole but he didn't turn up. More's the pity.

At one point, when I was umpiring at square leg, Dudley, the club secretary, sent someone out with a large vodka and ice for me. That was the act of a Christian and a gentleman. After that there was a hiccup. During a lull in the game and waiting for a new batsman to come in I sat down on the grass and couldn't get up again.

Such is the weakness of my thighs these days that I need something to pull myself up with or the arms of a chair to push down on. A couple of fielders pulled me to my feet and walked me to the pavilion. The humiliating incident was misinterpreted, of course. The next day the *Evening Standard*'s Londoner's Diary said that I had been overcome by the sun and I suppose many spectators assumed that I was drunk, which was unpleasantly far from the truth. I did manage a couple of drinks, though, in the Young's brewery marquee with Graham Lord of the *Sunday Express* and that was a nice tea break, so to speak.

The man who interviewed me for the *Evening Standard* asked me what it was about cricket that makes it my favourite game. I was lost for words and told him that it isn't a game but a way of life and I couldn't even explain that statement. My father, who loathed cricket, called it 'organised loafing', but he obviously couldn't see or grasp the subtleties of it. The interviewer also asked me did I ever fantasise about cricket. Unceasingly. The times I have square-cut Dennis Lillee for boundaries and knocked Don Bradman's middle stump out of the ground are countless. What depresses me is to have become an umpire thanks to ill health.

One of the memories I most cherish was an occasion playing for art critic David Sylvester's team. I had bowled about seven overs and he took me off saying that I was spoiling the game which he wanted to last until the pubs opened. I couldn't go wrong that day and even got off with the scorer's daughter in the evening. Happy summer days and daze. As a schoolboy I had the honour and privilege of being coached by the great Maurice Tate on a few occasions and I shall be wearing the whites my second wife didn't give away to Oxfam in the hope of an emergency telephone call from Graham Gooch at the Oval to replace someone or other.

But it is good to be living near the Chelsea Arts Club again. From West Hampstead it was £9 each way in a taxi (the legs can't cope with public transport any more), which made a drink cost £20, assuming one went there for 'just the one'. So I am resigned to have been relegated to being an umpire now. But it does feel horribly like *Goodbye Mr Chips*. If the *Spectator* plays the Coach and Horses soon I shall sit that one out. And today sees the return of that playboy and cricket expert, Norman Balon, who thinks that Test matches are played at Wembley. God save our souls.

Rice with everything

At long last the Westminster Hospital has fixed me up with some home help. The said help is a very pleasant woman, originally from Grenada, who comes in every morning at 9.30 to wash me, dress me and clear up whatever is lying about. She is very valuable, as are my nieces and the bombshell from the Soho Brasserie, Roxy Beaujolais. Try putting on a pair of trousers, tucking a shirt in at the same time, with one hand. You can't. When Josey finally zips me up I find it depressingly symbolic of the age I have reached. There was a time… Oh well.

Anyway, the minor inconveniences that go with broken arm and elbow are getting me down. I can't peel a potato, although Josey would if I could carry some home, so it is rice with everything. Also I got stuck in Wandsworth last Monday when I should have been meeting David Gower for a drink in the Groucho Club. What a glorious batsman he is. I was choked that we didn't meet up. Apparently he sent me his regards and told them that he hopes I recover soon, although he doesn't know me. He reads the *Spectator*, however. I wonder what Ian Botham reads. The *Sun*? Perhaps that conjecture isn't fair but he sometimes bats as though he does.

But apart from providing home help the Westminster Hospital is driving me mad. Everything they do takes two hours, right down to the trivial business of getting a prescription for pain-killing tablets. I am afraid that vodka doesn't work for pains worse than the petty ones of divorce, bereavement or moving house. And the tablets don't go with vodka, although I am trying to teach them to do so.

The last time I wrote here I forgot to tell you about the strange chat I overheard in the West Suffolk Hospital in Bury St Edmunds. In the next cubicle a small boy was having his ears syringed out and being quizzed by a doctor. It transpired that while he had been fast asleep the night before, his brother had crept into his room and filled his ears with peanut butter. I knew there must be some use for the stuff. But it is rather extraordinary how our various orifices fascinate children and I thank God that I am not a banana.

Meanwhile, Norman's mother – the poor old thing is ninety-three – is in hospital with a broken hip caused by a fall. That can be a serious business at her age, but she seems to be coming along okay. What tickles the number one son is the fact that she thinks she is in an hotel. She swears she will never come back to it and that it is not as good as the Miami Hilton. He has offered to look after her rings but dementia stops there and she will not let go of the £50,000 job that we have all had our eyes on for some time now.

Norman is a kind but sometimes embarrassing hospital visitor, paying calls as he does to every bed in the ward and then announcing in a loud voice gloomy prognoses on the doomed inmates. 'He hasn't got long,' is his usual verdict. He should wear a black cap on his hospital rounds.

And now Josey has just left, telling me that I am very brave. She should hear me moaning in the night. I am just a baby in long trousers with what she takes to be a glass of water in one hand. I wish I could take her on full-time.

Biter bit

A friend of mine, a journalist and novelist, has taken it upon himself to write a biography of me. I am not quite sure how I feel about the project. In a way it is quite flattering but it is also faintly ridiculous and it will be extremely hard work for him since he reckons he will have to speak to about a hundred people on the subject, ranging from relatives to ex-wives and unknown enemies. I can only think of about two enemies but I have it on the good authority of friends that I have colleagues who don't even know me who simply detest the idea of me.

I gather that there are people outside *Private Eye* who work on the up-market newspapers who are extremely snooty about my lifestyle. Dreadful phrase that, lifestyle. It is true that I live a lot in the past and idle away hour after hour reminiscing, but confronted with a biographer I can only remember trivialities that I wouldn't have thought in book form would interest anyone other than a man or woman who has led the most achingly boring life imaginable. It is that more than anything that has made me opt out of four commissions to write an autobiography. I see no point whatsoever in an autobiography, or a biography for that matter, that isn't a hundred per cent honest and that reveals the sordid nittygritty of the years since 1948 when I left school.

People are so childishly and easily shocked by any owning up that has to be done, and nowhere have I found that more so than when writing for the *Sunday Mirror* whose readers, nearly all of them, write me letters signed, 'Disgusted housewife, Scunthorpe'. The nice letters come from people whose grass I make look greener.

I fooled myself for a couple of days when I told the erstwhile author that I couldn't think of more than a couple of enemies, and he wants more to balance the book. A friend in the Coach and Horses overheard me say that and immediately said, 'Don't kid yourself, you should hear the backbiting that goes on about you when you're not here.'

Well, I do a bit of backbiting myself. We all do. But it slightly puzzles me that I upset these backbiters, because I can't see that I'm anything more unpleasant than a cantankerous, bad-tempered, short-fused old bastard, with the bad habit of uttering false truths when I am drunk. There are thousands of such people, but I must have been born with a silver knife in my back.

I suppose I wouldn't give a damn about anything my friend will write about me but I have to own, and it disgusts me, that I want to be liked, as a little boy wants a pat on the head from Mummy. It is a strange thing but a racing certainty that my ex-wives will not be bitchy. At the most all they can complain of was my absenteeism, but they can't ever say that they thought they were looking at a meal ticket when they first saw me walk into the saloon bar. I used to think that it was I who defused ladies and rendered them harmless but, of course, it was they who made this squib a damp one.

Oh well, if he thinks that he can get a book out of it then good luck to him. We are good friends now but I fear that in six months' time he will be sick of the sight and thought of me.

Memories of the Master

The death of George Barker is a sad blow for those of us who had the pleasure of his company and particularly those of my generation who more or less grew up under his wing in Soho in the late 1940s.

I first met him in 1949 and he soon introduced me to poetry. The sort he gave me to read made a welcome change from the stuff I had been forced to memorise at school. He threw me in at the deep end, so to speak, by giving me a volume of poems by Ezra Pound. It was as though I sat at his feet in those days and they make me think of that painting, *The Boyhood of Sir Walter Raleigh*, in which youth sits at the feet of the old mariner and listens to his stories of distant lands. In fact George was teasingly but affectionately referred to as 'the Master'. He liked that.

On my eighteenth birthday my mother gave me £3 which enabled me legally to go into the Swan in Notting Hill Gate where I had been drinking with George for nearly two years. That day Robert Colquhoun and Robert McBryde were there as usual and also W.S. Graham who was always rather pleased with himself. Roy Campbell was a regular there too. Anyway, at closing time George, the Roberts and I all went down to Lewes for the weekend where the Roberts had rented a charming house. George kindly made me feel accepted and for a moment I felt quite grown-up. I wonder what sort of a picture we cut as we rolled over the Downs in the afternoons.

But the big treat for me was to be invited on occasion by George to his cottage near Haslemere, called Herne Cottage. He said that the legendary Herne the Hunter had lived there when he was one of Henry VIII's game wardens, but I suppose he was romancing again. In any event it was in a stunning setting on the edge of a wood with meadows stretching out before it. We would drink bitter in the local, George being very funny the while, and in the evenings he would read poetry aloud. I remember one of his favourites was the anonymous Quia amore langueo.

One thing I thought sad about George was that he never really got his fair share of money. But he wouldn't write crap for cash. In spite of that I very well remember a day in 1950 when he took me to his bank in South Kensington, drew out some money and handed me £3. In those days I used to sit in his mother's kitchen and sip whiskies with her, she being in George's words 'seismic with laughter' for most of the time. Perhaps some of George's more serious fellow poets would have been surprised to know of his liking for sport, in particular running. We watched the famous race between Chris Chataway and Vladimir Kutz one night in the Swiss pub. He lost ten shillings to me on the outcome and paid up saying that I was 'an evil boy'.

The last time I saw George was at his house in Norfolk at the beginning of the year. We all had lunch, George, his wife Elspeth and my brother Oliver. It is a fond memory. I wish, for selfish reasons, that he hadn't gone to live in Norfolk years ago. It is a remote spot and so I did not see enough of him. His rare visits to London were a treat for me.

Up the wall

I have been harping on about my disgust with the Soho mural elsewhere, but my anger and fury is such that I can think of little else. In case you don't know about it, Westminster council, some people called Free Form Arts and another group called Alternative Arts have put up a damn great mural near Carnaby Street called 'The Spirit of Soho'. It depicts a large group of people who have either lived in Soho or been closely involved with it. There are Mozart and Canaletto, Hazlitt and the fool who invented television in Frith Street, and then they come right up to the present day. I am at a table with Dylan Thomas, Brendan Behan, Jessie Matthews and George Melly. In the catalogues – they must have printed a couple of thousand of them costing £5 each – I appear as 'Geoffrey Barnard'.

This bloody mural isn't up here for five minutes: it is supposed to last. If my name is incorrectly spelt on the key to the mural – I haven't seen it yet – and if it has not been corrected by the time I get back from Barbados next week I shall personally vandalise the wretched thing. Then the incompetent wankers can take me to court.

I am grateful for small mercies, though. At least Michael Corkrey, the man who is painting me, hasn't given me black hair and three arms. In fact the portrait is coming along very nicely and, talking of portraits, I had lunch with Graham Lord, the *Sunday Express* literary editor, one day last week at the Chelsea Arts Club and how that place has changed over the years I have known it. Where were the artists? Ever since Michael Heath invented his strip 'The Suits', men are looking and behaving more and more like that tailor's dummy John Major. There were some rather dashing painters of the old school at one time in the Chelsea Arts Club. They are all dead. I miss Loris Rey particularly, whom I used to drink with when I lived around the corner from the club. I didn't exactly live around the corner, I was taken prisoner around the corner by a woman I couldn't escape from until the day I backed Fred Winter's Anglo which won the Grand National at 50/1. For me that was like the relief of Mafeking.

Later on I wrote a piece about the Arts Club for the *Sunday Times* magazine and David Montgomery took a splendid group picture of all the old rogues. Francis Bacon figured prominently in the foreground, although he never used the place much. I gather that my father used the club as a sort of refuge as long ago as 1930 if he and my mother had a tiff.

Anyway, what with a mural and a portrait I feel as though I have paint coming out of my ears. Meanwhile Graham Lord has had some strange replies from people he has written to about me to help him with his biography. He tells me he received a nice letter from John Osborne, and that reminded me of how good it was to see him on the *South Bank Show* recently. Seeing and hearing Osborne again was tremendously reassuring. Thank God there are still a couple of his ilk left. Definitely not one of the 'Suits'.

The trouble with being caught up in a time warp is that I don't particularly want to meet anyone new, although I look forward to speaking to the barman tonight in the Sandy Lane Hotel, Barbados. The taxi driver will be here in ten minutes to take me to Heathrow. He used to drive Norman's mother to and from the Coach and Horses every day and even went to her funeral. I hope he isn't a jinx.

Home, sweet home

From where I am sitting, facing south and from right to left, I can see the Regent Palace Hotel, the Swiss Centre, the Odeon Leicester Square and the clock on the tower of St Anne's Church, Soho. From the bedroom window I can see Centrepoint. Am I already dead and in heaven? I have seen the Rockies, steamed up the Mississippi, down the Nile, entered the temples of Thailand, the Hermitage in St Petersburg, walked on the gallops by Lambourn at dawn, seen storms at sea, sunsets in the West Indies, women who could break your heart from a hundred miles but never ever have I seen anything quite so stunningly beautiful as the rotting fruit and vegetables in Berwick Street Market just outside the front door of this block of flats. Home, sweet home. At last.

Not even Ulysses had to live out of carrier bags for five years. Neither did he have to put up with the landlords, landladies, neighbours and household pets that I have had to endure. There was a dog in Kentish Town that used to evacuate its bowels every morning on the lupins in the garden. That was as painful as seeing a work of art destroyed. There was the woman in the basement in West Hampstead whose screams of ecstasy made my bedroom windows rattle. In Covent Garden I was cheated out of £1,000. Then there was the Peeping Tom of Maida Vale and the landlady who disappeared with my £650 deposit. After that there was the tower block in Westminster whose windows persistently beckoned me to jump.

As I have said before, it has only been the joint efforts of Keith Waterhouse and Peter O'Toole that have prevented me from going quite bananas. And what strange spin-offs there have been from the play. Yesterday, a company that makes films for television telephoned to ask me if I would be willing to recite, so to speak, my obituary to camera. Since they pay properly I said I would be willing but I am horribly superstitious about it. One more trip down a staircase or off a pavement could do it for real.

I shall sit here and stare at the backside of the Regent Palace. My brother Oliver sent me a card yesterday saying, 'There's no place like home so don't go out for a few weeks.' He is very likely right, but it is tempting and like a breath of fresh air to me to step outside into the squalor of Soho. No more taxis, thank God, and no more thanking me for not smoking.

The only cloud I can see on the horizon is the prospect of another six sittings for the portrait. I don't suppose it ever occurred to anybody that having your portrait painted entails wearing the same clothes for every wretched sitting. And now the man who commissioned the picture wants my daughter to sit for the artist, Michael Corkrey. I am sure she will but the trick is to find her. I am damned if I can and I need her help to unpack some things that have been in store for an age and to open the champagne I have on ice. I shall never be able to open a bottle of fizz again thanks to the bust arm and elbow and I won't miss it much, but a flat in Soho needs a christening. So Isabel, if you are reading me loud and clear, for God's sake telephone me. Where? In the bloody Coach and Horses.

Thank God it's all over

Soho was almost dead at Christmas. The most unlikely people went away to visit their parents. I say unlikely, because I don't believe that some of them were ever born or were ever children. I feel that they first materialised walking through the door of the saloon bar when I first met them years ago, or whenever. They all sounded like reluctant travellers, and the few who stayed at home to be visited by their parents were dreading the occasion. In the days leading up to Christmas everybody was talking about family reunions as though they were so many dreaded dental appointments. Last year my daughter came round to where I was living and I carped like Scrooge about the amount of my Remy Martin her young companion consumed.

This year an old friend and drinking companion from the Coach and Horses came around for lunch, and I'm afraid I snapped at him after he said, for the hundredth time, 'Is there anything I can do?' There was. Stay out of the kitchen and drink your bloody whisky. He had very kindly brought me a present of an anthology of essays on cricket called *Cricket Heroes* and I was very surprised to see, when I first opened the book, that one of the all-time greats had committed suicide. That, somehow, seems so very unlike the action of a cricketer. You can expect almost anything of a boxer but cricket and suicide seem strange bedfellows. Fielding at silly mid-on for a lousy bowler is just about as near to it as they come, or so I had thought.

Anyway, we had 'the one' in the pub before lunch and, as usual, Norman's two daughters had been recruited to serve behind the bar. I am not sure whether or not that is a Christmas tradition in the pub or whether it is a device of Norman's to avoid paying a barman double time. One of them, Natasha, brought her fiancé along for public inspection, and he had the good sense to lose a game of chess with his future father-in-law. All the time he was complaining about the cost of Natasha's wedding reception this coming August. He says it will set him back some £3,000, and that fact was broadcast every five minutes. But what intrigued me was why wait until August? Natasha told me that there were a lot of things to 'arrange'. What? Whenever I have wanted to get married I have done it straight away like a sprinter off the blocks.

So Christmas Day passed and the leftovers were consigned to soup. The crowd in the pub is a human leftover soup of a kind and I am getting weary of the reheating process every day. A cheque is cashed, a round is bought and Chorus enters stage right declaiming, 'You should have been in here last night.' I squirm uneasily on the imprints my pelvic bones have made on the bar stool, and suppress a gigantic yawn for fear of dislocating my jaw. Somebody got drunk, somebody else got barred; Christmas turned out to be jolly good fun after all and thank God it's all over. The rings of vodka left by my glass on the counter drift out of focus and I can only be woken up now by a beautiful, brand-new person, but where the hell is she? Making soup with her leftovers presumably. But at least, now that all the office parties and secretaries in England are abed, normal service will be resumed. And now, next Thursday, the play opens in Perth. I shall be sitting with clipped wings at the bar, listening to Chorus droning on and praying that the show will not be just a leftover from the West End. And a happy New Year to you.

Read all about it

Perhaps hate is recycled love. Graham Lord, now 45,000 words into my wretched biography, tells me of a woman I lived with for nearly seven years who refuses to speak to him about me, describing me as a 'closed chapter' in her life. Funny that. I think we should be told just why I am a closed chapter. It certainly wasn't a Bank Holiday the last time she needed some money. Any other women wishing to air their grievances should contact Graham at the *Sunday Express*. He spoke to my second wife, bless her, as well last week and she said, 'You can see what you're getting when you look at him.' And there was I thinking that I looked rather jolly thirty years ago. Anyway, I met the one who calls me a closed chapter in a ghastly pub in the Portobello Road, which should have given her a clue.

When this book comes out I think I shall look at the last page first. I want to know if it has a happy ending and if I get the girl. If I do I hope it isn't the girl next door who is seventy and who told me off yesterday for smoking in the lift. But I have opened all my chapters for Graham except for those that remain for ever shut owing to amnesia.

There must be some good reason for having such a miserable face as I have and I don't want to know it. When I had the penultimate sitting for the portrait being painted by Michael Corkrey I remarked on that and also the wrinkles he has ascribed to me. He said he has made me look a lot better than in fact I do. Well, I suppose if you get set up you must expect to get shot down in flames. What with being a closed chapter of wrinkles I feel a little gloomy and I see from the flag flying at the top of the Swiss Centre that the wind is blowing from the east. That doesn't bode well. There are no strains of Sibelius on it or even a single measure of Finlandia vodka.

And that brings me to another point and a serious one too. One day last week a restaurant charged me £5 for a vodka and soda. I don't suppose a restaurant writer would notice that but I was paying and it turned me to ice. And that was in Chinatown. Which reminds me, I hit the bonnet of a car last week that was being driven by a Chinaman. He was driving along the pavement outside the Coach and Horses and he nearly knocked me down, so I gave the bonnet a whack with my *Spectator* walking stick. I fully expect to hear more about it. The last time that happened I kicked a car on the pavement outside Kettners. The woman driving it reported me to the police at Vine Street nick. She told them that her awful vehicle had been assaulted by a man with grey hair who was obviously fond of a drink. Quick as a flash they said, 'Oh, that'll be Jeff Bernard.' Shades of Sherlock Holmes and I must be careful not to be seen the next time I murder somebody. On that occasion they photographed me as well as taking my fingerprints. And you know that business of them destroying records after a time? They don't. Sherlock pressed a couple of buttons on a computer and reminded me that I had been Absent Without Leave in 1951. I thought that was a closed chapter too. Maybe I kicked my tank and went off in a huff, which would be a good name for a smallish tank.

And now the wind is veering from the north-east. Norway. What a dreadful place. Grieg and £3 for half a pint of lousy lager. You would have to be a millionaire to be an alcoholic there. I confined myself to the cruise ship after that experience and drank in my cabin with yet another woman who told me that I made her sick. I think of her whenever Radio 3 puts on the Holburg Suite. Not often. She is almost a closed chapter. That hurt.

Grog blossom

I dozed off after a lunch in the Groucho Club one day last week and when I awoke I found that Sue Townsend had left me a nicely inscribed copy of her book *Adrian Mole: From Minor to Major*, by my side. I opened it at random and read one of young Master Mole's entries which was a one-liner saying, 'I am having a nervous breakdown. Nobody has noticed yet.' Oh, I know the feeling. Or at least I used to know it years ago.

The next morning we had a farewell drink together. Sue lives in Leicester, and we said we both felt that one's childhood was one long nervous breakdown. Mine lasted until I was able to escape school. It is odd that most parents assume that their children are more or less blissfully happy. There is such a lot they don't notice.

And talking of childhood we discovered that we had been and still are addicted to rivers and streams. Sadly for Sue, somebody has dumped a rusty old car in her stream, as people will. Mine probably dried up years ago. It ran by a ruined Norman castle near Peterchurch in Herefordshire. The edges of it were all watercress and buttercups and even on the hottest summer days it ran icy cold and clear and we cupped our hands and drank deep of it. Where could you or would you dare to drink from a stream today?

And the great game was to build dams. I still think of drinking that water now when I wake up in the heat and anxiety of the night and light my umpteenth cigarette of the day. How odd it seemed to be sitting in a club bar and talking to Mrs Mole about playing and picnicking by streams.

Something Sue said reminded me of a childhood daymare almost as bad as a nightmare, which was to imagine I was doomed to spend my life serving behind the counter in an ironmonger's shop. You have to wear a brown coat for that and put up with the smells of creosote and turpentine. 'A pound of three-inch nails? Certainly, madam. And here is your galvanised bucket.' I wonder why ironmongers should have first struck terror and boredom into me. But I waffle, and we did, and a nice change it made from the usual bar talk.

The day hadn't started all that well. I received a letter from the Health Education Authority about an anti-alcohol campaign they are launching to persuade young people not to take to it like so many ducks to water. They want a slogan or two for their posters and a black and white photograph of me looking awful to hold up to the youth of England so as to warn them about what 'just the one' can do to a man's face.

I don't mind. My appearance has become a source of copy to journalists and just a few days ago Peter Tory, writing in the *Daily Express*, headed his piece 'Facing the Awful Truth'. An old library picture was captioned, 'Bernard as he was in the

Sixties' and a recent picture was captioned, 'Now ... Bernard's decline is a sad sight'. Well, it may be a sad sight in the shaving mirror, but I don't see why it should be to anybody else.

But what is the point in warning young people about the evils of alcohol? They know them already and can see them every day in the streets or in the House of Commons when they are sitting. I have never taken a peek into the House of Lords but I should imagine there are a few grog blossoms in there too.

A load off my mind

I turned on the radio this morning at the crack of dawn as I always do to hear that an organisation called Mind has declared that millions of working hours are lost each year because of stress. So what? I couldn't live without stress. I cherish every hour that I cling to cliff edges by my fingertips.

The radio announcer then went on to say that there was something of an archaeological tragedy taking place near Bristol because of building something or other which would ruin traces of what happened 250 million years ago. I don't give a damn what happened 250 million years ago, just as it is too late to benefit me to know what won the 2.30 at Sandown Park on 7 March 1928. What I want is an archaeologist to tell me what happened last night. They could turn the Groucho Club into a dig. Archaeologists worry me a little, although I must admit to having been nigh transfixed by my walk through the Valley of the Kings and discovering or unearthing a small shed which dispensed ice-cold lager – something Lord Carnavon never found.

An old friend of mine, Bill Haddow, who I was in the nuthouse with twenty years ago, worried me last week by asking me whether I had considered what there was before the universe. I am now worried sick by that consideration. To hell with wondering whether or not there is life after death, I am now sleepless with wondering how it all started. Who created God? Who triggered the first explosion? All of this creates what Mind calls stress and it is just that which enables me to sit in a bar for three hours in contemplation without feeling bored.

All I know now is that there is life *before* death. This was confirmed yesterday at the diabetic clinic at the Middlesex Hospital. My sainted consultant has at last agreed for me to have an operation to cut out the two cysts on the back of my head. I thought his initial reluctance to have the deed done was because of the possibility of diabetics having heart failures or strokes under a general anaesthetic, but he told me that the only danger was liver failure. I fear not. I have been under a general anaesthetic for twenty years now and my liver and I are still on speaking terms. More than you could say for quite a lot of marriages.

But you should have seen the face of the surgeon my consultant fetched in to have a look at his forthcoming task. They get enormous job satisfaction do surgeons. He looked at my head as a salivating gourmet might look at a roast goose about to come under the knife. They love it. I felt almost sorry for a young Australian surgeon at the Middlesex ten years ago when an infected foot, poisoned by Bajan coral, got better and deprived him of the sheer joy of cutting it off.

But the removal of these two wretched cysts will be a weight off my mind and that is almost literally true. I do not wish to be incinerated at Golders Green looking like the Elephant Man. So if anybody here prints that awful phrase, 'Jeffrey Bernard is unwell', don't believe a word of it. I shall simply be having a deeper sleep in the Middlesex Hospital than the one I usually have in the Groucho Club of an afternoon.

Hack off

It came as no great shock to me to be fired by the *Sunday Mirror* last week. I was only surprised that the editor, Bridget Rowe, bothered to let me know. It was the first and only occasion in all her time at the helm of that ship on which she has bothered to communicate with me. Even Eve Pollard once took me to lunch. For all I know it might have been Ms Rowe who told Robert Maxwell to go take a running jump. It was a black day for me and many others when that man kicked Mike Molloy upstairs. So, goodbye Mirror Group Newspapers after twenty-seven years of on-and-off hacking. I must say that in the last four years or so I never wrote a single column that came anywhere near pleasing me, although I received three proposals of marriage from so many demented female readers, one free ride in a taxi from a driver who recognised me and a five-pound note from a reader who wrote to say that I sounded like a man in need of a drink. Cheers to that.

From time to time I would moan about the difficulty of writing for the *Sunday Mirror* and I always had the horrible feeling that I must write down to its readers as opposed to *Spectator* readers. I confided the fact to Keith Waterhouse one day and he said, 'A juggler doesn't change his act because he changes his venue.' How very right and true. But with Mike Molloy it was different and not quite so like defecating in public. In his time I never once faxed a column or dictated one to a copy-taker because it was always a pleasure to go to the office and deliver it personally. He always had the time to read it after telling me to help myself to a drink and he always had something encouraging to say, or a pat on the head, so to speak, for this little boy, who I am ashamed to say still needs one from time to time. But an editor who is always too busy to give you the time of day isn't on top of his or her job.

I first worked for Molloy in 1969 when he was the editor of the *Daily Mirror Magazine.* Jolly days they were too. Incidentally, Eve Pollard was the fashion editor and I worked alongside Bill Hagerty, Scarth Flett, Russell Miller and Colin Bell when I wasn't downing oysters in Wheeler's in Old Compton Street. When the magazine finally folded Colin Bell hit the nail on the head when he said, 'Gravy train derailed'. I think it must have been then when I took to drink.

The next job on what was then IPC was a twice-weekly column for the *Sporting Life*. That wasn't exactly a gravy train but it kept a pack of wolves from the door while ruining my pancreas. The letter of dismissal from the editor said my behaviour was unpardonable. And now, last week, it was called unforgivable. I would say it was unfortunate. I should never have taken time off and away from this awful machine, Monica, to go to Australia. It has resulted in a double kicking of sorts, since what I wrote for the *Sunday Express* who arranged the trip out there was postponed. Bridget Rowe's secretary told me I was forbidden to write for the *Sunday Express*, but why not? I was never ever under contract to the *Sunday Mirror* and Ms Rowe wouldn't have subsidised a trip to Notting Hill Gate.

But never mind all that; the bad news is that my daughter has just shaved a patch of her lovely hair and she was to sit for her portrait to be painted by Michael Corkrey in two weeks' time. And I have just heard that his portrait of me is to be exhibited in the National Portrait Gallery soon. I am delighted for him and Guy Hart who commissioned the painting. Perhaps Mirror Group Newspapers may buy it. Or slash it? From where I am sitting everything, but everything, is quite absurd.

Crying all the way to the bank

My last three winning bets have not pleased me as much as you might think. The results came in the form of relief only and I couldn't shout for joy, certainly not in the case of the Conservative Party winning the general election. My head shovelled far too much money on them but my heart was never with them. Next came Hatoof, the French winner of our One Thousand Guineas. I like to see English horses beat foreign invaders but I couldn't spot one after going through *Timeform*. The only consolation is that her trainer, Criquette Head, is one of the nicest Frenchwomen I have met. Certainly in Chantilly.

Then Stephen Hendry won the World Snooker Championship with a tremendous late run and I can't abide him. And you can't not like Jimmy White. What a strange business it is to take strong dislikes to people you have never met. I can't bear Hendry's face. He must have been a goody-goody at school, probably still is, and he probably helps old ladies across the road who don't even want to cross the bloody road. Jimmy White on the other hand looks like a man who has seen trouble. The prize money for the brilliant clearance of 147 should keep him in beer for the rest of his life. He went on the wagon for this year's championship and the strain may have told. He'll be back.

It is also to be hoped that my daughter will be back from Italy one of these days. She set out with her boyfriend last week to hitch-hike to Milan. Where are they now, I wonder. Will they come back when they run out of sandwiches? More to the point, will any lorry or car driver stop for them? They looked a mess when they said goodbye to us all in the Coach and Horses. The young man has his hair in black curly spikes, the shape they used to make sticks of barley sugar in. I

wouldn't stop for him and I would think twice about stopping
for her if I didn't know her. I don't like it. Hitch-hiking on the
Continent has become a dangerous business these days. They
are also daft enough to think that they will find odd jobs of
work on their journey like fruit-picking. In May? What do they
teach in schools today apart from how to roll a joint? I can't
think of many things worse than sharing a sleeping bag with
a punk in the middle of nowhere but then I suppose it is none
of my business any more what she does.

Heaven knows I have tried to be a good father and once
even took her to Ascot. She has also swigged champagne at
Brighton and Newbury races. She has had what you could
call every opportunity. And now she is in a sleeping bag
that is probably home to a million scabies. It didn't look like
a Harrods job, I can tell you. And will I get an SOS from
Italy? You can bet on it. If the Italians are anything like the
Italians who frequent the Coach and Horses then getting
out of the sleeping bag may be a jump from the frying pan
into the fire. I should have asked Taki for a list of Italian
millionaires.

Anyway, a portrait by Michael Corkrey is definitely on, but
I am worried slightly about our painter. Twice now since I sat
for him he has come into the pub in the morning for just the
one and stayed until about nine pm. It is not the way to land
a commission to paint the Queen.

Rattling old skeletons

There was a piece in last Monday's *Evening Standard*'s 'Londoner's
Diary' about my brother Oliver, to which my attention was
drawn by several layabouts and subsequently newspapers. If
you didn't see it I quote the gist of it:

In a forthcoming autobiography, *Getting Over It*, Oliver, a teacher and translator of French poetry, discloses for the first time how he became a rent boy, for six weeks, at the age of 15. 'I don't know, apart from loneliness and a kind of despair of human comfort, how I began my brief and unnecessary career as a male prostitute or rent boy,' he concludes. Bernard, 62, who has since established a more prosaic reputation as vice-chairman of Christian CND, continues: 'I'm not sure even how long it lasted. Perhaps five or six weeks. Eight or ten men and boys may have been involved, and I remember most of them.' The confession is extraordinary for its candour.

The diary went on to say that Oliver has notified both myself and my brother Bruce. In fact we have known that for ages and Oliver is sixty-six, not sixty-two, and he was not, repeat not, expelled from Westminster.

So, of course, the telephone lines began to buzz and I was asked what I thought about this amazing revelation. The answer was, not much. And what did I think about Oliver now? I think he is a bloody hero, is the answer to that. But poor Oliver in so far as the censorious *Guardian* and *Private Eye* will probably have a go at him. I think it was the *Eye* that first disclosed the dark secret that I drink. It will be Bruce's turn next – he has been a werewolf for sixty-four years – and our cupboards are crammed with skeletons. We have a sister too. Anyway, I thought I'd pass that on. Keith Waterhouse might get a couple of entertainments out of it all, but casting Oliver and Bruce could be tricky. Mind you, Dirk Bogarde could be a suitable rent boy, with *Das Lied von der Erde* in the background.

Anyway, these shock-horror disclosures have saved me from writing and you from reading about my memorable evening in the Pickwick Club with Marlene Dietrich in 1964.

Hot on the heels of Francis Bacon the obituary people have had a field day or fortnight. Also, you have to admit that I didn't bore you by writing about my Gay Hussar lunch with Frankie Howerd. And now, five weeks after it was transmitted, I have just seen myself on the *Obituary Show* for the first time. I was in Australia when it first went out. Predictably, Michael Heath and Jonathan Meades were very kind and predictably the female journalist and Richard Ingrams were seriously judgemental. Ingrams said I could have been a fairish hack if I didn't drink, without realising that I couldn't write a note to the milkman without a heart-starter. You can't win.

And now I am trying to draw up a guest list for a birthday party. If I wake up on 27 May I will have defied the obituary writers for sixty years. I am sure Geoffrey Wheatcroft can't wait to see his effort in print. What I don't want are judgemental guests, but I would like my diabetic consultant, Anthony Kurtz, and his clever nurse Belinda, the heroine who saved me from bleeding to death two months ago, to tear themselves away from the Middlesex Hospital and come along for a drink. Come to that, I would like to track down and invite the registrar from St Stephen's Hospital who told me in 1965 that I would drop dead if I touched another drop. But he is almost certainly dead himself by now. I wake up in the night and chuckle sometimes.

And now Norman has just telephoned to ask me whether he should accept a registered letter addressed to me. It is almost certainly a summons, but who from? The Inland Revenue or the Grim Reaper?

Happy birthday

Sixty at last. I can't quite believe it but here it is in today's *Times* alongside some oddballs who make me even more sceptical of astrology: Cilla Black, Paul Gascoigne, Henry Kissinger and Vincent Price, to name but four.

There must be members of the staff of the Middlesex Hospital who won't quite believe it too. I know Norman is quite incredulous and yesterday he told me that he was going to buy me a lobster. It will be much appreciated but I will have to scrounge some mayonnaise from the kitchens of the Groucho Club. Try making the stuff with the shakes. You can't.

Anyway, whether or not I can make mayonnaise is the least of my worries. My recent obsession with reaching this 60th birthday has given me a new recurring dream in which the walking stick the *Spectator* gave me turns out to be rotten and crumbles while I am leaning on it. Hot on the heels of the financial disaster of getting the bullet from the *Sunday Mirror* it is not surprising, and now the LEB are threatening to disconnect the electricity because I filled in some form or other incorrectly. I think it is a miracle that most of us are not completely mad. I no longer think of going to bed to sleep, I stagger to my bedroom thinking let's go and have a nightmare.

And the daymares are pretty bad too. That is why I shall now have an early glass of Stolichnaya. It is a birthday present from my friend Bill Haddow who I was in the drying-out bin with twenty years ago and considering he doesn't touch the stuff any more I thought it was a noble gesture on his part. When he presented me with it he apologised for it not being a very imaginative present. But it is, it is. It is a bottle of sweet dreams in which walking sticks don't crumble.

And now the telephone – no, not cut off yet – has been buzzing this morning with calls from surprised well-wishers. And the birthday cards in the post this morning have cheered and moved me. I even got a call from a forty-year-old woman who has claimed in the past to be my daughter. And now two people, one of them our own Jennifer Paterson, have just called to inform me that I can now get cheaper rail travel. This would be a good thing if only I could get on to a train without assistance.

This telephone doesn't stop. My ex has just called and I heard her children in the background, so she's all right at last. Well, it sounded like a pretty picture anyway. It's nice that they fall on their feet when they leave me. So for some, marriages do have a happy ending.

But I must not allow this birthday nonsense to obscure the great puzzle of what is going to win next week's Derby. I am still with Rainbow Corner and I am beginning to think that Silver Wisp might be the best outsider, although it must be years since an Epsom-trained horse won the Epsom Derby. But looking for dangers to my original fancy has often in the past led me to waste valuable ammunition.

I shall not be going this year, although the Groucho Club are having a splash of an outing for the day, and I shall never go to the Derby again. It is now, for me, strictly a television event as is a Test match. You can barely see a yard of the running unless you are at the top of the grandstand. Even Charles Dickens was complaining about Epsom 130 years ago. This drought, though, could make a mess of the form book. When Harry Wragg's horse, Psidium, won at 66/1 I seem to remember it was like concrete. As hard as the looks a young woman would give to a man who has reached sixty.

Taken short

The art dealer, Guy Hart, told me two remarkable, true stories last week. One concerns the ski slopes of Switzerland and the other a train journey to Sevenoaks.

It seems that earlier this year a group of English people went on a skiing holiday somewhere in Switzerland. One day they were at the top of a long run preparing to descend when their instructor warned them to go to the lavatory first, as it was going to be quite a trip down and back to the hotel. Those who wanted to did so. One young woman decided not to bother and then, as the group set off downhill, she changed her mind, detached herself from the others and went behind a tree for a pee. As she squatted down to do the business, her skis began slowly to move, as she was on a slope. In no time at all she had gathered momentum and was soon careering down the hill, her ski-pants around her ankles and peeing all the while. The next day she returned to England, and in the back of the aeroplane where she sat the crew had accommodated a man on a stretcher. Both his legs were in plaster and he had a bandage around his head. They started talking and she asked him how he had had such an appalling accident. He said, 'Well, it is quite ridiculous really, and you probably won't believe it. I was out skiing yesterday morning when to my utter amazement a woman came whizzing past me with her pants around her ankles and peeing the while. I was mesmerised and tears of laughter were running down my face, and I crashed straight into a tree.' End of story. Or is it? When I reflect on it, I like to think that they are now happily married and settled down and will be on the slopes together this coming season.

Telling me that story must have jerked Guy's memory because he then told me an even more bizarre tale concerning a young man, the son of an affluent bookmaker who had offices near Simpson's in Piccadilly. His father gave an office party one day and the son duly attended. He was green and inexperienced, ignorant of drink and its attendant dangers. For an hour he mixed champagne with whisky – disastrous. He lost control and inadvertently – how can I put it politely? – evacuated his bowels. With a mixture of panic and embarrassment he staggered into Simpson's and asked an assistant for a pair of trousers. 'What sort of trousers?' he was asked. 'Any,' he said, 'any at all. The first pair that comes to hand.' He left the shop with his purchase and hailed a taxi to take him to Charing Cross to get the train home. Once the train was moving, he went to the lavatory to clean himself up as best he could. Having done that, and as the train was speeding through the suburbs, he threw his dirty pants and trousers out of the window. And then, with what one can only imagine to have been a long sigh of relief, he put his hand in the Simpson's carrier bag to pull out his new trousers. The only thing in the bag was a V-neck pullover. He had been given the wrong bag. That is all we know.

Since I was told that story I have lain awake at night trying to picture the scene. I presume he put his legs through the sleeves of the jersey, but what I want to know is where did he put the exposed V of the jersey. To the front or his rear? I wonder, too, what the ticket collector thought, let alone the other passengers alighting at Sevenoaks. He is probably a broken man now and gets out of the train either at the stop before Sevenoaks or the stop after in order to go home by taxi. He is now almost certainly a teetotaller. There are holes in this story, but Guy insists that it is true. I am afraid I rather hope so. Poor man.

Standing joke

I was eating my weekly intake of chicken in orange sauce in the Ming the other day when Christine, the lovely lady from Hong Kong who owns the place, came over to join me at my table as she often does. After the usual pleasantries she leaned forward and said, 'I bet you £500 that you couldn't get an erection in a sauna.' Now of all the things that have crossed this restless mind over the years the possibility of that event is something that I have never considered. A natural punter, I pondered the challenge as I polished off the mixed vegetables. I reflected that I have been in states of considerable excitement in equatorial conditions from Mombasa to Bangkok and from the Nile to Singapore, but it also occurred to me that the Chinese, as a general rule, do not back outsiders. She must 'know something', as they say in racing.

Anyway, whether or not to pick up the gauntlet she had thrown down? I thought about it for most of the afternoon as I sat sipping vodkas in the Groucho Club with what must have been a slightly glazed look about the eyes. Sibelius almost certainly got it up before he went rollabout in the snow and if dear old Sean Kenny, the stage designer, were alive today he could earn himself an easy £500. Saunas were, in fact, his downfall. The last time I saw Sean was the occasion when we were both staying the weekend in Kevin McClory's rather posh house just outside Dublin. That was equipped with a sauna and you couldn't keep Sean out of it for long. But what amazed me was that he not only took his girlfriend into the steaming coals but also a bottle of whisky. Old Bushmills, I think, but her name escapes me. I warned him what the combination of the two could do to his heart but he laughed it off. About two months later and back in Soho he dropped dead in Shaftesbury Avenue of a heart attack. I doubt he had any regrets when he was met by his maker.

But Christine's bet can wait. What can't wait for much longer is the decision what to back in the big race at Ascot, the King George VI and Queen Elizabeth Diamond Stakes. At the time of writing the Irish favourite, St Jovite, looks to have it at his mercy. I don't trust racing certainties, but I would like to recoup my Wimbledon losses on Monica Seles. Looking for horses to beat 'good things' can be disastrous but it is always tempting. Doctor Devious couldn't get beaten in the Irish Derby and St Jovite spreadeagled the field. If Monday's rainstorms are to be repeated then I would take a chance with Sapience. I probably will anyway. His trainer, David Elsworth, is much more than simply the man who trained that chasing legend Desert Orchid. *Timeform* don't exactly rave about Sapience and he stands at 12/1.

My bookmaker friend who breakfasts in the Bar Italia every day, Alfie Edwards, certainly doesn't rave about my chances of winning the bet with Christine and I stand, if that is the right word, at 33/1. They say that bookmakers always have the best information and I wonder if Alfie knows something that I don't know. What a double that would be if it came up. In fact, it would pay 441/1. It could be a heart-stopper, though, if both events had to be determined by photo finishes.

Banged to rights

I have just received a letter from a former Coach and Horses customer, Patsy, who is at present resting in what he calls the Ford Country Club by Arundel in West Sussex. It is, of course, one of Her Majesty's hotels, Ford Open Prison. Some time ago, I warned Patsy, when he said he was off to Reading, not to end up where Oscar Wilde went and he has remembered that well, for he quotes Wilde twice in his letter, beginning it by saying, 'Anybody can be good in the country,' and ending by writing, 'We are all in the gutter but some of us are looking at the stars.' Well, as far as H.M. hotels go, the branch at Ford doesn't sound too bad. In fact it doesn't sound much worse than the Coach and Horses. I too, Patsy, am banged up with the same people day in and day out and that is my punishment for having decided to stray from the straight and narrow many years ago. I am glad that you were able to get away for a couple of days' racing at Glorious Goodwood, pleased that you backed Bonnie Scot and I hope that the lunch at the Avisford Park Hotel was up to scratch. I suppose some of you must have managed to go to Glyndebourne for a picnic and an aria or two as well. The sporting and cultural facilities here certainly can't match your own. Betting shops and television are a poor substitute for Mozart in the garden and the popping of champagne corks in the member's bar at Goodwood. All I wonder is how do you manage for drink and cigarettes? But I suppose you have that sewn up too. The screws where you are can't be worse than Norman, who still steadfastly refuses to serve a drink himself. Thank God for the Irish staff.

There was only one thing in your letter that depressed me a little and that was your remark, 'Crime in reality is a dull and tedious business.' What isn't? Blank sheets of typing paper don't exactly excite me. What they call 'job satisfaction' continues to elude me. And what work do they give you to do in Ford? Are you by any chance the man who puts the lumps into the porridge, or are you lucky enough to do the odd job in the gardens of the club? And that reminds me. I did once have a job I quite liked many years ago when I worked as a gardener of sorts in Holland Park through a summer and the autumn. Making bonfires out of autumn leaves was pleasant enough and I met a few nannies wheeling their gurgling charges about in that park. That was easy since a gardener is regarded as harmless. Anyway, our editor will be delighted to know that you and your fellow lodgers get the *Spectator* and enjoy it. A pity poor Oscar couldn't. And I am delighted to hear that some of your acquaintances there liked my column in the *Sunday Mirror*. A pity they didn't write to tell the editor, not that it would have made any difference.

Captains are obliged from time to time to make crew members walk the plank if for nothing else to show that they are in command. Would you believe that I am still awaiting payment for an article I wrote in April for another newspaper. Yes, April. Not that I should moan to a man in your hotel. But if I were just a shade more cynical, I might advise you to stay put. At least your accommodation and food problems are taken care of and I can assure you that neither has the taste of alcohol improved in the last two years, nor has the ritual of sex. Not only is Goodwood adjacent but you also have Fontwell Park for the jumps in the winter.

Take some slight comfort in the fact that you are missing nothing of note. As leopards don't change their spots neither do pub bores. Sometimes, most afternoons, Norman gives me parole and I go to the Groucho Club. There are bores there too, as there are in any place that dispenses booze. They are just richer there. What you will need when you terminate your stay in Ford are 'ex's'. Even Norman's awful doorstep sandwiches are £2 each and I am sure you would rather choke on a truffle. Perhaps you could write a column with a facetious title such as *Inside Out*.

And now I am off to Dublin to record my hazy and vapid thoughts on that city which is a damn sight more *simpatico* than anything south of Hendon. Keep your spirits up and don't bother to escape into this.

Not a pretty picture

Last week I read the proofs of Graham Lord's biography of me, *Just the One*, and I have been feeling not a little depressed ever since. This is not Graham's fault, who has worked very hard and done a good job, it is just that it is not a nice story, not a pretty picture. I must have been mad to have looked forward to it. I wasn't daft enough to think that everybody Graham interviewed would be lovey-dovey about me – I wasn't even that myself – but some of it still came at me like a bucket of cold water in the face when I read it in the sober light of day. Being as vain and self-preoccupied as any man, I thought it might be required reading for me from cover to cover every day for the rest of my life.

I shall be interested to see what the book looks like when it comes out – it is illustrated – and then it shall be kept closed for ever after. Was Dorian Gray in the habit of looking at his revolting portrait? I wouldn't know since I have never read the book. I would guess that he took the odd peek at it. I was happily surprised, though, to discover that a couple of ex-wives and the odd ex-girlfriend had been fairly pleasant about me, although even they couldn't remember much beyond the fact that I had blue eyes when they met me. (I have just looked at them and they have faded like an overexposed watercolour. What with the pink in them now they remind me of Sir John Astor's racing colours.) Of course, to me, the book reads like an obituary without pulled punches: I wasn't 'convivial', I was as pissed as a rat. And it should be required reading for any boy stupid enough to think that a glass of whisky will make him an instant Jack the Lad.

Anyway, when I finished reading *Just the One* it occurred to me that now I live with a potted palm tree I have arrived at an anti-climax. Or maybe it is a climax in disguise. There are, of course, a few things that are mildly irritating to me and that is only to be expected. Yes, I have ignored my sister in the past and I do now because I have never liked her and I couldn't

suddenly feel any warmth for her when she was certified years
ago, just as I wouldn't feel sudden affection for somebody who
was diagnosed as having cancer. It would just make one think
a bit. I do that all right.

It has also stirred memories and muddied a pond which I
thought was becoming clearer. I had nearly obliterated my
memories of the horrors of early family life but they have been
brought back to the surface. My brother Oliver's forthcoming
autobiography, *Getting Over It*, also slightly depressed me for that
reason. I used to argue with Frank Norman that his being taken
into a Dr Barnado's home was a blessing in disguise but he
would have none of it. Nevertheless it can be a terrible thing to
be a child and discover that you have inherited a mother. And
as for my daughter Isabel, she came round last week to see me
and read a chapter or two which opened her eyes a little. She
wasn't shocked but she didn't exactly laugh. But now that she
is twenty-two years old it won't do her any harm. I wish I knew
more about my father, whom I strangely miss although I never
knew him when he died and I was only seven.

I see now that what I have said looks very much like self-pity
but I am not much given to that nowadays since I see that it
has all been rather absurd. What Graham Lord's book has
done has been to rekindle some guilt and remorse and that is
my own fault. Remorse is horribly negative, as is envy, and I
was surprised to read an undercurrent of envy in some of my
friends and enemies that Graham interviewed. How anybody
can envy a faintly breathing cadaver is beyond me.

Oddly enough, the book has a comparatively happy ending
when Graham Lord writes of the opening and run of *Jeffrey
Bernard is Unwell*. Was it really such a nightmare up until then
and did Keith Waterhouse simply invent me? I shall never know.
But I can't help smiling at a remark made by a woman in the

book who says of years ago that I wasn't very good at cuddling because I got so instantly randy that it led to closer contact. And that is meant to be a put-down? Those were the days.

A walk on the wild side

A minor but nevertheless unpleasant spin-off of some accidents and illness is the attention drawn to the victim by physiotherapists. These strong, starched, no-nonsense women can give you hell and on the two occasions I have had pneumonia, once with pleurisy, my chest and back were given pummellings far more memorable than anything I ever suffered in a boxing ring. They had me walking on crutches and almost screaming only three days after the master mechanic, Mr Cobb, bolted his titanium plate into me and yesterday a physio called in to my flat to take me walkies. As it turned out, I gave her a walk if not a run for her money.

We set out in the rain, dangerously slippery, with the intention of my walking the one block to Berwick Street market. I was greeted there nicely by the stallholders whom I hadn't seen for nearly four weeks, and we paused for the usual cockney badinage. After a while I told the physio that I thought I could make one more block and I hobbled and staggered to Wardour Street. It was then that I got the scent. I realised I was only a block and a half from the Groucho Club, and she looked at me with something like admiration when I gamely suggested that we should press on still further. Outside the club I feigned exhaustion and said, 'How odd, I know this place. Let's stop for a rest.'

We sat down on a sofa, she concerned that I wouldn't be able to get up from it, and me thinking that if I couldn't it would not be for want of bone and muscle, and I got stuck into a large vodka while she sipped coffee. Of course, I have drink at home, but taking it alone is like swallowing medication. By the next time she calls I think I should be able to make another two blocks and have a rest at the Coach and Horses. Some members of the medical profession are good at dangling carrots – they were pleased that I smoke in the hospital because it forced me to walk to the landing outside the ward – and I wouldn't be at all surprised if Theodore Dalrymple encourages his convict patients to jump over walls.

Speaking of prisons, Patsy is on parole again. He is supposed to be coming to see me today and I hope he makes it via the lift and not the drainpipe. Last Friday, Sister Sally and a nurse called Mary who looked after me in hospital came to see me and we went out for supper. The girls seemed to enjoy being taken out and what they ate must have been a nice change from the hospital food. We even had a jolly chat about pain and death before they took this exhausted body home and put it to bed. Perhaps one day they will lay it out.

Meanwhile I await a postcard from Vera, who is languishing in St Raphael. That I would dearly like to see. She probably washes up the dishes after they have eaten in a restaurant, such is her habit. Her stand-in is not the harridan I had feared but a gentle Irish girl called Claire. What she makes of this place and Monica's tapping out a column God alone knows but she shies like a nervous horse. This morning she poured a vodka down the sink supposing it to be an old glass of water. She stands corrected and I have told her to let me sniff, sip and test all waste matter in the future. She will return to headquarters and doubtless tell the council that I am 'difficult'. The Middlesex Hospital had me down on their files as being difficult and I can only suppose that it must mean being slightly more lifelike than a cabbage. I once watched a nurse there put me on a dextrose drip and not a saline one, pointed out to her that I was a diabetic and asked her then how many people she killed on average every month. Vera knows exactly what to put in a drip and I hope she brings some of it back. And now Deborah is coming to take me walkies. My tail should be wagging but it isn't. Maybe it needs a titanium plate in it. Everything else seems to.

Heartbreak hotel

I was right to be apprehensive about staying in the refurbished Adelphi Hotel in Liverpool. It was dreadful. Any lingering echoes of the past there may have been have been drowned by piped music. It is everywhere. There is also no way whatsoever in which a disabled man like me on crutches or anybody in a wheelchair can negotiate any of the awful facilities. If Graham Lord hadn't been there to give me a helping hand I would have been kippered.

The place was full of what are now called reps – travelling salesmen to me – all wearing striped shirts and soaked in cheap aftershave but still with dirty fingernails. You just know that they regard an overnight stay in such a place as a treat and they probably even boast about it when they get home to their unfortunate wives. They are in a purgatory for those halfway between lager lout and yuppie.

We kicked off with my being interviewed by a young man from the local *Daily Post*. That took place in the lounge which, with its marble arches and chandeliers, still has a vague splendour, now faded. The hack seemed nice enough but I didn't much like his piece when I saw it the following morning. The wrong word here and there, put in for some literary effect, can completely distort the picture. Apparently my camel overcoat is 'threadbare'. By the end of the piece it seemed that he had interviewed a drunken tramp. Maybe his editor asked him to do just that. What was threadbare was the upholstery in that lounge. There was little chance of getting drunk either, thanks to paralysed waitresses.

After the interview we drove off to find a pub and did in fact find one which was potentially one of the best I have stumbled into in ages. A Victorian job called The Lion, it has been ruined by muzak and a fruit machine. Otherwise it is quite stunning: brass and glass, not monopoly brewer's Formica. The end of the evening back in the Adelphi was a sort of hell that I am beginning to think you can only find in England, or maybe in a war-torn country. On such jaunts as this one I put my trust in room service and now, on crutches, even more so. Mistake. I ordered something to eat and a couple of drinks and waited, and waited. After half an hour I suddenly remembered that Sir Jock Broughton of Happy Valley and now *White Mischief* fame had committed suicide in the Adelphi. After another fifteen minutes of hunger and thirst it occurred to me that he had done the deed out of sheer desperation.

Eventually two maids arrived, one carrying some dried-up lasagne and the other two glasses of vodka and soda, but no ice. Why do maids and waitresses have to make everything they serve smell of talcum powder? Women at home don't. It was the waitress-only service that put me off eating at Sheekey's years ago. Anyway, I lay there for an age trying to get some sleep but I couldn't stop thinking about the Happy Valley lot in Kenya and what a happy time I had out there. It occurred to me that the Groucho Club and the Muthaiga Club could come to a reciprocal arrangement and become twin clubs. Then I slept and dreamt of murder.

Gone with the Wind

There were a few of us in the bar of the Groucho Club the other day talking about Camillagate when, during a pause for reflection and a sip of our drinks, a lurking waitress suddenly said, 'I wish I was a suppository inside Prince Charles.'

I couldn't afford to choke on my drink, not at £4 a shot, but I did pause to think that my own ambition to be an engine driver when I was not that much younger than she was a pretty meagre and unambitious dream. Some strange dreams and fantasies have been manufactured in this head of mine but I have never hoped to be medication in an orifice, royal or not, to melt and then be gone with the wind. To want to be the bee in Saddam Hussein's bonnet would be reasonable enough, or to have been the bullet that killed Hitler in the end would have been a worthwhile dream, but to end up as a fart is an appalling thought.

I didn't realise that women waited on tables thinking such things. Oh well. There was a man once who said that he would like to be stabbed in the back by Carlo Ponti and you can see his point, but how could a seemingly sane Liverpudlian girl want to go for a dip in brown Windsor soup? Our obsession with royalty really does know no bounds. I remain content to know that the Queen used to read my column in the *Sporting Life* every Wednesday and Saturday some twenty years ago and that was as close as I ever wanted to get to the Palace.

Meanwhile, life ticks by for this commoner and pretty boring it is too, although letters from readers in Australia of all places would indicate that they think I live in a bowl of cherries. Last night was OK, though. I went to see Peter O'Toole in *Our Song*, liked it, liked him, and went around to his dressing room after to have a drink with him. He autographed a picture of himself for the sainted Vera, who is about to turn up at any minute. She will be well pleased.

So will I be to see her. Her stand-in last week was a young man, unsuitably named, I think, for a home help, Craig, who wears a Russian fur hat while he washes the dishes and who studies fine art in Holland when he isn't elbow-deep in the sink. He is rather formal, as befits a Craig – a Tom, Dick or Harry would tell me to get stuffed – and he says he doesn't mind working his way through college at fairly menial tasks. I don't get that. Washing up dishes and hoovering for crocks can't be fun. By the same token he finds it hard to understand that thumping Monica electric de luxe is loathsome to me. I think Olympia typewriters should bring out a new model and call it Camilla electric de luxe. I would like to be the ribbon in her.

Anyway, last Friday I had to buy a sofa in the sales. It is essential. I haven't actually sat next to anybody in this flat since I moved here a year ago. It is a very flashily upholstered job, as bright as a Henley Regatta blazer, and bloody expensive too. I moaned and whinged about the price of it for hours and the very next morning I received a cheque in the post covering the cost with a little bit over. To my amazement the cheque was for royalties for a short run of *Jeffrey Bernard is Unwell* in Copenhagen. What on earth could the Danes have made of it? Keith Waterhouse and I must speak in Esperanto. Gabby who runs the delicatessen in Old Compton Street tells me he read good reviews of the play as well in the Italian paper he buys. Considering the Italians are tantamount to teetotallers I should have thought it would be absolute Greek to them.

But it bodes well. I need a new cooker as well as a sofa on which to chat up young gullibles. Perhaps 1993 might not be as disgusting as I had thought. And don't tell me about small mercies. The big one is not being a suppository.

Not a drop to drink

The case of the woman who won £15,000 damages from her employers because of the suffering she endured at work from passive smoking has sickened me somewhat. You only had to see pictures of her in newspapers, or watch her on television, to see that what she is really suffering from is the most awful obesity. Even my own doctor, a non-smoker herself, thought it 'quite disgusting'. It is no wonder that the victim of office smoke has difficulty in breathing. Every time she takes a breath she must have to raise about 50 lbs of mammary gland and I would wager that most of her £15,000 windfall, or smokefall, will be spent on custard cream biscuits, Mars bars, treacle tarts and chocolate cakes.

The case is the thin end of a very sinister wedge and I speak, of course, of passive drinking. That will be the next target on the list of liberties we shall be robbed of. My last wife, dear thing, divorced me because of the suffering she had to endure through passive drinking and she was quite entitled to do so, but I am not married to this lousy Government. And thank God for that, for my dinner would never be in the oven and my cigarettes and corkscrew would be confiscated.

When I mentioned the passive smoking woman to my doctor, she, the doctor, had called on me to check me over. She has the good sense not to tick me off and tell me to give up my two remaining comforts but she did smilingly remark, 'You know you're destroying yourself, don't you?' She then took my blood pressure and said, 'Extraordinary. Your blood pressure would be the envy of a twenty-year-old.' Swings and roundabouts. Last week I didn't appear here because of an entirely new complaint. I think my intestines might have taken early retirement.

And here's a funny thing. Last week a magazine asked me
to test several vodkas for them and nine bottles of different
vodkas were duly delivered. I haven't been able to do it yet and
I have been staring at my review bottles on the shelf feeling a
little sick. It is a form of passive drinking. If I don't get better
soon I might have to farm the job out and get it written by
a ghost. And there are several of those around here sitting
on the pavements, poor sods. One day recently such a man
called out to me from the other side of the street asking me
for the price of a drink. I beckoned him to come over for it
and he waved me away. That has to be the Everest of laziness.
I am not going trotting after winos with my bust hip. In fact
yesterday I even had to get a taxi to the Coach and Horses
which is a mere four blocks away. The doctor offered to get
me a wheelchair when she called but that would be an awful
surrender. Anyway, who would push the wretched thing?

So here I am staring at those nine bottles of vodka
wondering more than ever what it can all mean. It is drizzling
and the London Electricity people are coming to cut the stuff
off because I forgot to pay. They don't know about amnesia
and why should they? They don't sit about in bars for most
of the day trying to blot out pub talk with pure grain spirit.
So there might be blackout in this flat tomorrow. They wrote
also to say that if they do cut it off there is a reconnection fee.
What they don't seem to understand is that if they don't cut it
off in the first place then the fools wouldn't have to reconnect
it. Well, that seems quite logical to me anyway.

School for Soho

I have been invited by Pangbourne College to go down there
next week to talk to the sixth formers. They expect me to talk

about the low life, but at the moment I am damned if I know what to say to them. After all this life of mine isn't particularly low and consists mainly of loafing around. The fact that I do most of that with a glass in my hand does not, in my opinion, make it reprehensible. A few days ago Taki took me again to Aspinall's for lunch. Had he arranged for us to meet at a greyhound racing stadium for a sandwich I would have called that pretty low. The boys and girls are in for a disappointment.

Yes, they have a few girls there now and my old masters must be turning in their collective graves. I was born into the wrong generation. But what surprises me about this invitation to give a talk is the fact that they know full well that I loathed the Nautical College, Pangbourne, as it was then, and was extremely unhappy there. One of my clearest boyhood memories is of the occasion when I tearfully begged my mother to take me away from the place. She must have been very disappointed in her would-be officer and gentleman.

The invitation from the college sadly coincided with the tragedy of the boy who hanged himself the other day. Newspapers had it that bullying was the reason for his dreadful end, but I do not believe that that was necessarily so. I never saw the slightest hint of bullying in my two years there, although my divisional tutor (housemaster) was a sadistic, slightly deranged homosexual who taunted me from time to time because I was there on a grant and not family money. Of course we had fights, prearranged to take place in the squash courts, but it was Queensberry Rules stuff and never reminiscent of Tom Brown's schooldays. There can be plenty of other reasons why a boy should commit suicide. They must be horribly upset at Pangbourne now.

I gather that the school is vastly changed for the better forty-five years on from my days. It couldn't be anything else.

Corporal punishment is strictly forbidden, for one thing, and the introduction of a few girls sounds nicely civilised. They were mysterious objects slightly to be feared when I was a boy and it is awful that most of us grew up nervous to meet the female of the species. I was lucky there. Ken Russell was also at Pangbourne, three years or so before me. I suppose the two of us reacted against Pangbourne in our different ways and I am glad to say that it threw me into the arms of Soho, Sandown Park and Smirnoff and not into making bizarre films about the likes of Wagner.

Perhaps I owe the school a debt after all. It certainly made a large chunk of life seem like something of a holiday ever since and my small stint of national service seems no worse in retrospect than having been forced to take a holiday in a Butlin's holiday camp instead of Barbados. The Coach and Horses cricket team have asked me to try to arrange a match against Pangbourne this coming summer but I fear the boys and masters would blanch at the sight of our troupe seemingly straight out of Shakespeare's Boar's Head. A pity that, for it would be an education of a sort for the boys, who would anyway undoubtedly win the game. Perhaps the Coach and Horses should stick to playing teams of their own class and calibre, and with that in mind I shall try to get a fixture against the England team when they return from India.

Old school ties

At last I have laid the ghost that had haunted me for forty-five years. My return visit to Pangbourne College to speak to the sixth formers went very well, as far as I was concerned, and I don't think the boys were too bored by our question and answer session. The atmosphere of the place has changed beyond all recognition since my days there and my hosts were charming and I even felt some warmth in their company. The boys I spoke to were very pleasant and I may have to rethink my attitude toward teenagers.

It is all something of a puzzle. Could it all have been as terrible as I have always remembered it, or did I bring my own unhappiness to school with me at the start of every term? It could have had its roots at home where there was always some tension and some danger of a row or drama of some sort, my mother and even my sister being what they were. I am no longer sure that I can go on blaming Pangbourne for my being such a miserable bore, although the masters did not serve me vodka and Perrier as they did last week. How odd it seemed somehow to be sitting in a classroom and the headmaster's quarters sipping and smoking.

The day started badly enough. It was the coldest I can remember this winter and in my rush to catch the right train from Paddington, I left my flat having forgotten to take my insulin. I was met by a master at Reading by which time I felt at death's door and yet could not feel my legs or feet. A master with diabetes later saved me from crashing out by kindly getting me some insulin from the village, and after the headmaster's wife had given me a couple of drinks without looking shocked at my request for them I was almost back on course.

What a friendly bunch they are. The Captain Superintendent when I was a boy, Commander Skinner, could have put ice in a vodka just by looking at it, or maybe that is one more thing that is in my imagination. Anyway, the chat with the boys and four girls went on for a little more than an hour. There were about sixty of them and they kindly refrained from trying to shoot me down in flames. I can't remember now much of what I said, but I do remember unwittingly slightly depressing one girl when I said that it is slight odds against ever being really happy. I shall attempt to make amends by sending her a copy of John Cowper Powys's *The Art of Happiness*. Sorry about that, Liz.

I later discovered that they had videoed the whole proceedings and they will probably show it to boys of the future as a warning as to how you can end up looking on fifty cigarettes and a few vodkas every day. After a good buffet lunch, a vast improvement on the cabbage of 1947, we said goodbye and to my astonishment I was genuinely sorry to be going. I could have hung about all day. I felt comfortable and at ease and all the way home to Soho I kept wondering whether it could all have been so awful all those years ago. If it was, perhaps it was just as well if it toughened up that miserable boy who was so reluctant to stray far from his mother's apron strings. Not that the diva of Holland Park would be seen dead wearing an apron unless it had been designed by Chanel. I think I shall go back to Pangbourne this summer, and maybe watch them play some cricket or row on that so pretty stretch of the river. In my present mood I may even start recommending the college to the parents of fourteen-year-olds.

What I do now, though, is to extend an invitation to the boys and girls to drop into the Coach and Horses some time during the holidays. Norman needs their pocket money.

Pelvic moan

I didn't in fact break my hip again. I slipped up and fell on it, agony enough, and I cracked my pelvic bone. One of these days somebody is going to sue Westminster Council over their uneven paving stones. Smirnoff are not responsible for all the accidents that happen during the long hobble to the grave.

Anyway, in the morning I could not move and if I hadn't had an extension to my telephone put by my bed I should probably be rotting in it now. My doctor fixed it for an ambulance to take me to University College Hospital and I was admitted as being in need of what is now called 'pain control'. Pain is too bland a word for what I felt. The nurses on the orthopaedic ward welcomed me as an old friend, as indeed I am with two of them who have been to my flat on occasion for a drink ever since the initial hip fracture last October. They like the Groucho Club too, which should make them honorary members in order to sedate members such as Jay Landesman and Julie Burchill.

On day two I was helped into a wheelchair and wheeled out to the landing so that I could smoke. That landing by the lifts is what the hospital calls a 'designated smoking area' and it is the pits, an awful alternative to lying in bed and staring at the ceiling. The wheelchairs of the amputees huddle around a large ashtray which is ignored by most patients and the windowsills are lined with old paper cups and empty fizzy drink cans. You could sit there for a year without having a conversation. The only subjects discussed are the hospital routine, going-home dates and details of individual ills, operations and pains. At night an old wino would lurch about in search of dog-ends. The security must be almost non-existent. These tramps creep in through the casualty department in search of warmth and a pinch of tobacco and they could easily rob most patients on that floor who are physically helpless.

But it is the patients who get up my nose the most: readers of the *Sun*, football fans, moaners and men who would take an oath on *Reader's Digest*. I sometimes wonder if it is only the ugly and mindless who get sick. I must have looked pretty sick myself because one day a visitor approached me and asked if I could direct her to the mortuary. There was one man on my ward who was so incoherent that after a while I asked him not to bother to speak to me. At first I thought his mumblings were of East European origin but it turned out that he came from Edinburgh. It took him fifteen minutes to explain to me that he couldn't speak properly because he had never bothered to make the effort. That is appalling, although there are those I know in Soho and the Government who, likewise, should never have bothered. He chain-smoked, stared into the distance and then would make a noise like an animal. His pyjamas were glued to him with sweat, but I couldn't feel sorry for him. He probably couldn't have been bothered to feel sorry for himself.

One consolation during my stay was that the registrar on my ward allowed me to drink, saying that he would rather I did than prescribe for withdrawal symptoms. But the food was so awful that I ignored my diabetes and ate a mountain of digestive biscuits. My blood sugar went very high but it was better than hunger. There was an American woman in my ward who had foolishly come over for a holiday – Sarajevo or Belfast would have done. She broke a wrist when she arrived at Heathrow and was presented with half a slice of cold toast for her first breakfast. For that she was paying £160 a day. I thought the toast was interesting in a way, being what I imagine a slice of carpet that had had some butter smeared on it the day before must taste and feel like in the mouth.

There were reassuring aspects about my stay, though. Mr Cobb, the consultant surgeon and the man who sculpts with titanium, told me with some irony that I should make myself at home. There will always be a bed and I think he expects me to return. Looking at X-rays of people he has operated on, which are pinned to the notice board, I can't help but think of him as being the Isambard Kingdom Brunel of surgery. And I mean that in the most complimentary way. I am saving my left hip for him.

Over the odds

Sometimes weather forecasters end their summary by saying, 'There is a risk of thunder.' Why risk? Thunder is music to my ears. In Andalucia they don't announce that there may be a risk of nightingales singing and the wretched things used to keep me awake all night when Simon Courtauld was kind enough to lend me his pied-à-terre just outside Tarifa. The editor here doesn't announce that there may be a risk of Julie Burchill writing a piece next week, but there usually is.

The English seem to me to be reluctant to take risks, although they go to the races in droves. But taking risks gives me a buzz of sorts and if this were 1815 I think I would risk having £100 with my bookmaker, Victor Chandler, on the French to win Waterloo despite our good away record. If it hadn't been for that outsider, Blücher, getting up in the closing stages we might not have had the railway station of that name.

But would you risk £1,000 on Tenby to win the Derby at 2/1 on? I never trust certainties and, come the day, may risk a little on the 'long fellow' to win the race on Fatherland, awful name for a horse. I fear that my brother Bruce may never forgive me for risking a hefty sum on Australia to win the forthcoming Test series, but that is how I now see the outcome. England don't bowl very well but I should be overjoyed to lose my money, especially since Dennis Waterman might pay Victor Chandler. I am in fact disgustingly patriotic.

The one risk I didn't take this week was to go to the Chelsea Flower Show. For years and years I have tried to get a ticket to the first day, and at last got one this year, but I didn't go for fear that with my weak legs and leaning on a stick I would fall again in the crowd. Weeded out, so to speak. I particularly wanted to see the water garden and avoid the press tent.

And now I have suddenly remembered that it is Deborah's birthday, of course, because it is the day before mine. The press had a tiny field day writing about the two of us and Richard Ingrams. It would appear that I lost a battle of love to the Cyrano of Aldworth, but I am happy for them both and I hope that Deborah will enjoy pumping Richard's organ for years to come.

So I sit here now in a wheelchair in my flat languishing in a warm breeze watching my palm tree waving. Taki claims in last week's 'High Life' that he invited me to Greece which he didn't and my new neighbour, the woman next door, says I am rude. My doctor told me on the telephone yesterday that my legs will get progressively worse and not better but the Vintage House have just delivered a case of vodka, so not all is lost. Just my memory.

Vera will arrive any minute and tomorrow the Groucho Club are kindly sending someone to help me stagger out for a birthday drink. And as I write this Vera has just appeared and with a birthday present and a card, which is beyond the call of duty for a home help. Her portrait should be on the back of a banknote, but I suppose the Royal Mint will put Julie Burchill there soon. I don't know what the world is coming to and I certainly don't know what is coming to me. But I can guess.

Grandstand view

I daren't have a bath these days for fear of slipping when I get in or out, so I have to get help, otherwise it is a strip wash in front of the basin. Yesterday an old flame came to my flat and bathed me and it took me back thirty-odd years. Looking down at my skeletal frame I asked her, 'Do you recognise this body?' and she said, 'No. I've never seen it before.' It is

very nearly depressing but I am slowly coming to terms with
disability. If she is an old flame then she must regard me as a
dying ember.

Oh well, at least I am not in some ghastly NHS home.
Friends have been good to me recently, keeping me company
and fetching me the odd bits of shopping, and what with Vera
calling in on three mornings a week I am getting used to being
confined to barracks and this isn't a bad one as barracks go.

Now it is five a.m. and soon I shall be helped to the
Groucho Club to get on to the coach for the annual Derby
Day outing. Very soon, I suppose, a few of the Arab owners
will be waking up and licking their lips with anticipation. They
can't seem to go wrong except for the one who sold Dancing
Brave to Japan. Even more disastrous than Charles St George
selling Saumarez to France just weeks before winning the Arc.
Goodbye a few hundred thousand.

Charles took it very well, although I could almost hear him
shrugging when I spoke to him on the telephone the day after
and he was pleased that I had put £50 on Saumarez at 20/1.
On Derby Day in 1979 he slipped a security man a few quid
who then allowed us to watch the race from the grandstand
roof. It was a sight I shall never forget. It was also only a
couple of weeks since I had got married for the final time and
I think that day might have given my wife some inkling of
what she had let herself in for.

Anyway, from where our coach is parked it will be difficult
to see much of the race, but there is always something of a
buzz on the Downs on Derby Day. I shall resist the temptation
to have my fortune read by some phoney gypsy as a lot of
people do. I am afraid I know what my fortune is. And that
has just prompted me to pour the first drink of a long day
although it is still an unearthly hour.

I must say that I wouldn't mind going to Epsom today as a bookmaker. Not many people have enough money to have a serious bet on a red-hot favourite like Tenby (awful place to name a horse after), and it is human nature and folly to try to pick a rank outsider usually. But whatever the result no doubt the enemy will moan and complain that they have suffered large losses.

Sadly, I will not be making a book, although I would dearly love to. I suspect that some of those gypsies on the Downs will be Customs and Excise men in drag. Hopefully some awful member on the coach from the Groucho, an advertising John Major look-alike, may have a portable telephone so that I can get in touch with Victor Chandler, my man on the rails. Otherwise I shall need a runner and I have never seen a member of the Groucho Club run unless it is his or her turn to buy a round of drinks.

But I do look forward to tomorrow, when I shall glue myself to the television set and watch the first Test Match. I have had a basinful of racing which will last me until Royal Ascot and I had to retire hurt from the recent York meeting, although I backed a couple of winners at Sandown Park last Monday. Horses have no regard for one's cardiac problems. Both horses won only by a head.

What I shall miss tomorrow will be the presence of David Gower. Two swallows may not make a summer but one Gower can make my summer. Mind you, it depends what you're swallowing.

Staying the course

The Derby Day outing to Epsom on the Groucho Club coach was a day to remember and I only wish I could remember more of it. The start of it was as awful as Captain Brown's start to the Grand National. I got up at six a.m. to write something and Monica and I needed two or three vodkas to get going. Sometimes she needs oiling. That done there was a champagne breakfast at the club at eight a.m. The bosses didn't offer me a glass, which niggled me slightly although I don't drink the stuff, but I suppose it is on the bill. Never mind. Absolut is excellent.

I told anyone who cared to listen that Commander in Chief would probably win and I think a couple of receptionists who stayed behind backed it. Of course most mug punters backed Fatherland because that man was riding it and, although I mentioned the horse, I had gone right off it when the words were barely out of Monica's big mouth. Fatherland was out of his class.

Once on the coach the drinks appeared as though on a conveyor belt, thanks to the helpful and willing staff. So many people resent their jobs nowadays. Can you imagine the nightmare of going to the Derby on the Dumpling Inn coach and being served by Chinese waiters? Only the Ming could handle it. So for lunch we had fresh salmon followed by strawberries and cream and that is blotting-paper that went to Eton.

Then the racing and the betting commenced. What odd horses the uninitiated back. In fact, there was an American woman on the coach whom I had never seen in the club who irritated me somewhat by picking five out of six winners while not knowing a horse from an ostrich. It is luck enough to be a woman in the first place but that is pushing it. My old friend Gordon from the Coach and Horses whom I had taken had no luck at all, but at least I saw to it that the level in his whisky tumbler didn't fall below the obligatory two fingers. I suppose we must have looked like two old codgers to the others, being as we were firmly stuck to our seats for the entire day. It is a small fringe benefit of drinking spirits that the dehydrating effect enables you to go for hours without having to pee.

But there was one strange bet struck by one of our party, Jim Baker. In the last race he backed all nine runners to win in the hope that the eventual winner would be returned at 8/1 or more. In the event he lost. Oh, lucky Jim. He is best remembered by me for being the man who introduced me to my last wife after a considerable amount of nagging on my part. 'Please introduce me to the woman who owns those legs I keep seeing walking along Old Compton Street,' I used to plead. Pathetic really.

It was an exhausting day, what with the combination of a steady flow of Absolut and the bore of mental arithmetic, working out people's bets. By the time we got back to the Groucho for 'just the one' I was out on my feet. At last I was escorted home and crashed out only to wake up at some unearthly hour bathed in sweat. I had dreamt that Mia Farrow had won custody of me in the High Court. That had me groping in the fridge for ice and more vodka. Should it ever come to it that I get adopted or taken into care I hope to God it is either by Anna Haycraft or Beryl Bainbridge. In either case life would be what racing people call a gas.

Explosive mixture

I should have known that breaking my foot was on the cards when I dropped two lamb chops on the carpet that morning. Usually God's little warnings come by my dropping toast on the floor, marmalade side down. But that Monday was black. At the time of my fall I didn't think much of it but when I woke up in the morning and saw a foot like a purple balloon I was not a little scared wondering whether or not I had got the dreaded diabetic gangrene.

A friend took me to the Middlesex Hospital and even those battle-weary people tut-tutted a bit at the sight of the awful pedal extremity. Anyway, it doesn't pain me any more and I can hobble to and fro from the kitchen dropping chops and chicken legs on my pristine carpet. My new and expensive sofa too is suffering from toast fall-out and cigarette ash, and Vera seems like Canute when she brings out the Hoover.

On the way back from the Middlesex my friend and I stopped in the Groucho Club for just the one and after we had sunk that he walked round the corner to Old Compton Street to get me a taxi to take me the two blocks home. He found one, rather unusually driven by a woman who said to him, 'If it's for that Jeffrey Bernard and he's drunk, I'm not taking him.' Now how on earth could she have guessed it was for me since I was a hundred yards away and well out of sight? It is a mystery to me, as was the fact that I overtipped the old harridan at the end of our brief journey. Since then I have been confined to barracks, so to speak, and have come into my second childhood or dotage.

Thirty years ago when I had a long spell on the wagon I took to making model aeroplanes to while the time away and I have started again. The other day I asked my friend to get me a Fokker DR1 triplane. He somewhat cynically remarked, 'From fucker to Fokker,' but he got it for me. And now I find that I can't put it together because it is so small and my hands shake too much. It should be red like Baron von Richthofen's Fokker but this one is grey and is the model of the triplane flown by Werner Voss, whoever he was. It doesn't matter anyway since my friend was daft enough to forget the glue. What with these shakes I must stick to monoplanes in future and today I shall send him out to buy a Flying Fortress or a Thunderbolt or Spitfire.

If this flat were bigger I would buy a train set and if I could walk I would go to the park to sail model yachts. During the war years I took a particular dislike to a boy who sailed very posh yachts on the Round Pond in Kensington Gardens. I vowed to sink one. To this purpose I designed a torpedo. The warhead was a twelve-bore cartridge with the shot removed and with a small nail directed at the firing cap and it was to be fuelled by sodium. Theoretically it seemed sound and if it failed I could always hit him over the head with a brick when our nannies weren't looking.

Unfortunately sodium is tricky stuff. It doesn't burn from rear to front when contact is made with water, it blows up willy-nilly and anyway is extremely hard to buy or obtain. I had exactly the same trouble when I tried to make nitroglycerine to blow up the London Musical Club in 1944. The nitric acid was hard to come by and anyway you need some fairly sophisticated equipment to remove the residual water from the mixture. I had to make do with firing rockets down the chimney whenever they held parties or dances.

On one magnificent and for all I know spectacular occasion, which I couldn't see since I was on the roof, one of my rockets shot red-hot coke all over the dance floor, sending the slow foxtrot into a quickstep. Oddly enough my mother grassed on me to the police. I think I was a little angry about something in those days and the mood is returning what with my imprisonment here. I may send out the home help soon to buy me some iodine crystals, aluminium filings and ammonia.

Sober in Soho

I was paid a visit yesterday by Vernon Scannell, a good man and an excellent writer, who called with a BBC producer who taped us talking about Fitzrovia in the 1940s and early 1950s. We soon decided that there never was such a place as

Fitzrovia. There was the Fitzroy Tavern and Fitzroy Square, but to all of us it was always Soho, although it lies just a few yards north of Oxford Street.

We reminisced about the people who used to haunt the Black Horse and the Wheatsheaf in what now seems another age. So many of them are now dead, which is not surprising considering its heyday was round about 1948. I was sixteen then and passing myself off to assorted publicans as being of an age to drink legally.

But it was a bad interview on my part and I shall very likely be cut from the programme. I had woken up as sick as a dog with gastritis and had been vomiting on and off for three hours before Vernon turned up, so I didn't dare have a drink and I need exactly three large ones to go on television or the radio. It isn't a question of nerves, it is just that I find it difficult to communicate without oiling my tongue, so to speak.

Anyway, we spent two hours talking about Soho and Fitzrovia and it left me feeling a little depressed. There are parts of the legend I would like to forget. For one thing, most of us were very broke for most of the time. The amount of drinking that went on is greatly exaggerated by writers today. We hardly ever had the money for the hard stuff. Dylan Thomas, for example, drank halves of bitter and so did John Minton. They broke out into whisky rashes later. Nina Hamnet (I had forgotten that she once lived with Modigliani) somehow always managed to have a gin in her hand although she was past work of any kind.

But I preferred the rougher Duke of York which was much more of a sawdust-on-the-floor type pub and not so packed with painters and writers. Quite a good number of Greek Cypriots used the pub and occasionally there would be some horrendous punch-ups. Another hang-out was Tony's Café at

92 Charlotte Street. The café was always changing ownership between Tony and his chef depending on how their games of gin rummy had gone the night before. I can't see that situation now except in Chinatown. Things have quietened down. I can't think of a single person today who could be described, even loosely, as being a Bohemian.

And now the only good baker's shop in Soho has just had to close down because they could no longer afford the rent. In a twinkling of the eye it became a dirty book and video shop. The butcher opposite is also finished. So am I.

Well, nearly. I haven't been out of this flat now for a month. There are very few places you can be pushed to in a wheelchair in this city. For example, the gents in the Groucho Club is in the basement two flights down, and the staircase down to the Academy Club is like a precipice. When I did go out after I broke my hip and my legs gave up, I noticed steps everywhere and very few sloping kerbstones. There are consolations, though, and one of them is Vera arriving like the Queen of Sheba every morning to present me with a cup of tea and a bacon sandwich. I have become addicted to them all.

On the rack

At last I have reached the age where it is almost impossible to be unhappy. It is true that anxiety and boredom walk hand in hand through this flat and nightmares lie waiting in the dark, but love hasn't wrung a tear from these tired eyes for some thirteen years now.

Anyway, I have run out of love and I am far more concerned these days that I might run out of cigarettes. My misery this morning was caused by shirtmakers who make the buttonholes too small for the buttons. And I was not a little irritated to have it confirmed yesterday by my physiotherapist that the foot I broke nearly three months ago was set crooked. The biggest metatarsal sticks out, but at least it doesn't pain me, so I do not intend to have it rebroken and put in plaster for another eight weeks.

And last Sunday was a mess. Hot on the heels of the drama student who was standing in for Vera and who told me she couldn't hoover the sitting-room floor because there was already a plug in the wall socket I had a visit from two schoolgirls who also drove me to distraction and who lit my short fuse.

You would be surprised at some of the people who read the *Spectator*. The first girl, a sixth-former, didn't know how an answerphone works. She buzzed me for an age, went away for a while and came back to do it again. Eventually someone else let her in. When I eventually stopped shouting at her she explained that she didn't know how an answerphone worked because she goes to school in Cumbria.

But the second schoolgirl on Sunday took the biscuit. I asked her, because of my various disabilities, to help me with my supper by seasoning a chicken, putting some butter on it and then banging it in the oven so that I could turn it on later. This she did and later I found that she had put it straight on the rack *without* a baking tray. I burned myself getting it out with one hand while the other hand was holding on to the dresser for support. In the morning, the substitute home help kindly washed the fat off the kitchen floor, and my hand is blistered. As an added bonus she left the milk out of the fridge so I had no tea on Monday morning.

This particular schoolgirl is sweet and sixteen. She is reading for her A-levels and studying history, English, the classics and philosophy. What she ought to be reading is domestic science and learning how to roast a bloody chicken, but I suppose we should be grateful for the fact that she is not studying nuclear physics or medicine. What bombs, what crooked bones we could expect then.

And now Monica is at death's door and I am a little distraught. The typewriter mechanic who called said there was very little life left in her, but worse still she has no sisters because electric typewriters are obsolete and they only make electronic jobs now. How I curse modern technology. If any London reader knows where I could get a replacement I would be grateful and relieved to know. I cannot work much that is modern and I am still not yet on intimate terms with my microwave.

But where shall I bury Monica? I don't think she deserves a rubbish tip and I think I shall get someone to bury her with full honours, whatever they are, in Soho Square. Another marriage ended.

Lesser evils

How odd it is that one of the few bits of Latin that I can remember from my schooldays, 'Iam veniat tacito curva senecta pede' – 'Then came bent old age with crooked foot' – should have at last become so applicable. I am also reminded, when I see my face in the shaving mirror, that 'Seges est ubi Troia erat'.

But the crooked foot annoys me. I suppose I shall never be able to wear a left shoe again. My piffling accidents turn out to be mini-disasters. I am going away for the day next week and that means I have to find an escort to take me from this flat and put me on the train itself at Paddington. God knows how I shall get back.

That is just one complaint of the week. The other is the implication behind my being asked to review a book about vice. I am glad of the work, of course, but why me? It is true I like a drink, enjoy a day at the races and get great pleasure from the company of women, but I don't think that is deserving of being typecast as some sort of monster, which is what I am told I am.

But whether or not something or other is a vice depends very largely on just who you are. The royal family's days at the races, Sir Winston Churchill's brandy-swigging and Errol Flynn's womanising are and were regarded with great affection by most people, even envy and admiration. At what point do these things become vices and not games that people play? Well, when they are too good for the servants, for a start. It was all right for Edward VII to be an adulterer. One of the Queen's trainers, long since gone, was once overheard to remark that racing was far too good for the working classes and that only he, his ilk and the royal family should be allowed to watch it. But I suppose the working classes would be allowed to go to Southwell on a wet Monday afternoon to watch a few selling platers getting bogged down in the old days.

And it was always all right for the man wearing a top hat and carrying a cane, so beloved by the music hall, to be so drunk he had to hold on to a lamp post for support, but never come back from lunch and tell the boss what you think of him. I did that once or twice in bygone days and now look at me. I must say that Harry Evans was remarkably tolerant towards me when he was editor of the *Sunday Times* and after I had called him by a rude name. I saw him the following day and he simply said, 'Swear at me if you must, but please don't in front of my secretary.'

Of course the business of being typecast is originally self-inflicted and God knows I have written about drinking enough, but from thereon the exaggerations blossom like something tropical and well-watered. I have heard at least six versions of why it was that I got the sack from the *Sporting Life* in 1971, the most extraordinary one of the selection being that one day I put my genitals on the editor's secretary's desk.

The truth of many matters is far too boring for some. In fact, I was simply drunk when it came to giving an after-dinner speech at one of the *Life*'s soirées for the denizens of National Hunt racing. It is true that I once phoned the same story over to them three times in one afternoon from Newmarket, but I would call that an instinctive dedication to duty come what may. So now I have ended up by having to write about vice while I know of seriously evil men who go undetected in Fleet Street.

I should have gone to live in Ireland years ago. They know the difference there between the sound of a man having a gargle and the sound of a rattlesnake winding up to strike. And that reminds me of the good news this week: *Jeffrey Bernard is Unwell* is being put on in Dublin in January, with Dennis Waterman in the title role. We live again.

Visiting hours

My doctor, a good Irishwoman, spent all of half an hour in this flat yesterday. That is quite a hefty chunk in a day in the life of a GP. It seems that my nervous system is in tatters and that I must stop sitting on my sofa and staring at the sky and get out and about more before atrophy sets in.

She says that this sitting about all day is a form of depression. I am not so sure. I think I am at last bored and up to here with what is downstairs and outside. Mind you, children confuse boredom and depression because at an early age they don't understand what depression means. Since I know almost exactly what is going on and being said in my old haunts it matters not a lot. My precious visitors are my lifelines. Even the district nurses.

Yesterday, Christine, who owns my favourite Chinese restaurant, the Ming, came up with some orange chicken and mixed vegetables and in passing told me that she had been brought up in Hong Kong a Protestant. In spite of being aware of missionaries it hadn't really occurred to me that anyone Chinese could swallow the Bible. Deborah came along too, having been given a leave pass (compassionate?) by Richard Ingrams, and Irma Kurtz arrived with some grub for me having been to our only fishmonger for miles. And the postman brought me two postcards from the Duchess.

Vera is away on holiday this week, but Juanita comes every morning and sets me thinking of the Fisherman's Bar in Barbados where she comes from and where the fishermen play dominoes, banging them down so hard it makes the windows rattle. The flowers that Sue Townsend brought me last week are now dead but I still keep them on the table as a souvenir of sorts of a visit from a delightful woman. It is good to know Sue, Alice Thomas Ellis and Beryl Bainbridge. They are so much nicer than hackettes. Then, on Saturday mornings, my friend Bill who I was in the drying-out bin with twenty years ago calls in and my brother Bruce comes along to tell me that he can only stay for three minutes. Sometimes my daughter Isabel comes along and cooks me lunch. With all of that who needs to be pushed along Old Compton Street in a wheelchair?

I must say, though, that I would like to be reminded of what a tree looks like and I wouldn't mind being escorted to Ireland or Barbados either. Meanwhile, readers have responded very kindly to my request for a replacement for Monica who is in intensive care and slipping away. This could be her last bit of work. If she doesn't want to go on I suppose that is my fault. She never got around to writing a novel. But I can't sit here moping, so I shall pour myself a vodka and ponder the amount of the stuff the medical profession think excessive.

The medical establishment's hysteria about drinking will soon be on a par with the hysteria about smoking. I think it was Mrs Thatcher who pronounced in so many words, shortly after she came to power, that it was obligatory that we should all live for ever, but that would be extremely expensive and mean that one day I would be sharing my bachelor pad with about twenty geriatrics. No thanks. We should be allowed to fade away like Sue Townsend's flowers have done.

And I have been told that an aspirin in the vase will keep flowers going longer and with that in mind I have wondered whether to lace my drinks with Baby Bio, the stuff that feeds plants. I certainly shouldn't mind looking as healthy as my palm tree. My rose tree is dead, as is my fern, and perhaps the liveliest thing in this flat is my plaster bust of Nelson.

The unkindest cut of all

I have been brooding about the man whose wife cut off his penis and I have been doing my brooding with my legs crossed. Thank God I don't live in America. The cheering of American females came across the Atlantic after the deed was done and it is still ringing in my ears. Even the few harridans who have visited me these past few days have had a spring in their step.

But there are aspects of this penisectomy which puzzle and intrigue me. The husband has been found not guilty of rape. If he had been guilty then he should have been punished severely, but I think that parting him from his member was a little over the top. The man must be a fool as well. If a woman climbed into my bed with an eight-inch kitchen knife I think I would get the hint. It would be a clue of sorts, anyway.

Then, why did she drive off with the severed organ? She could have flushed it away or given it to the dog, but she drove off with it and threw it in some long grass, wasting valuable police time in the search for it. Apparently a severed penis will last for eighteen hours if it is kept cold. Don't I know. You could add a few weeks to that. But while he waited in the hospital for the wretched thing to be returned it seems that he bumped into an old chum and they fell into conversation. He should have been bleeding to death, but luckily for him a clot formed which saved him. But to stop for a chat in that condition does, you must admit, take some balls.

A couple of surgeons who must be quite brilliant managed to sew it back on and it is to be hoped that they sewed it back the right way round. My man at the Middlesex Hospital would have put a titanium plate in it as he did my hip to make sure it couldn't happen again. But what with the nerves having been severed the idiot will get no joy when he next pulls it out for a trial run and it serves him right. Mind you, his wife should have left him and gone back to Ecuador. Her drastic measures speak volumes for the Latin temperament.

Women here, though, don't need knives. I know female scribblers who can emasculate a man with one withering glance of contempt. But a major worry and anxiety for me now is that when it is my turn for an old flame to perform a penisectomy on me it will not be sewn back on because I am a smoker and we know how doctors feel about helping smokers. Oddly enough, Central Television telephoned yesterday to ask me if I would consider going on a show in which they are to discuss teenage smoking. I said I would but mulling it over in my mind last night I have decided that I would have little contribution to make to the show. I do think that smoking is silly and bad, but I also think that telling people what they can and cannot do is wrong in some ways. The Government's aim to keep everyone alive for ever while at the same time ruining the National Health Service is a mad contradiction.

Edwina Currie was bad enough, but she has nothing on the awful Virginia Bottomley, who would have made an excellent health minister in the Third Reich, although storm troopers were notoriously heavy smokers. She would willingly throw a bucketful of penises into the long grass like the Ecuadorian wife and we would all end up grovelling in that long grass arguing about which one belonged to whom. In that event there would be some whopping lies told, with Norman probably foolishly laying claim to a large black job. Yes, I fear the lady from Ecuador might have started a new fashion which will become all the rage.

Bed of nettles

Ten days ago I was flattened by one of the infections that are doing the rounds. It was and is a particularly virulent one and it called for a week in bed with hardly a visitor and only Vera keeping the teapot hot and bothered.

The only thing that aroused me from my semi-coma was a piece in *The Times* about the unfortunate Marquess of Bristol. I feel sorry for the man. The English man-in-the-street won't, however, since he is largely envious, vindictive and punitive. Bristol got through £7 million, lost an annual income of £350,000 and had to sell the splendid house at Ickworth.

That mess has been attributed to his taking drugs and I don't believe it is as simple as that. I certainly don't believe that keeping him in the company of prison warders for ten months will be of much help to him. I also read that he was made to wear long white gloves as a child and was forbidden to eat in the company of his parents. I read more into those two facts than just the print itself. You get a whiff of his upbringing if you stop thinking about retribution for a moment.

And now it is the turn of the Prince of Wales to get some stick. That man in the street again knows what is best for the royals. He knows little about himself, would not even understand the recent Budget but, by jingo, he knows what is best for other people. It is a mercy that there aren't more referendums in this country. They would be hanging children.

But now, sitting up in bed with my nose running and unable to stop coughing in my fifth week on the wagon, I still can't stop thinking about this Marquess of Bristol. I thought my own childhood was a bed of nettles, but it must have been a rose garden. I know that at school they thought I would go what they called to the bad and you don't need £7 million for that, but I am glad I fooled them and only skated on the fringe of disaster.

What, I wonder, will the man do when he comes out? I have smoked a hundred cigarettes pondering that one. There is nothing quite so daunting and boring as a new leaf. I have turned over more of them than I care to remember, starting the day after I lost the first advance I ever had on a book at roulette in ten minutes thirty years ago. Oddly enough, the book, *Soho Night and Day*, done with Frank Norman, was published and I heard to my amazement that a shop in Charing Cross Road was asking £60 for a secondhand copy of it last week. Who knows, it may become a collector's item.

It doesn't matter and won't do me any good anyway, and neither will the visit from the district nurse I am expecting at any minute. She is coming to help me in and out of the bath and it is a racing certainty that I will catch another cold and have a relapse in spite of the central heating. When she last came here she asked me about the play opening in Dublin next month and in an aside she remarked that although she liked Dennis Waterman she couldn't fancy him because he was too old. That brought me down a bit, since I am sure Dennis can't be more than forty-six. Not much anyway. So what does that make me? I know I have no legs, a broken hip and a broken foot but my heart still beats and my GP vouched for that yesterday.

And I am to eat as much as possible. Red meat is the order of the day and as I chew the sirloin my thoughts turn yet again to the Marquess of Bristol, feeding, I suppose, on porridge. My brother, who has done time for his CND activities, says they don't put enough salt into prison porridge. If that is so I hope Bristol sends it back.

Scratched from all engagements

I was amazed and deeply touched last week by a visit from Peter O'Toole himself. I never thought the great man would bother but he appeared on Wednesday afternoon all smiles and with a bottle of Bollinger in case, as he put it, I was in need of a bubble. An old windbag, a hip replacement patient – why do these people talk so much? Perhaps they are not ill enough to shut up – introduced herself and started talking to Peter. At the end of her chattering she said, taking her leave, how thrilled she would be to be able to tell her friends that she had met Richard Harris.

Peter insisted on coming down to watch me in the gym being put through my agonising exercises by the physiotherapist. He seemed to be very curious about my struggles at hopping along between parallel bars and he asked the physio some most technical questions about amputations. My stump seemed to interest him although the sight of it makes me feel deeply depressed. When we came back to my room a young woman from the University of East Anglia presented herself and me with some beautiful lilies which must have made quite a hole in her student's grant. She said that she had always wanted to meet me because she is a reader of this column, and meanwhile Peter persuaded her that he was my brother. She swallowed that and would have taken any other bait flowing about that day.

The next day I came back down to earth with a ghastly visit by ambulance to the Charing Cross Hospital in Fulham to be measured up for an artificial leg. They took a cast of what is left of me, which they said was pretty good going on a first visit since it showed that I was healing well and quickly. These legs I saw looked to be fairly cumbersome and I am sure I will make the most awful clumping sound when I learn to stagger around my old haunts again. But at the moment I sit here thinking, as I chain-smoke and stare out of the window, that I will never ever return to those places. It has taken years, but at last I think pubs bore me. It is a pity that half the membership of the Groucho Club – more than half in the evenings – bore me too. So perhaps home really is where the heart is and always was.

I was reminded of it last week by a visit from my last wife and it made me think what else I have thrown away apart from an old leg. And now the council want me to reconstruct my bathroom so that I can manoeuvre my wheelchair in it. This will cost me an arm but not, I hope, a leg. And I get no grant from them, in fact a private surveyor is going to charge £40 an hour to look the place over. I shall now sit in a shower when once I lay soaking in hot baths nursing ice-cold vodka and orange as I simmered away. That wretched blister I got

on my foot some three months ago will have cost me dear by
the time Derby Day comes round again, and by that time I
will have been, as my trainer might say, 'scratched from all
further engagements'. Which reminds me, if a horse had to
survive on what I eat it wouldn't win a lot. There is a limit to
how much mincemeat and scoops of mashed potatoes a man
can swallow. But at least I have been given permission to have
the odd nightcap. I would like more than the odd one, but
the idea of facing the gym and my physio with a hangover of
sorts is too much to bear the thought of. Completely legless is
something else.

My fellow inmates

I was re-apprehended last week by two storm-troopers
claiming to be ambulance men after three weeks of having
been AWOL from the Middlesex Hospital. They caught me
in flagrante in bed with pancreatitis and there was no escaping.

They took me first to the casualty department at University
College Hospital where, thanks to the awful Virginia Bottomley,
I had to wait on a stretcher in a corridor for five hours before
getting a bed, and another two hours before getting a shot
of the mighty painkiller, pethidine. For three days and three
nights I retched and would have given another limb to have
been able to vomit successfully.

As luck would have it, the miraculous Messrs. Cobb and
Sweetman of titanium fame walked past my stretcher, and
I yelled and they promised to rescue me and move me to
their workshop in the Middlesex. Their ward is run by Sister
Sally who looked after me and befriended me two years ago
when I broke my hip. My pancreas stopped screaming after
a while and as I was on the mend I got the shock horror of

my life when I passed a pint of what looked like claret into a urine bottle. The staff thought nothing of it, but I haven't had such a scare since almost the same thing happened after a lovely Sunday lunch with the Courtaulds once when Philippa Courtauld served a delicious meal that included hot beetroot.

And then a most horribly self-important businessman with a broken leg was put alongside me. He spent all day on a portable telephone talking pompously to his secretary. He reminded me of some of the people that I've listened to in disgusting provincial hotels who are nearly always reps selling anything from ladies' bloomers to garden gates and who put on the airs and graces of managing directors.

In contrast there was a very nice old lady on the other side of me who works in the British Library by King's Cross. She has a fascinating theory that the library has been built over an enormous German Second World War bomb, a posthumous calling card from the Luftwaffe.

Another saviour on that ward, a male nurse, Roger, saw the pained look on my face although he was giving me pethidine every four hours, and twigged that our businessman was boring the arse off me and he kindly moved me to a bed at the end of the ward situated opposite two old dears suffering from dementia who talked all night in their sleep. I had been warned about them but at lights out I pricked up my ears and spent an age listening to what you could call a better programme than *Book at Bedtime*. One of them was the unconscious narrator of what I was certain was her autobiography. She started with, 'Daddy, Daddy,' in a pleading voice then she went on, 'Oh Betty, how could you, Daddy will kill you if he finds out... Come in out of the rain, George... you revolting man. Go outside if you want to do that... you think you can come round here and knock on my door any time you want something.' And so on. The woman in the next bed who was, I guess, Viennese and also suffering from a sort of dementia, insisted with old-world charm in trying to pay and tip a nurse for giving her two sleeping pills.

Anyway, by the time you read this, Mr Cobb will have given me a few more weeks' leave before rearresting me and I shall be at home writing my *Good Hospital Guide*. The Middlesex gets four stars in spite of the fact that Mr Cobb has failed to return the leg I lent him, but the nurses are amazingly kind. How hospitals have changed since 1965, the first time I ever suffered from pancreatitis. It is now mixed wards, Christian names and cups of tea whenever you want them. There seems to be no restriction these days on the amount of visitors one is allowed to have. Last night on our smoking landing I counted twenty-two Jamaicans and it was like a carnival in Kingston. No wonder, the bastards have won the Test Series.

The Bottomley line

The media have the natural knack of making anything, however awful, however serious, however tragic, into a bloody bore unless, with some exceptions, the events are taking place on one's own doorstep. I now switch off the news when it concerns Ulster or what was Yugoslavia, although I am aware of the misery and unhappiness generated by both theatres.

It is quite selfish of me, but I react more nowadays to news of the disgusting Virginia Bottomley. Two weeks ago I waited for no less than five hours on a stretcher in casualty before seeing a doctor. People have died in corridors waiting for attention, so it is not to be wondered at that such matters should be uppermost in my mind in spite of ever-present death in Ulster and Sarajevo.

Party politics in this country don't just bore me, though, they make me sick. I shall never bother to vote again. Somebody in the *Observer* once wrote that I use the word 'boredom' too readily but most of life is a bore. As Maurice Richardson once said to me, as he turned the pages of *The Times*, barely glancing at the obituary page, 'Even death has lost its charm for me.'

I have to admit to rather liking the obituary page, but then I always did like reading biographies. I still have a yen to read my own obituary, which I am told has been written by a friend for the *Daily Telegraph*. I am sure it is bitchy and will be full of words like 'convivial', meaning alcoholic. It was said of the late Lord Rosebery that he did not suffer fools gladly. In fact he was the most overbearing, irascible, bad-tempered bully that ever rode to his wretched hounds. I wonder how Virginia Bottomley's obituary will read. Not that I wish her dead but just to suffer a little. To this end I would willingly marry her.

For some strange reason it reminds me that, were I not writing to you today, I am supposed to be collecting the finished artificial leg this morning from Charing Cross Hospital. There will be less excuse for lying about watching the wretched news on television. We need another government scandal to keep the smiles on our faces and it is high time a female MP was caught with her hand in the till. Virginia Bottomley's scandalous behaviour is not rated as a scandal and a few people dying from waiting for attention is not really newsworthy.

Neither is it newsworthy to tell you that I have been invited by the Oxford Union to speak to them next month. They tell me that past speakers have included President Reagan and Mother Teresa. Following Reagan doesn't worry me in the slightest, but how the hell do you follow Mother Teresa? I have nothing to say and I am not given to lectures, so I hope I can kick off by getting the undergraduates to fire some pertinent questions at me. Apparently it was their idea to ask me and the only thing that worries me is that I shall have to come off the wagon to get hold of some Dutch courage. It annoys me that I sometimes feel almost inferior because of never having been to even a red-brick university. I'm not quite sure why that should be, because the world is full of idiots who went to universities, but I suppose I regret having spent too many years in prep schools and at Pangbourne thinking about sex instead of working. Not that I would have read English. I can think of better things to do than spend three years writing essays about *Pride and Prejudice*, but it would have been nice to have won a blue at something or other, even Monopoly. When I spoke to one of the biggest schools in England at Sevenoaks, the headmaster gave me one glass of sherry. I hope that the Oxford Union cellar runs a little deeper than that. I shall certainly drink to forget the entire episode when I get home.

My Oxford day

I spoke to the Oxford Union last Tuesday and I wasn't very pleased with myself, although the organisers and the undergraduates who questioned me seemed satisfied enough. Before going into the library to speak, Robert Palmer, the vice-president, took me into a bar where I wouldn't have minded sitting all day, although most of the talk I overheard was about politics. Is there no escaping that boring subject in watering holes? Never mind, I wasn't there for the conversation only some Dutch courage.

The library in which I spoke is a lovely round room with a ceiling decorated by pre-Raphaelite artists. I started off by telling them that I had absolutely nothing whatsoever to say to them and that unless they wanted forty-five minutes of silence then they had better start by asking me some questions, which they did. At first I was nervous of the young women in the audience and I thought they might start sniping at me because of my past record with the female sex. But since nearly all of them were *Spectator* readers and know that this is where I hang out the dirty washing every week they were very friendly and quite delightful. In fact no one took a metaphorical swing at me and I was grateful for that. They asked me a load of questions about journalism, Soho, drinking, my family and marriage. I think I may have caused a tiny bit of antipathy when I said that I thought nearly all poets are mad and then, when asked to name my heroes, I included Byron in the list. But then I hardly ever think of Byron the poet, but nearly always Byron the hero. All this waffle went on for quite some time and it was the first time I have not resented being in a No Smoking area, but then the vice-president rescued me halfway through the talk by fetching me a large vodka and soda.

At the end of it I would guess that I didn't get as many laughs as President Reagan and Mother Teresa must have got, but I must have got as many as my predecessor – I noticed in the visitor's book that it had been Yehudi Menuhin and he is a dour character who is, among other things, a health food fanatic. Thank God Jane Fonda doesn't play the violin.

Anyway, after a couple more drinks, Robert Palmer kindly took me to a very pleasant restaurant for lunch. It is called Gee's and is housed in a conservatory. I would like to live in a conservatory and then be reincarnated as a lizard living on the edge of the Mediterranean. But Gee's is worth a visit if ever you're in Oxford.

One of the blessings of that day, apart from the hospitality, was the fact that the only person who did not want to speak was the taxi driver who brought me to and from home. One and a quarter hours in a taxi held prisoner by a football fan or a Tory-voting driver can be sheer hell, but the man on Tuesday was as miserable a bastard as was his passenger.

I really must sit down one day and write a speech concerning something other than Soho. I sometimes think that perhaps Soho is all that there has been to my life in which case it isn't surprising that it is a bit of a mess. Still, how much worse it would have been to have been educated in Chelsea. It isn't just aging that makes me think these places were better many years ago. It is the awful decline of the quality of life itself and I feel pretty sure that favourite places like Bangkok and Barbados have also been on the skids even without the help, as in the case of Soho, of the awful Paul Raymond. I live in dread of him buying my block from the Westminster Council and putting all the rents up to £1500 per week.

Rocky rides

The girl I am dictating this to is about to go to university to read English. I can't think of anything more boring, except for reading physics, than to be force-fed on the likes of Virginia Woolf or even Thomas Hardy.

Once upon a time, I regarded going to Oxbridge as the acme of a young man's life, but then I was still under the influence of *A Yank at Oxford*, starring Robert Taylor as the all-conquering undergraduate, athletic, handsome and a dab hand at sticking chamber pots on the top of church steeples. I thought it was all punting down the river through the waterlilies and scoring a century at Lord's in the Varsity match. Work never crossed my mind and, anyway, I wouldn't have had the self-discipline to do much of it, left to my own devices. Thinking about it now, I have a hunch that it might be more interesting to read anthropology than Henry James. I don't know of much work more tedious than reviewing a book that one doesn't want to read in the first place, but it is useful work and cannot be turned down.

And today could prove to be hard work as I have to entertain an American ex-girlfriend whom I first met on a freebie trip up the Norwegian fjords on a luxury cruise liner. She was the only American on the ship without a blue rinse and the only one not so greedy as to queue up for a second breakfast. That sort of thing explains why so many Americans have got excessively fat arses. She said I first came to her attention because I was just about the only passenger to be seen sitting in the ship's bar. She said the same thing again a year later when she cleverly fixed up for us to have four days going up the Mississippi from New Orleans to Memphis, Tennessee, on a paddle-steamer. Before that I stayed in her house just outside Boulder, Colorado, where we had some great screaming matches that must have been heard from one end of the Rockies to the other.

Most of my biggest and best rows have started in the kitchen and not, as you might think, in the bedroom. One day she got quite hysterical when I ground out a cigarette with my heel in the middle of a field and, somewhat over the top, she screamed that I could set the entire state of Colorado on fire. On another occasion, there were screams and tears when I reacted to being called an English pig because I don't like my bacon to be crispy as all Americans do. In the end, she would drive me into Boulder, deposit me in the bar and leave me there all day until she was ready to collect me in the evening. We only had one row in New Orleans and that was thankfully drowned by the ubiquitous jazz. Looking over the battlefield at Vicksburg I had another row, this one with the woman guide who, like a lot of other Southerners, described it almost as a Confederate victory, and it took an Englishman to put her right about one of Ulysses S. Grant's greatest victories. Some Americans are still fighting that civil war, particularly rednecks. Ten years ago, she came to visit me in London. She could barely afford the return fare and I was yet again in the Middlesex Hospital, in and out of comas and suffering from pneumonia. The temporary impotence that caused me annoyed her far more than me not liking her crispy bacon in Boulder, and we ended up having yet another row. And now this morning she phoned me out of the blue and is coming here for a third-rate lunch that would not satisfy a greedy American.

As it is Rory Knight Bruce is here to inspect my flat for the *Evening Standard*. The sainted Vera has only to have left the premises for five minutes and it is somehow like a flat in which the IRA have thrown a party. When the American lady appears later I shall be able to find out whether or not these walls are scream proof. But she is a good woman and she turned the boredom of that giant mud slick called the Mississippi into something of a private party. It was good for a while to be called a Huckleberry Finn.

One-legged nightmare

I was interviewed three times last week and I should be pleased to be flavour of the month, so to speak, but I found it very embarrassing, and the questions put to me simply served as a reminder of what a narrow life I lead. Racehorses, vodka, Soho and a sprinkling of disgruntled women seem to be the ingredients of a life made even more boring by the fact that at last, after five months, I am getting desperately fed up with existing on one leg.

Yesterday, my wheelchair got stuck in the narrow doorway of my kitchen and I could have screamed. I am also wondering where the ladies are who I was told would still like me for myself – horror of horrors – and not give a fig about my only having one leg, or at least one and a half legs.

Anyway, Paul Callan came up here from Classic FM to record an edition of *Celebrity Choice*. It was much the same as the *Desert Island Discs* I did with Sue Lawley three years ago, but this time I included Elgar's Cello Concerto. Callan kindly brought with him some excellent claret plus a bottle of Absolut vodka, which I think is the best. I heard the programme last Sunday at noon and was fairly embarrassed. I didn't realise I had a radio voice which consists of talking proper.

Then a nice bloke from the *Telegraph*, Robert Philip, a sports writer from Glasgow, arrived to question me on the eve of Royal Ascot about my likes and dislikes on the Turf, and how big a fool I have made of myself. Philip also brought with him some excellent claret, but I do wish newspapers and the BBC would get it into their heads that I don't pay the rent or the shopping with bottles of booze.

I also have the feeling, and it made me quite paranoid, that press photographers quite delight in the fact that I now look like the physical has-been that I am, and now I dread the *Evening Standard*'s forthcoming piece about this flat which is more like a prison in which the food and drink is better than Dartmoor and in which I am allowed to smoke. This old lag no longer puts many bums on the sitting-room seats. The committee downstairs thinks otherwise. I call them the committee and what they are are mostly a few harridans and a couple of men who are residents of this block and who sit about just inside the front door in the hallway. They sit in judgement. My niece tells me that when she was let in the other day by one of them,

she was asked, 'Who do you want to see?' and when she said
'Jeffrey Bernard' the reply was, 'Bloody hell, this place is getting
like Lourdes.' A slight exaggeration.

The fact that I write this a couple of days before Royal
Ascot reminds me of the awful behaviour of some busybody
concerned with the Westminster Health Authority. Apparently,
this man followed one of our angelic District Nurses on her
rounds one day and then reported her to those on high for
having gone into a betting shop on her travels. He claimed
that she spent all of four minutes in there and, apart from
the fact that she may have been putting a bet on for one of
the people she cared for, there is no law against going into a
betting shop, neither is it unethical.

That in turn reminds me of being watched by the Customs
and Excise people for six weeks when I was illegally taking bets
in the Coach and Horses. Surveillance is an expensive business
and on Saturdays I presume it pays time and a half. There is a
betting shop next door to my front door and it wouldn't surprise
me if one of the people downstairs on the committee is a grass.

Not in front of the nurses

Unhappiness is one of the best kept secrets in the world,
although sometimes the truth is blurted out by people having
nervous breakdowns and becoming insane.

I thought about it a lot last week on my fourth and very
nearly my most depressing visit to the Middlesex Hospital this
year, which is why I was away last week. Hot weather abroad
is to be savoured and soaked up, but here that recent spell of it
ruined my appetite and I went three days without a bite to eat.
In the end, I had to phone the police in the middle of the night
to come and bring me some insulin from the sitting-room to

my bed just ten yards away. They thought I looked so awful that they sent for an ambulance and thus it was that I ended up in the Middlesex's worst ward contemplating the misery I mentioned at the beginning of this column. It was the same ward that discharged me too quickly in January, saying that the infection in my right foot was cured, only for Mr Cobb to add it to his collection two weeks later.

Last week was the first time I have had a proper row in a hospital. I got more than a little angry when they kept ignoring the same infection I now have in my left foot, inaccurately nowadays described by the medical profession as being my 'good' leg. I raised my voice to the staff sister and said to her, 'You have been promising to clean and redress my foot for three hours now. What the hell is going on?' At the time, she was remaking an empty bed. I said, 'For fuck's sake, do something about it.' She said, 'Look here, Mr Bernard, we've had a very busy morning and two patients have nearly died since breakfast.' I said, 'I'm not in the least bit fucking surprised.' She came back with some nonsense about not swearing in front of her students and I said that if they were grown up and going to become nurses they had better get used to the occasional swear word and I told her she also should never go to the cinema again or watch television after nine p.m. if so-called bad language upset her too much. And I also said that I wanted to hang on to my left foot and leg although they didn't help the spontaneity of life that I used to enjoy so much.

The smoking area, the landing by the lifts, was just as it always has been for years, but with a different cast. These horribly regular visits to the Middlesex are becoming like quarterly outings to see *The Mousetrap*. The dialogue is always the same, as are the characters. There is always the stoic making light of having cancer – the poor sod on this occasion had carcinoma of the oesophagus – and all those awful old women with tarty nighties designed for the young are still sitting about like old dragons who have had their teeth pulled and whose flames have been snuffed out. How odd it is that the only nice doctors there are Mr Cobb's team who are collecting pieces of me bit by bit. Mr Sweetman, Mr Cobb's registrar, came to see me a few times to see if I was all right and I was rather touched considering I wasn't one of his patients this time. And now I'm home again and have finally lost faith with Prozac and all the other wretched pills that are supposed to stop you from feeling wretched. I repeat to nit-picking readers that I have barely an ounce of self-pity but it does depress and irritate me to think that I can't simply get up, walk across the room and open or close a window.

Another thing I find depressing is the business of Taki's yacht having been blown up in Piraeus by some lunatic shit. The fact that Taki is not short of a few shillings does not diminish the plain nastiness of the deed and, anyway, to blow up a really beautiful yacht is as pig-ignorant as slashing any work of art except for one entered to win the Turner prize. My own wild guess is that the yacht was sunk with envy being the main ingredient of the deed. It so often is the motivation and I even have friends who can't bear the odd occasions when life is going smoothly for me. Well, they needn't feel envious at the moment and a couple of them will be pleased to hear that I sent a shirt to the laundry last week that had £100 in the pocket. Just another one of God's custard pies.

More sex, please

A certain amount of loneliness is beginning to creep into my life – very different from being alone, which I like – and it has prompted me to put an advertisement into the personal columns of this journal stating quite simply, 'Alcoholic, diabetic amputee seeks sympathy fuck.' I'm not sure that our editor would wear this final 'cry for help' and I suppose that anyone who might answer it would be as daft as a brush.

I have been pushed out this week a couple of times and have to run the gauntlet of banter from the barrow boys in the market, usually about the prettiness of my nurses who do the pushing. Little do they know what bossy boots these pretty girls mostly are. They usually dump me in the Groucho Club and it is there, while sipping Absolut vodka, that I torture myself talking to and looking at two beautiful women, one of them a customer and the other a manager, and pointlessly wonder what might have been. A fruitless pastime.

It amazes me that Charlie Chaplin was able to bed such beauties in his seventies, especially considering that he wasn't very funny. Perhaps I am now considered to be harmless but it was quite a lot of fun, some time ago, to be dangerous.

And talking of sipping Absolut, the English agents for the stuff invited me to be one of the judges in a cocktail-making competition, the contestants being twenty-two cocktail barmen from all over London. I was well aware that it could have been both foolish and dangerous for me to accept the invitation and that my pancreas might scream at the touch of just one of them. So I determined to take the smallest of sips – enough just to taste the mixtures – and that way thought I might get away with it. But, however small the sips, just imagine drinking twenty-two cocktails, some of them quite foul, on the trot. Also, thanks to being stuck in my wheelchair and considering the length of the queue at the barbecue, I went all day without a bite, which was stupid for a diabetic.

With no more than three exceptions that I can think of, the cocktail is a fairly disgusting invention. Anyway the next day I was sick as a dog. Surprise, surprise. Perhaps it served me right for attempting to go slightly bent and award too high marks to the Groucho Club barman simply because he's a kind, helpful young man who lifts me up the two steps into the bar. Then two days later, Smirnoff sent me the gift of a bottle of their new black label vodka, because a picture of me appeared in the *Evening Standard* with a bottle of their stuff in the foreground. I haven't tried it yet and I may at last have lost my nerve since those twenty-two successive cocktails.

It occurs to me, while I am polishing off the last of their red label vodka, that I should make more use of my friend, Irma Kurtz, who comes to see me every so often. She is, after all, an agony aunt and although I am not in agony but just discomfort, I should make more use of her advice. Francis Bacon once put it in a nutshell when he advised me, 'Just regard everything as being totally unimportant.' That was bullshit though and there were many things that he regarded as having great importance and significance and not only his work. Perhaps Irma and I should swap problems although I don't think she has many, but how does anyone ever know about anyone else? Perhaps I should set up as an agony uncle except for the fact that the people who edit and run magazines, particularly women's ones, have the idea that men don't have any problems. They should be in my boot.

And now, to get my daily dose of injustice, I shall get the sainted Vera to push me to the Groucho Club so that I can look yet again at those young women who have the bad judgment to consort with advertising agency creeps. Bitter? No more than angostura.

Afternoon men

Nothing has happened here during last week of the slightest interest to me, except for a visit from yet another nutcase who wants to write yet another biography of me. One is enough in any language and I am sick at the idea of going through, yet again, one of the most boring stories I can think of; that of my life. I could dislocate a jaw with yawning at the idea of it.

The would-be biographer is called Jeremy Lamb and he recently wrote an excellent book called *So Idle a Rogue – the Life and Death of Rochester*. I have already pointed out to Mr Lamb that it will be a waste of his time since he'll be lucky to sell a dozen copies of this book, but he is determined to go ahead with it. It is a big jump from the great Lord Rochester with whom I have nothing in common, not even the ability to write erotic verse or to have ulcers in my bladder, which took the great man away in the most agonising way. But *So Idle a Rogue* is highly recommended and I wish he'd saved that title for his book about me.

Idle is the key word, since I have done nothing since 8 February when Mr Cobb carved me up. Sometimes I get pushed around the corner to the Groucho Club to have a drink amongst those dreadful businessmen I call 'the suits'. But at least the club no longer allows portable telephones in the bar, and so now all that it remains for the club to do is to withdraw members' rights to talk business and shop in the club, when they should be renting offices for that. The last straw was seeing the other day an advertising bore with a word processor on his table. Such people would be as nothing without their gadgets and dreadful television commercial scripts.

But on my last visit to the Groucho there was so trivial an episode that irked and depressed me so much that I am almost ashamed to mention it. I was talking to one of the more attractive female members of the staff and she began with some harmless banter about how we should elope together – presumably at my expense. The next day she said, 'Think of all the money we could make from the most awful of the tabloid newspapers. I can see their headlines now, "Attractive young woman elopes with old man."' The more I thought about it, the more it annoyed me. Old is seventy plus and I am sixty-two turning sixteen in my head. What's more, I am only dead from the knees down, whereas most of the women involved in the Groucho are dead from the neck up.

Such is life nowadays, but I can actually sit on my sofa all day when I don't have friendly visitors and waste my time brooding about such unimportant things. It is, I suppose, symptomatic of the boredom I am feeling and which will eventually drive me out of this country for a while, even if it means being stranded in a bar for a few days unable to push myself up a couple of steps to a lavatory. My ex-wife, who lives in Majorca, has invited me out there for a few days and says she will look after me. God knows why she should want to stir up old memories, and she was quoted in a magazine last week quite inaccurately as having said, 'Jeff only behaved so badly all those years ago to test me to see if I really did love him enough to put up with him.' This is rubbish and the only things I believe to be true in newspapers now are the football results that I don't give a damn about anyway. Perhaps she extended the invitation out of curiosity to see what it might have been like to push somebody in a wheelchair into the sunset.

I am not Michael Foot

Four or five years ago, I was sitting in the Groucho Club one afternoon wiling away the time with a vodka, when one of the few men I've ever seen paralytically drunk in that club lurched over to where I was sitting and punched me in the face. He was too drunk for it to be very effective and, anyway, I was very resilient in those days, so I just said to him, 'What was that for?' He said, 'You're Michael Foot, aren't you?'

I have always admired Michael Foot, duffle coat and all, and he is an excellent writer. So, in a way, I felt quite flattered but also quite irritated, considering that I am just over twenty years younger than he is. The mistaken identity cropped up again last week when another customer came over to my table with a large vodka saying, 'That's for you.' I said, 'That's very kind of you, but I don't even know who you are.' He said, 'Maybe, but I know who you are. You're Michael Foot, aren't you?' If Michael Foot happens to read this, I hope he isn't too upset. As for myself, I'm getting slightly fed up with mistaken identity, although thanks to it I have brought considerable happiness into a couple of lives.

Quite a few years ago I was having a drink in the Queen's Elm in Fulham Road, standing near a bit of a look-alike when a woman suddenly screamed at him, 'You're that shit Jeff Bernard, aren't you?' and promptly threw a pint of beer at his face. He ducked and I got the lot which gave me something of a drenching. When the misunderstandings, all of them apart from whatever it could have been to make her think I was a shit, had been cleared up, the angry woman and my look-alike fell instantly in love and are, to this day, living happily in a fairyland castle that I can see in my mind's eye surrounded by sunshine and cherry blossom.

There was a time when I would tell bookmakers, bailiffs and the police that I was my twin brother but both of my brothers have two legs each so I can't get away with that any more. What I do puzzle about is what on earth I could have done to the beer-throwing woman in the Queen's Elm. It certainly must have been more complicated than going to bed with her and then not telephoning her the next day, otherwise I'm sure that I would have remembered her, but I must admit that my memory started failing me years ago and has done so frequently ever since. Perhaps I was born with premature Alzheimer's syndrome. There is usually some way of talking oneself out of such messes but I am still trying to think of an excuse to offer my wife of twenty-two years ago who, one Sunday, came into our village pub wearing a black wig which someone had lent her for fun. She looked rather sensational and I'm afraid that I started talking to her – and I have never been in the habit of talking much to women without having had a formal introduction – when she pulled me up short by suddenly calling me one of the rudest words in the dictionary.

Lunch was difficult to swallow that day and another pint of beer in the face would have been more welcome, or even some of the whisky I used to drink before I was mistaken for Michael Foot. Probably the worst one, although happily they kept it to themselves at the time, was a man in the pub who thought I might be Herbert von Karajan. Now there was a shit of the first order and I don't think that Taki would be pleased to have seen and heard a man looking at a picture I have on the wall of the two of us who said to me, 'I didn't realise you knew Bob Monkhouse.' I wonder where the next punch on the nose or large vodka is coming from. Perhaps I should try getting up in drag. That could spread the rumour that Dame Edith Sitwell is still alive.

On the wagon

The absence of last week's column was due to the fact that I had another attack of pancreatitis which I was told is now a chronic condition and one from which there is no longer any escape. I had even been on the wagon for a week before, and non-stop nausea is very nearly as bad as pain.

Anyway, the one thing that can be said about what is tantamount to being an honorary patient of the Middlesex Hospital is that it keeps me firmly in touch with reality, which I like. The days of dreaming are over. Taking up my usual position in the smoking area of the landing, I fell into conversation one morning with a disconcerting-looking Indian gentleman in his sixties. I say disconcerting because, his *café au lait* colour apart, he was an absolute ringer for James Joyce. So, sitting there feeling dejected and a little sorry for myself, I asked him what was wrong with him, as patients will ask each other when they meet. He told me that he had cancer of the pancreas and then he added, 'This morning they told me that I have six months to live.' It seems that his cancer is inoperable and even Mr Russell, the surgeon who is ace with the pancreas, can do nothing. After a while, I asked him did he feel bitter about it and, although he spoke excellent English, he said he didn't understand the word 'bitter', but he answered the question later by repeatedly saying, 'Why me? Why me?'

It occurred to me, not for the first time, how large a part good and bad luck play in health and medicine. (I wonder how I should be now if I had not had such an obsessive presentiment about having one or both legs amputated as long as three years ago. Someone in *Antony and Cleopatra* says, 'He who is was wished until he were'.) But apart from James Joyce, as I began to think of him, another incident that gave me food for thought was when I was being wheeled out to the smokers' landing, I passed a side ward – a single room – and I said to the nurse pushing me, 'Who's the lucky sod with the room to himself?' The nurse said, 'He's not so lucky. He'll never come out of that room.'

After my release and a day at home, I was beginning to feel well again until I watched *Timewatch* about the people involved in one of the last executions in this country. It made me feel physically sick. Albert Pierrepoint being dead, they filmed his assistant, a slightly self-righteous and very ordinary artisan who was only doing his job, wouldn't you know. At least one of the warders who kept the condemned man company at the end had the good grace to have had nightmares for some time after, but details of the drop and the mechanics of hanging a man were quite chilling. It took a good two hours to regain a little of my composure only to be made sick again by accidentally switching over to *The Generation Game* and seeing the revolting Bruce Forsyth. To cap it all, I got a bill this morning for £84.50 to renew my television licence.

I keep looking back on that *Timewatch* episode and remembering that, when I worked in the cutting rooms at Ealing Studios, we spent three days with Pierrepoint. Like his assistant, he too was just doing a job, but if he hadn't pulled himself up just short of saying, 'Somebody's got to do it,' I think I would have hit him. After he retired he took a pub with the gruesome name of Rest the Weary Traveller, and put up awful notices on the walls of the bar with jolly quips like 'No hanging about'. He continually spoke about how brave the objects of his bread and butter were. Without admitting it openly, he implied that most people went to the gallows fortified by a glass of brandy. I bet they were doped up to the eyeballs, just as I have to be to watch the aforementioned idiot, Bruce Forsyth.

Nine weeks without a drink

I wish I could cope half as well alone in this flat as Joanna Lumley did on her desert island. At least she had a camera crew nearby for emergencies and to have the odd chat with, but she coped very well, cooking the most ghastly looking food out of SAS mess tins. I eat better than her and I have Vera but I have clothes moths like Ms Lumley had sandflies. She was entirely admirable, even looked marvellous in her nine-day old clothes and lack of a shampoo and I felt ashamed when I realised that all I do in this, my own desert island, is inwardly to moan and try to keep self-pity at bay. But at least tomorrow I am going to be joined by thirty-five friends who only cost £1.50 each which is cheaper than the few I have in the Groucho Club.

My new friends are fish for which I have had an aquarium built last week. They will live in water that is being acclimatised at this moment to reach the temperature of the Amazon and the water is also being oxygenated. How odd it is that my other friends all drink like fish but the aquarium will need no additives to make my Amazonian friends either roar with laughter or bore the arse off me. As I say, they arrive tomorrow with their plants that will make up the landscape, riverscape, or what you will. They have the reputation for being calming and therapeutic but already I find myself staring hypnotised at a tank containing just gravel and water. Oh, for a mermaid like Joanna Lumley. Another thing about her was the fact that the filming she did of herself was a lot better than the potshots that the professional crew took of her.

But I am going to an island myself pretty soon and although it is my favourite one, Barbados, that too will be a desert island since Mr Cobb nicked most of my right leg. If you stop to think about it, which you won't but I never stop doing, it will be impossible to use a wheelchair on a sandy beach and every bar and restaurant worth going to that I know in Barbados is approached by steps. Whether or not I can stay on the wagon out there is another worry. The place was made for long iced drinks and the silence of a waiter approaching you from behind broken only by the tinkle of ice in a glass plus that of the very gentle surf is the most exquisite music, compared to that of the electric saw outside my window here, plus that of the market stall-holders shouting out the price of their wares.

Incidentally, it is now my ninth week without a drink and I am still getting the odd present of a bottle of vodka. I am not complaining. I could throw a party for the staff of the Russian embassy. Along with the vodka, I have also had presents of the odd tin of caviar, since which three girls who work in the Groucho Club have offered to wheel me home. I suppose I've had a tendency to be slightly cynical ever since I was a schoolboy. Now I'd go so far as to say that if I wasn't a mite cynical then I might have an extremely low IQ. That idiot footballer, Paul Gascoigne, was once told by a colleague after he had made a terrible mistake, 'You've got an IQ as low as the number on the back of your shirt.' Gazza ruminated for a couple of minutes and then turned to his colleague and asked him, 'What is an IQ?'

But if someone had told me during a break for 'snapping' in the mines forty years ago, 'One day you will be loved for your vodka and caviar,' I would have pooh-poohed the idea and gone on reading my copy of *The Times* which I always wrapped my sandwiches in. I think I told you once before that it was during a break one day that a fellow miner accused me of being a Tory because I read *The Times*. I explained to him that I got *The Times* primarily for the sports pages and then made it worse by, without thinking, saying that I also got it for the crossword. I tried to talk my way out of that at the end of the shift but he gave me a bit of a shellacking when we got to the surface. Oddly enough, it was the Poles who were the nicest of the miners in that pit and they are supposed to be mad. Not so.

A paw for Mr Webber

I have just received a letter from an inmate of HM Prison, Cornhill, Shepton Mallet, Somerset. The convict in question is S.J. Webber (NJ0735). He is, by all accounts, desperate to have his name in the *Spectator*. So there you are, Mr Webber.

The letter, itself, would fascinate Sherlock Holmes and he would probably learn a damn sight more about Mr Webber than I can. In the first place, his handwriting is that of a well-educated man but, at the same time, it is very affected. He says he misses the *Spectator* but that it is beyond his present financial means. Although I am addressed in the beginning as 'Dear Mr Bernard', he goes on to call me 'my dear' all through the letter. He ends by saying 'and so to bed, but without my teddy bear who is in Brighton. Such a bundle of charm. Goodnight, sleep innocently. Yours etc.' By the way his resolution for 1995 is to get hold of a copy of the book of collected 'Low Life' columns. Not a very ambitious resolution and I'm not sure I trust a man who can be separated from his teddy bear for longer than a three-month sentence.

I have a teddy bear myself – a present from my niece. He arrived one day in the post with a label stuck to one paw which read, 'My name is Byron and I want to be your friend.' Heaven forbid that I should go all the way to Somerset to cheer up a man who for all I know might, as his handwriting suggests, be fairly bright; he might also be a psychopath and might be serving time for abusing teddy bears. The original Byron might even have welcomed it but his namesake will remain safe overlooking my bedroom. I fear that my other

contact who was a resident of Ford Open Prison, which he
referred to as the Country Club, might have renewed his
membership. God knows why. I see no excuse or very few
indeed for going to prison. I can't think of one crime I could
commit that would improve my lot here which is a prison of
sorts. The Middlesex Hospital sentenced me to a life term
nearly a year ago and although Vera sometimes lets me out
on parole to push me to the Groucho Club I am, for the most
part, banged up here with just my new fish to look at and
Byron to talk to.

I have been watching my fish for a while now and then
and they are slightly different although they are all brainless.
Every pub has its bore and maybe every aquarium has its
bully just like every school. My resident bully I have called
Sally after a female writer with the same mental disorder. But
a strange thing I have never noticed before, which I should
have noticed on a fishmonger's slab a thousand times, is that
fish have no eyelids. So perhaps they never sleep but go into
a sort of floating trance like the ones I love in hospitals which
are produced by injections of that marvellous painkiller,
pethidine. This being England, of course, only a third of
the fish and the plants that I paid for in advance have been
delivered. Apart from their love of queueing, the English of
whatever trade have a nasty habit of making you wait in all
day for a repair or delivery and then don't turn up.

The exception in this flat is the Collector of Taxes who
I am far too nice to. I wonder if I could claim for him on
expenses. The last time he was here I went to the trouble of
making him both tea and toast and, needless to say, burnt
myself doing so from my wheelchair. I ought to get a stove
made for midgets or dwarfs and I am assured that there are
such appliances. Ideally I should be living in a doll's house and

I am quite used to people staring in at me just as I am used to the banal and stupid gossip about me that goes back and forth between the old residents who sit around inside the front door of this block and who I refer to as the 'committee'. I suppose that S.J. Webber (NJ0735) is the subject of as much gossip in HM Prison, Cornhill. Thank God the committee downstairs simply regard me as a drunk on the wagon. But a drunk with a teddy bear called Byron would be too much.

In search of happiness

The next person who tells me that there is always somebody worse off than myself is going to get a crack over the head. It is of no consolation to me nor is it a cure for chronic pancreatitis to be told that somebody in Bangladesh has cancer of the stomach. And I am also getting a little fed up, having been on this wagon for twelve weeks now, with people who keep telling me that I look well. I know exactly how I look. Awful.

I have been thinking about all this and kindred things ever since reading Robert Byck's piece in last week's *Spectator* about the attempt to define happiness – so far without success. It doesn't really bear thinking about but it is extraordinary how people continue to think that they have the right to inherit it like an old age pension or any other government hand-out.

When I was a boy I somewhat naively thought that this thing called happiness would be something I would wake up to find every day once I could smoke, drink, fornicate and when all authorities like my mother, school and national service were dead and buried. I suppose that one cure for unhappiness might be the chemistry that could make one stop thinking altogether and to live only by instincts, which is what I suppose the fish in my new aquarium must do. I have yet to see or meet an unhappy village idiot and that very nearly goes for all the city idiots that I know.

I have also noticed during the time I have spent drinking in pubs and clubs that very nearly all bores are quite happy or at least content, and contentment is my idea of happiness. But I think a lot of people, like children, confuse unhappiness with being bored, or children say they are bored when they are, in fact, depressed. I am confused about it all myself. My fellow traveller on this wagon is called angst but then when he isn't obviously sitting next to me he is simply lying in wait around the corner. Even if Robert Byck and other psychiatrists ever find a drug to cure the general malaise of being unhappy, they will surely never find a cure for specific components of it such as remorse and guilt and yea, though I run through the valley of death I am running straight into its arms.

I wonder if the suicide rate goes up at Christmas? I should think it does. If somebody as free from care as I should be feels a little down in the dumps, God knows how many people involved with and in families must feel. I can't remember many Christmases as a child that were particularly happy ones but then I believe that most unhappiness starts with what can be a ghastly institution – the family. In many ways I am glad I am no longer involved deeply in my own. My daughter is going to spend Christmas in Spain with her mother and I shall spend mine wallowing in my television set and *Mary Poppins* but, unlike most children, I shall be ogling Julie Andrews who I suspect in reality is nearer to being a raver than *Mary Poppins*. I have had some invitations to go away for Christmas and people kindly but erroneously think that a quantity of self-pity will ooze into this flat on the day itself. It won't. Although my goose will be cooked by two p.m. and always has been, I shall just miss that Christmas card I sometimes got telling me that my dinner was in the oven, and I shall wonder if they yet have written new scripts for their present husbands. I doubt it.

One of the biggest rows I have ever had began and ended soon after one Christmas Day morning with my mother-in-law triumphantly sweeping out of my house and victoriously declaring, as though it was a bullet through my heart, 'You must be a very unhappy man.' Not to see the end of her, I wasn't, but I did cry later on that very cold day when I saw that not only had I run out of wives but logs too.

And a happy New Year, whatever that means, to all my readers.